CHRISTINA ROSSETTI IN CONTEXT

ANTONY H. HARRISON

Christina Rossetti in Context

University of North Carolina Press

Chapel Hill and London

© 1988 The University of North Carolina Press
All rights reserved
Manufactured in the United States of America

92 91 90 89 88   5 4 3 2 1

Library of Congress Cataloging-in-Publication Data
Harrison, Antony H., 1948–
  Christina Rossetti in context.
  Bibliography: p.
  Includes index.
  1. Rossetti, Christina Georgina, 1830–1894—Criticism
and interpretation. I. Title.
PR5238.H37   1988   821'.8   87-10773
ISBN 0-8078-1755-4
ISBN 0-8078-4211-7 (pbk.)

FOR LINDA

CONTENTS

PREFACE

INCE the early 1930s, only one major critical book has been devoted to the work of Christina Rossetti. This astonishing fact has its roots deep in the history of the modern critical tradition, which was until the 1970s dominated largely by the "new critics" in the academy. In the last fifteen years, however, the range of available critical methodologies has expanded enormously, and we have begun seriously to question the standards of literary taste and value, as well as the literary canon, established earlier in this century.

To recover what has been lost in the meantime requires, at the outset, a project of retrieval—an archaeology that will eventually expose the complete and particular contexts surrounding the production, publication, and reception of literary works. If we proceed with an awareness of our own (historically dictated) biases, we may by means of such a project come to see literary works as they have truly operated throughout the history of their existence. As has been recently argued by critics as diverse as Jerome J. McGann, Herbert Lindenberger, Marilyn Butler, and Robert Weimann, without the dialectic of an historicist approach, any literary investigation "must remain purely intersystemic."[1] Such an approach is especially crucial with a poet like Christina Rossetti, whose ideology— that is, whose social, moral, amatory, religious, and literary value system— is largely uncongenial to the ideologies of the academic scholars who are most likely to study her today. This book, therefore, attempts to extend the process of retrieval that truly began in 1979 with the publication of Rebecca Crump's first volume of a variorum edition of Rossetti's complete poems. Here I attempt to reclaim and delineate the various contexts of Rossetti's work in order to understand more fully its operations. The following chapters examine the contemporary reception of Rossetti's poetry, the historical relation of her work to that of the other Pre-Raphaelite poets, the connections between her own and Ruskinian as well as Tractarian aesthetics, and her transvaluations of the Neoplatonic traditions of amatory poetry that reached their highest level of achievement in the Renaissance with the poetry of Dante and Petrarch.

Discussions of such contexts and of the intertextual qualities of Rossetti's work lead to a focus on the culturally important tension that emerges in her poetry between aestheticism (as defined by Walter Pater in his 1868 review of the poetry of William Morris) and asceticism (Rossetti's Victorian adaptation of the dominant impulse of the Middle Ages). In Rossetti's poetry the interaction between these two ostensibly opposed modes of behavior and modes of discourse is powerfully reciprocal. Both lead finally to a solipsistic withdrawal from any active life in the world in favor of a life committed to poetic and religious idealities. Imagined forms of spiritual fulfillment become "aestheticized" and are often expressed in sensuous images, while the desire for sensory and erotic satisfaction is elided or transmuted into traditional religious aspirations and language. Ultimately, Rossetti's poetry enacts a wholesale renunciation of this world not only because it is intrinsically evil or fallen, but also and consequently because all that it can offer is "never enough" for the "craving heart."

We might easily conclude that such a radical withdrawal into the "narrow chamber of the individual mind" would have been, for an intelligent, middle-class Victorian woman, the only available escape from a corrupt and inhospitable world, one that denied her the possibility of true independence, unqualified professional achievement, or the retention of complete integrity in marriage. But fully understanding the values espoused in Rossetti's poetry and comprehending the implications of that poetry's everywhere implicit turning upon itself (as the exclusive habitation of craved idealities) also requires a detailed knowledge of the value systems available and acceptable to her in forging a literary ideology.

ACKNOWLEDGMENTS

Y greatest debt in writing this book is to Jerome J. McGann, who initially stimulated my interest in the Pre-Raphaelite poets and who has been a constant source of ideas and assistance of all kinds. Jerome Bump, William Fredeman, David Kent, and George Tennyson read the manuscript in earlier versions. Its present content, I hope, reflects the influence of their keen perceptions. Portions of the manuscript were discussed by members of the Literary Criticism seminar at the National Humanities Center in 1981–82. Their suggestions for improvements have been helpful. To Marcia Colish, John Hodgson, Benjamin Hrushovski, Stephen Marcus, and Anna Nardo I am especially grateful for useful criticisms. I am indebted to the National Humanities Center for providing ideal research facilities and release time from my normal teaching duties. I would also like to thank my students George Cox, Tamyra Davis, Dana Dewit, Robin Parsons, Muri Pugh, Betsy Rowland, and David Teal for asking dependably provocative questions about Victorian poetry and for working assiduously to answer them. Sandra Eisdorfer and Pamela Upton of the UNC Press have been model editors—hard-working, efficient, perceptive, thoughtful in all matters. I cannot adequately thank them for their helpfulness. Chapter 1 appeared in different form as "Christina Rossetti: The Poetic Vocation" in *Texas Studies in Literature and Language* (1985), and I am grateful to the editors for permission to reprint portions of that article. Unpublished letters by Christina Rossetti appear with the permission of the Pierpont Morgan Library, the Princeton University Library, and the Yale University Library. I regret that Dolores Rosenblum's *Christina Rossetti: The Poetry of Endurance* appeared too late for me to benefit from it in the writing of this book.

ABBREVIATIONS

Bell   Mackenzie Bell, *Christina Rossetti* (London: Thomas Burleigh, 1908).

Face   Christina Rossetti, *The Face of the Deep* (London: Society for Promoting Christian Knowledge, 1893).

Fact   Herbert Sussman, *Fact into Figure: Typology in Carlyle, Ruskin, and the Pre-Raphaelite Brotherhood* (Columbus: Ohio State University Press, 1979).

FL   *The Family Letters of Christina Georgina Rossetti*, ed. William Michael Rossetti (New York: Scribners, 1908).

NER   Jerome J. McGann, "Christina Rossetti's Poems: A New Edition and a Revaluation," *Victorian Studies* 23 (1980): 237–54. Reprinted in *The Beauty of Inflections: Literary Investigations in Historical Method and Theory* (Oxford: Clarendon Press, 1985), 207–31.

Poems   *The Complete Poems of Christina Rossetti*, ed. Rebecca W. Crump, 2 vols. to date (Baton Rouge: Louisiana State University Press, 1979–).

RML   *The Rossetti-Macmillan Letters*, ed. Lona Mosk Packer (Berkeley: University of California Press, 1963).

RP   Jerome J. McGann, "The Religious Poetry of Christina Rossetti," *Critical Inquiry* 10 (1983): 128–44. Reprinted in *The Beauty of Inflections: Literary Investigations in Historical Method and Theory* (Oxford: Clarendon Press, 1985), 232–52.

Sambrook   James Sambrook, ed., *Pre-Raphaelitism: A Collection of Critical Essays* (Chicago: University of Chicago Press, 1974).

SF   Christina Rossetti, *Seek and Find: A Double Series of Short Studies of the Benedicte* (London: Society for Promoting Christian Knowledge, 1879).

VDP   George B. Tennyson, *Victorian Devotional Poetry* (Cambridge, Mass.: Harvard University Press, 1981).

WJR The Works of John Ruskin, ed. E. T. Cook and Alexander
      Wedderburn, 39 vols. (London: George Allen, 1903–12).

Works The Poetical Works of Christina Georgina Rossetti, ed. William
        Michael Rossetti (London: Macmillan, 1904).

CHRISTINA ROSSETTI IN CONTEXT

CHAPTER 1.

INTRODUCTORY:

CHRISTINA

ROSSETTI AND

THE POETIC

VOCATION

To William Edmonston Aytoun, the satirist of Spasmodicism and contributing editor of *Blackwood's Magazine*, Christina Rossetti on 1 August 1854 forwarded six new poems, along with what most students of her work today would perceive as a startlingly self-assertive cover letter. In it she disingenuously describes herself as an "unknown and unpublished" writer, a "nameless rhymester." But speaking, as she says, "to a poet," she takes the liberty of insisting that Aytoun consider her works seriously. She stresses her own true identity as a poet, explaining: "I hope that I shall not be misunderstood as guilty of egotism or foolish vanity, when I say that my love for what is good in the works of others teaches one that there is something above the despicable in mine; that poetry is with me, not a mechanism, but an impulse and a reality; and that I know my aims in writing to be pure, and directed to that which is true and right."[1]

Despite Rossetti's deliberate assertions that a commitment to the poetic vocation was of primary importance in her life, critics until very recently have been reluctant to view her as a writer fully devoted to her craft. She was, in fact, a determined and careful artist whose unremitting ambition was to fulfill her potential to generate perfected poetic artifacts, "pure" creative works "directed to that which is true and right." This passage further points to what emerges as *the* pivotal tension of her existence, arising from a conflict, not always easily resolved for Rossetti, between aesthetic and moral (indeed, often ascetic or even prophetic) impulses. Evidence from this letter written when she was twenty-three, and also from earlier and later letters, confirms Rossetti's unrelenting belief in her own vocation as an artist. Yet critics still have not fully acknowledged her drive for aesthetic fulfillment, and, as a result, they have frequently been misguided in evaluating the precise aesthetic qualities, effects, and implications of her work. With the first two volumes of Rebecca Crump's projected three-volume variorum edition of Rossetti's poetry now available, however, we can begin a decades-overdue revaluation of Rossetti's methods of composition, her aesthetics, the value of her poems, and her true position in relation to the other major Victorian poets.[2] But first, we must establish the proper sociohistorical and literary contexts in which to view her work.

Easy access to the previously scattered manuscript texts of Rossetti's poems, and to the emendations of those texts after their initial publication, at last provides an opportunity to scrutinize the artistic procedure of an enigmatic poet. For almost a century Rossetti has suffered severely from the critical approaches of biographical scholars who have frequently read her verse to lay bare the nature of her unfulfilled passions or to discover the identity of her innominate lover.[3] Readings of Christina Rossetti's works by such critics have depended on the fallacious assumption that her poetry is written for the most part in a confessional poetic mode, as that mode was reinforced by the atmosphere of earnestness inescapable for middle-class Victorians.[4] Such, however, is by no means predictably the case with Rossetti's often experimental verse. Her poems are exploratory, presenting notably different views—from poem to poem and even from one version of a poem to another—of a given set of social, psychological, amatory, and artistic issues. Moreover, as only the most recent commentators have begun to indicate, her aesthetic values often derive from extremely diverse and sometimes ostensibly incompatible literary sources.[5]

In light of the misplaced emphases of past scholarship (as well as the dearth of genuinely useful criticism), a full reassessment of Christina Rossetti is in order.[6] Such a reassessment has profound implications that may well force us to revise currently accepted approaches to Pre-Raphaelite poetry as a whole and to see more clearly than ever the Pre-Raphaelites' importance in providing aesthetic documents that constitute the transition between Romantic and modern literary modes.

The most important piece of work to propagate the myth of Rossetti's "romantic" sincerity and her artistic innocence is William Michael Rossetti's "Memoir," which appears in his collected edition of her *Poetical*

Works, published ten years after Christina's death. There he promotes and extends a previously generated image of her poetic practice. He explains that

> her habits of composition were entirely of the casual and spontaneous kind, from her earliest to her latest years. If something came into her head which she found suggestive of verse, she put it into verse. It came to her (I take it) very easily, without her meditating a possible subject, and without her making any great difference in the first from the latest form of the verses which embodied it. . . . What she wrote was pretty well known in the family as soon as her impeccably neat manuscript of it appeared . . . but she did not show it about as an achievement, and still less had she, in the course of her work, invited any hint, counsel, or co-operation. (*Works*, lxviii–lxix)

William Michael was simply wrong—or at least significantly misguided— on both of the major points he introduces here. His sister revised in very important ways and, during her mature years, consistently sought criticism of her manuscripts from Dante Gabriel. In his memoir William Michael is, however, in part transmitting an image of his sister—as a pious and ascetic woman unconcerned with worldly achievements—that she herself had been at some pains to cultivate, especially after 1870. This image suppresses half the truth of Christina Rossetti's values and aspirations. Once dislodged, assumptions of her artistic innocence—that is, of the spontaneity and therefore craftlessness of her poetic production and the selflessness of her pursuits in general—must be radically qualified. We may then begin to discover the kind of values—emotional, social, and psychological, but especially literary—that inspire and inform Rossetti's poetry. From analysis of her texts and her revisions of them, along with epistolary and established biographical evidence, we can place Christina Rossetti with greater precision than before on the stage of rapidly changing aesthetic values in England from 1860 to 1900. We can also begin to understand more fully that the ways in which she diverges in her poems from the artistic practices and values of her brother, Dante Gabriel, and the other Pre-Raphaelites are more subtle and limited than we might expect, given the traditional image of Christina Rossetti as a withdrawn and highly religious woman who appeared to devote her life almost exclusively to her family and her God. In fact, for the most poetically productive years of her life—that is, until 1871—she devoted it, equally and irrepressibly, to her art.

ANY revaluation of traditional portraits of Christina Rossetti's artistic procedures or of her complex sense of vocation as an artist might usefully begin with exploratory readings of one of her most heavily revised poems. "Maude Clare" is a poem with what is, for Christina Rossetti's works, a not unusual textual history. Her procedures for revising "Maude Clare" and the effects of her major changes in its text are similar to those of "Song," "Echo," "Bitter for Sweet," "The Poor Ghost," "A Royal Princess," "An Immurata Sister," "Cor Mio," and dozens of other poems in her published volumes.[7] Rebecca Crump concludes that the first (and only extant) manuscript of "Maude Clare" was produced "probably after December 8, 1857, and before April 14, 1858" (*Poems*, 1:244). The manuscript version of the poem contains forty-one stanzas.[8] However, by the time it appeared in *Once a Week* on 5 November 1859, the work had been radically shorn to fifteen stanzas. Rossetti carefully pruned it once more before printing it as a poem of twelve stanzas in *Goblin Market and Other Poems*. In this 1862 version "Maude Clare" is a balladic narrative consisting entirely of dialogue except for the first stanza, which describes the poem's two central female characters, and the fourth stanza, which depicts Lord Thomas's reaction to the appearance at his wedding of Maude Clare, his jilted lover. The narrator's sympathies at the start of the poem are uncertain:

> Out of the church she followed them
> With a lofty step and mien:
> His bride was like a village maid,
> Maude Clare was like a queen.
> *(Poems*, 1:44–45)

Introduced in the second stanza is Thomas's "lady mother," whose words suggest the central theme of the poem (fidelity versus betrayal in love) and raise questions crucial in evaluating the characters. Ambiguously, "With smiles, almost with tears," she pronounces this benediction upon the newly married couple:

> "May Nell and you but live as true
> As we have done for years;

> "Your father thirty years ago
> Had just your tale to tell;
> But he was not so pale as you,
> Nor I so pale as Nell." (45)

At this point in our (first) reading we may well wonder if there is any extraordinary reason for the apparent tension between the mother's smiles and tears; whether the marital fidelity she cherishes might be an illusion; what beyond the usual anxieties might have caused the father to be pale on his wedding day; and what causes Tom's and his bride's pallor now. The narrator immediately provides the puzzling explanation that Tom "was pale with pride." As for Nell, we are told that "Tom gazed long on pale Maude Clare / Or ever he kissed the bride," an action that might distress any woman in the midst of nuptials. In the next three stanzas Maude Clare presents her wedding gifts "To bless the hearth, to bless the board, / To bless the marriage bed," but the gifts are bitterly ironic because they include an amulet and another love token formerly given her by Tom: "'My half of the golden chain / You wore about your neck'" and

> ". . . my half of the faded leaves
> We plucked from budding bough,
> With feet amongst the lily leaves,—
> The lilies are budding now." (45)

By this point the reader perhaps feels little sympathy for Maude Clare because of her bad timing, the arrogance of her ironies, and her queenly mien, which suffers in comparison with the implied humility and ingenuousness of the bride "like a village maid." Tom's inability in the next stanza to "match her scorn with scorn," his faltering speech, and his poignant sense of shame (he "hid his face") make Maude Clare look all the worse. So does her immediate verbal assault on Nell, which makes us question Maude's own potential for fidelity rather than caprice:

> "Take my share of a fickle heart,
> Mine of a paltry love:
> Take it or leave it as you will,
> I wash my hands thereof." (46)

If her indifference is genuine, we condemn Maude Clare for unjustly disrupting the occasion and for vainly upstaging the married couple. If it is a mask, then she is still doing little service by her tantrum to herself or to the man she would be thought still to love. In the poem's last two stanzas, Nell reinforces most readers' initial, positive impressions of her. Unlike Maude Clare, she shows courage and tenacity along with her previously implied humility:

"And what you leave," said Nell, "I'll take,
    And what you spurn, I'll wear;
For he's my lord for better and worse,
    And him I love, Maude Clare.

"Yea, tho' you're taller by the head,
    More wise and much more fair;
I'll love him till he loves me best,
    Me best of all, Maude Clare." (46)

Nell has the last words, and they significantly reflect our comparative valuation of Tom's two lovers. Many readers would retain little sympathy and perhaps even feel hostility for Maude Clare by the end of the poem.

I stress these points because the thrust of the manuscript text of "Maude Clare" is entirely different from the greatly reduced, austere, but powerful version I have just described. In the manuscript poem Maude Clare appears without question as the most sympathetic figure in the work, a woman betrayed and victimized by a capricious lover who chooses to marry for money. Throughout this version, narrative description of the setting and events dominates over dialogue, and as a result, the poem lacks the dramatic intensity of the 1862 version. Its discursiveness also detracts from the poem's emotional power, and much poetic energy is sacrificed—in narrative descriptions and additional dialogue—to provide signals for evaluating the characters.

Our sympathies are initially guided by conventional symbols that obtrude in the first manuscript stanza and that become relevant once the central characters are introduced:

The fields were white with lily buds,
    White gleamed the lilied beck,
Each mated pigeon plumed the pomp
    of his metallic neck.
                    (*Poems*, 1:245)

By the seventh stanza the reader retrospectively identifies Maude Clare, whose "cheeks were pale like pearls," with the purity and potential of the "lily buds" but also with their traditional symbolic resonances implying innocence and self-sacrifice. By contrast, we identify the soon-mated Nell with the detached and complacent, wealthily "plumed" pigeon of line four. Her "metallic" neck clinches our identification of her with money and further suggests insensitivity and invulnerability. Apparently Nell is like Thomas in her callousness. As early as stanza four Maude Clare identifies him clearly as " 'a false false love of mine.' " His behavior, we learn two stanzas later, has desolated Maude Clare, who now retains "never a sparkle in her eyes / That had wept the yesternight." Moreover, we learn in stanza seven that Tom has deserted this dazzling, lilylike maiden for "a new love frank and fair, / . . . who lacked the witching winning grace / Of his old love pale Maude Clare" (245).

In this version of the poem, as in the published one of 1862, Tom is desperately embarrassed by Maude's presence at the wedding, but here he suffers guilt for a much clearer reason:

> He cared not to meet her eyes again
> And he dared not touch her hand,
> For Maude Clare for all she was so fair
> Had never an inch of land. (245)

Tom's guilty behavior contrasts with the stalwart and heroic demeanor of Maude Clare, who, decked in jewels, is virtually deified by the narrator: "Lady Maude glittered" in the train of the bride and groom "Like a star of the firmament." She, rather than the married couple, attracts the admiring attention of the audience at the wedding:

> Then one stood up to pledge the bride
> With hint and waggish smile,
> Yet tho' his words were for the bride
> He glanced at Maude the while.
>
> "Health to the bride and length of days
> "And hopes fulfilled and wealth." (246)

Even Lord Thomas "turned to young Maude Clare / Before he drank the health." But despite her success in drawing the attention and sympathies of those about her, after all the feasting, singing, gift-giving, and benedictions, Maude Clare suffers unspeakably as she turns to address the couple: "But oh her heart must ache," we are told by the narrator in a line that anticipates and undercuts any suspicion that Maude is arrogant or unjustified in her recriminations. After her words to the couple (the same as those of the 1862 version), Maude Clare—as if to emphasize an already clear point—adds that Nell "has purchased" her husband "with gold," words that might well have reminded Victorian readers of Tennyson's *Maud*, published only two years before Christina Rossetti's poem was first written.

The manuscript poem ends with three rather than two stanzas of response from Nell. These differ entirely from those of the 1862 version. In them Nell's indignation seems tellingly lame, her protest too much taken up with advice delivered safely after the fact:

> But "Fie for shame . . . [my] Lady Maude,"
> Nell cried with kindling cheek:
> "It's shame on me who hear the words,
> "It's shame on you who speak.
>
> "I never guessed you loved my Lord,
> "I never heard your wrong;
> "You should have spoken before the priest
> "Had made our tie so strong;
>
> "You should have stood up in Church
> "To claim your rights before;
> "You should have parted us in the Church
> "Or kept silence evermore." (246–47)

Here Nell displays only callousness in her defensive, legalistic reply to Maude Clare, rather than the tenacity and boldness that make her the more attractive of Tom's lovers in the 1862 version.

These two texts of the same poem by Christina Rossetti tell us a good deal about her habits of composition and make clear the inadequacy of merely thematic approaches to her poems. The differences between the manuscript poem and the 1862 version also reveal much about Rossetti's rigorous aesthetic values, her central concern with artistic efficacy, and her ability to compose with a sense of artistic detachment that belies assumptions of her poetry's sincerity as well as critical propensities to interpret its contents biographically. Arguments that this poem is dramatic rather than lyrical, and thus not subject to "sincere" impulses, are irrelevant, for Rossetti's ruthless artistry was applied impartially to every kind of poetry she wrote.[9]

Rossetti's famous "Song" ("Oh roses for the flush of youth"), for instance, appears in its published form as a lyric lament acknowledging the speaker's resignation to an unfulfilled life and an early death, aptly represented by her choice of "withered leaves" of ivy as a memorial, rather than any traditional floral symbol of a more meaningful life (roses, laurel, violets, or bay). Our attention is focused finally, not on the barely sketched character of the speaker or her fate, but on the tradition of flower symbolism itself, especially as it is employed in literature of "the old time" (*Poems*, 1:40).

Although the title of the original version of the work, "A Song in a Song," suggests the self-conscious literary concerns of the poem, the stanzas themselves (the first three of which are deleted in the final version) draw attention away from the issue of traditionary symbolism and its proper uses. The poem instead erects a dramatic relationship between a different speaker and his dead beloved; he now loiters (like Keats's knight at arms) in expectation of his own death: "I sit and sing her song, / And muse upon the past." The first two stanzas emphasize the beloved's former beauty and her lover's despair at her unexpected death. The poem's final version is thus radically reformed and refocused upon predominantly aesthetic issues rather than those of elegiac or courtly love poetry.

Revisions of "The Bourne" demonstrate an even more drastic redirection than those of "Song." A devotional poem first written in 1854 in twelve stanzas, the work was reduced to two stanzas by the time of its first publication, nine years later, in *Macmillan's Magazine*. The published version contained only the second and fifth of the original stanzas. The first version is clumsily entitled "There remaineth therefore a rest," and with a good deal of overwriting it describes a soul's experience during what was known to Victorian millenarians and Anabaptists as "Soul Sleep," the waiting period between a person's death and resurrection at the Second Coming.[10] In this version Rossetti tediously rehearses the details of anticipated experience during Soul Sleep: the "cool" bed of the grave; the slumber and renewal that take place there; the equality of all the dead in this condition; an end to physical suffering; and the incipient process of fulfillment and perfection that culminates with the soul "Struggling panting up to God" (*Poems*, 1:280).

The published version of 1863 has been radically pared by means of simple but careful selection among the earlier stanzas. The altered title itself is a brilliant addition that reflects a new semiotic concern in the poem. As a pun, it is multivalent, at once suggesting continuity ("a stream or brook") and division ("a boundary"), an ending ("goal") and a beginning ("born"). The text retains from the original a thematic emphasis on the transitoriness and vanity of earthly life, but that emphasis surprisingly dissolves in the closing third of the poem. There we learn that, in the grave, "a very little girth / Can hold round what once the earth / Seemed too narrow to contain" (*Poems*, 1:142). The emphasis in these lines upon form and dimension, of course, introduces an insistence on spiritual infinitude and the impossibility of its full realization during earthly life. At the same time, however, the reader's attention is directed to the potential for a corollary expressional infinitude inherent in the medium of the poem itself. Like the remains of the originary body (poet or speaker), the poem is "a very little girth" (in the new version) and yet "contains" our transcendent spirituality. Indeed, expression of the latter is demonstrably dependent on the existence of the former. The "bourne," at which the powers of spirit and language meet and the one becomes embedded in the other, is the self-reflexive poem. Thus, as a symbol of the boundary between physical and spiritual worlds, as a locus for knowledge of eventual spiritual fulfillment, as an imaginative space where sensations of such fulfillment might be generated, and as the vehicle for transmuting all perceptions of prospective rebirth into material form, the poem itself is "The Bourne."

In an unpublished letter of 1888, responding to questions from an anonymous admirer, Rossetti retrospectively explained one aesthetic principle that was central, during her early years, to the developing poetic style revealed in revisions of such poems as "Maude Clare," "Song," and "The Bourne." She also forcefully acknowledged the importance of her brother Dante's tutelage. She explained: "Perhaps the nearest approach to a method I can lay claim to was a distinct aim at conciseness; after a while I received a hint from my sister that my love of conciseness tended to make my writing obscure, and I then endeavoured to avoid obscurity as well as diffuseness. In poetics," she concluded insistently, "my elder brother was my acute and most helpful critic."[11]

Rossetti's attempt to approach her ideal of "conciseness" is manifest in the revisions of "Maude Clare," "Song," and "The Bourne" that I have reviewed, but it is everywhere visible in her best poems as well. Pursuit of that single ideal, however, leads directly to ostensibly subordinate characteristics of her poetic style as well as to corollary aesthetic values that dominate the poems. It leads to tautness and a directness of expression, a deceptive simplicity of poetic surfaces that contrasts significantly with the "arduous fullness," the density and involutions of Dante Rossetti's style; it leads to dramatic intensity, to deliberate ambiguity, and, even more notably, to Christina Rossetti's often open-ended symbolic modes of expression (for instance, in *Goblin Market*, "A Birthday," "Up-Hill," and *The Prince's Progress*). It leads, also, to a thematic structure in her poems that is densely, though often ambiguously, allusive. The quest for conciseness often compels her to generate meaning by manipulating allusions to Plato, the Bible, Saint Augustine, Dante, Petrarch, Herbert, Crashaw, Maturin, Coleridge, Keats, Tennyson, and to troubadour traditions. One typical thematic mode of her poetry, then, is intertextual, directing her reader away from the apparently simple surface meanings of her poems and toward historically layered literary statements and traditions, consideration of which complicates, amplifies, and reifies the meanings of her own verse. Unlike her brother's densely wrought poems, the diffusive effects of Christina Rossetti's poetry come as often from explicit or implied literary allusions and parodic procedures as from recurrent image patterns, symbolism, or play with language. The demands her poetry places upon its readers, therefore, are hardly best served by approaching her works as veiled autobiography, or by neo-Freudian interpretations of them, or by single-minded new-critical—rather than critically pluralistic—methodologies.[12]

AT this point, one might well ask how criticism of Rossetti—and, by implication, discussions of other ostensibly autobiographical poets—is to proceed if exclusively thematic, psychobiographical, and noncontextual readings of her poems are proscribed. Some progress has been made already by recent critics who suggest the importance of purely literary considerations in reading Rossetti's poetry (and, by implication, some of Dante Rossetti's important poetry). From their earliest adolescent days, during which they wrote poetry and fiction in an atmosphere of sibling competition encouraged by their father and by their grandfather Polidori (who promised publication on his home press), the Rossetti children all possessed a highly literary self-awareness. It is no coincidence that all four children, including the Anglican nun, Maria, published major literary or critical works during their lives. Significantly, all published on Dante, and, of course, both Christina and Dante Gabriel allude repeatedly in their letters and works to Dante and the literary tradition he subsumed and perpetuated.[13]

There are a number of potentially fruitful approaches to the Rossettis' poetry. One, already touched upon by Jerome McGann, Barbara Fass, and Joan Rees among the major critics, is to look at the Rossettis' productions as self-conscious attempts to appropriate and extend specific literary traditions. One of these is obviously that of medieval French love poetry, which began with the troubadours and culminated with Petrarch, Dante, and the Renaissance sonneteers.[14] Analysis of their works in this context would expose the Rossettis' self-conscious and detached use (and pastiche) of specific forms and conventions of love poetry. Another approach especially relevant to Christina Rossetti's work is sociohistorical and uses incontrovertible biographical data and historical contexts to illuminate her works. Her letters, hundreds of which remain unpublished, are an invaluable source of information, for they reflect and comment specifically upon her artistic ambitions, her poetic methods, her reading, her acquaintances, and her responses to political, social, and religious issues of the day. A third approach to Rossetti criticism would investigate her use of the set of traditions surrounding Romantic "sincerity," especially as these appear in Blake, Keats, and Coleridge and as they are absorbed by Romantic and Victorian novelists. These traditions very often deliberately mask the detachment of the writer who, largely through his or her artificially "sincere" tone, elicits specific emotional, moral, intellectual, and aesthetic responses from the reader.

Concern with this latter tradition introduces a fourth, complementary approach to the poetry of both Rossettis, one that perceives the primary purpose in their literary efforts to be the generation of the most beautiful and affective artifacts possible. At the base of such efforts in every case are clear aesthetic values, which may vary in emphasis from work to work. In the case of the 1862 text of "Maude Clare," for instance, the values that dominate are dramatic and emotional intensity, ambiguity, and irony.[15] In all of Rossetti's significant poems, however, thematic (or "moral") considerations are coterminous with, if not subordinated to, aesthetic ones: sometimes even the possibility of deriving clear themes or ideas from a work is undercut. Art, comprehensive of relevant traditions, becomes the supreme value, as Dante Rossetti suggests in his introductory sonnet to *The House of Life*, in "Love's Last Gift" from the same sequence, and even in such apparently polemical poems as "The Burden of Nineveh." At the center of the latter work, transcending the histories of specific men's passions, fears, ideals, and ideologies (as well as those of their civilizations), is the winged beast of Nineveh, an infinitely interpretable work of art.

As we know, Dante Rossetti, the reluctant aesthete, was the most frequent and effective critic of his sister's manuscript poems. Christina alluded to him repeatedly as her mentor, and, as the revisions of "Maude Clare" suggest, she was, like him, ultimately more interested in the quality and effectiveness of a poem than in conveying themes or in being sincere and self-expressive. The extent to which artistic perfection was the preeminent concern in Christina Rossetti's poetry, as it was in her brother's, was perceived by early commentators like Arthur Symons, Virginia Woolf, and Justine DeWilde but has been ignored by most of her critics for the last fifty years.[16] Yet her irrepressible concern with the artistry of her works and with her own artistic vocation is unmistakable in her early letters. After her grandfather Polidori printed two volumes of her childhood poems, one in 1842 when she was twelve years old and one in 1847; after she succeeded in placing two poems in the *Athenaeum* in 1848; and after seven of her works appeared pseudonymously in *The Germ* during 1850,

Rossetti subsequently endured a frustrating hiatus in her publishing career. From 1851 until 1861 she saw only two of her poems and one short story appear in print, despite the self-confidence of her letters of submission to potential publishers.

The sense of urgency with which she pursued artistic success is, perhaps, most powerfully revealed in the second half of the 1854 letter to Aytoun quoted earlier. In an emotionally intense conclusion, she remarks,

> I do not blush to confess that . . . it would afford me some gratification to place my productions before others, and ascertain how far what I do is expressive of mere individualism, and how far it is capable of approving itself to the general sense. It would be a personal favour to me if you would look into the enclosed with an eye not inevitably to the waste paper basket, and a further obligation if, whatever be the result, you would vouchsafe me a few words as to the fate of the verses. I am quite conscious that volunt[ary]eer contributors have no right to expect this of an editor; I ask it simply as a courtesy. It is mortifying to have done something sincerely, offer it in a good faith; and be treated as a "non avenue."[17]

A similarly solemn dedication to her art also surfaces in brief comments responding to William Michael Rossetti's queries in 1849 about progress with her poem, "Three Nuns." She responds that "my dreary poem is not completed, but a few appropriate stanzas have been added since my leaving town. You will easily believe that, whatever other merit it lacks, it possesses unity of purpose in a high degree" (*FL*, 6).

Despite such passages in her letters, however, and despite prevalent opinion among her critics and biographers, Christina Rossetti was by no means always as earnest as this letter or her later petition to Aytoun suggests. On numerous epistolary occasions she demonstrates irrepressible wit. Yet her humorous self-inflations or self-deprecations most often serve to reinforce perceptions of her sense of vocation as an artist. Writing to William in 1850, for instance, while still enjoying the glow kindled by her prospective appearances in *The Germ*, she gives this advice: "Do you know, I seriously urge on your consideration the increase of prose and decrease of poetry in the *Germ*, the present state of things strikes me as most alarming. Should all other articles fail, boldly publish my letters; they would doubtless produce an immense sensation. By hinting that I occupy a high situation in B——ck——m P——l——e, substituting initials and asterisks for all names, and adding a few titles, my correspondence might have quite a success."[18]

Three years later, in a similar vein, she fantasizes that the depleted family fortunes might be reconstituted if justice were truly done to her short story, "Nick," then circulating. This could be accomplished, she insists, if only the story were submitted along with her own portrait: "a first-rate business head perceiving at a glance its capabilities, has [the portrait] engraved prefixed to ['Nick'], and advertised . . . all over the civilized world" with wonderful success. She prophesies that "The book spreads like wild-fire. Addey at the end of 2 months, struck by a late remorse, and having an eye to future contingencies, sends me a second cheque for £200; on which we subsist for a while. At the publication of the 20th edition Mrs Addey (a mild person of few words) expires; charging her husband to do me justice. He promises with one suppressed sob. Next day a third cheque for £2000 reaches me. This I divide; assigning half to Maria for her dowry, and handing the rest to Mama. I then collapse. Exeunt Omnes."[19]

Letters such as these facetious ones, along with those earnestly soliciting publication of her works and yet others of the 1860s playfully expressing envy of her visibly more successful, rival "poetesses" (especially Jean Ingelow), expose a Victorian woman with a clear vision of her vocation; she was anxious, if not determined, to make that vision real. Yet, although Christina Rossetti lived until 1894, most of her best poems were produced (though not necessarily published) before 1871, when she nearly died of Graves' disease. Afterwards, she led a virtually cloistered life in London, where any foray beyond the bounds of her home in Torrington Square was, as she repeatedly explained to her correspondents, "formidable." After 1871 she published only one volume of new poems (in 1881). She expended most of her creative energies during the last twenty years of her life in writing seven books of devotional prose or religious commentary. In 1874 she explained in a letter to her publisher, Alexander Macmillan, who was urging her to compile a new volume of poems, that "the possibility of your thinking proper some day to reprint my two volumes [*Goblin Market* and *The Prince's Progress*], is really gratifying to me as you may suppose; but as to additional matter, I fear there will be little indeed to offer you. The fire has died out, it seems; and I know of no bellows potent to revive dead coals. I wish I did."[20] The insistently prosaic echoes here of Coleridge's lament in "Dejection: An Ode" would not have been lost on either "the staunch Mac" or Christina herself. But what is also forcefully apparent to later readers of this letter is Rossetti's refusal in any way to compromise her artistic integrity for fame or profit.

In William Michael's memoir of his sister, he remarks, this time without any mistake,

> It may be asked—Did Christina Rossetti consider herself truly a poet-ess, and a good one? Truly a poetess, most decidedly yes; and, within the range of her subject and thought, and the limits of her executive endeavour, a good one. This did not make her in the least conceited or arrogant as regards herself, nor captious as to the work of others; but it did render her very resolute in setting a line of demarcation between a person who is a poet and another person who is a versifier. Pleadings of *in misericordiam* were of no use with her, and she never could see any good reason why one who is not a poet should write verse in meter. (*Works*, lxix)

The extent to which Christina Rossetti did insist upon the unique capabilities of the artist, as well as the autonomy of the artist's imagination and creative powers, is clear from her commentaries on her own poems. Paradigmatic is a passage from a letter written by her on 13 March 1865 to Dante Rossetti, who was at the time supervising her revisions of poems that would appear in *The Prince's Progress* (1866). Her comments in the passage concern the poem "Under the Rose" (in 1875 retitled "'The Iniquity of the Fathers upon the Children'"). Some readers might incorrectly assert that this is a surprisingly worldly poem for Christina Rossetti. It is a 545-line monologue spoken by a young woman, Margaret, who, in recalling events of her past life, has concluded that she is the illegitimate daughter of a kindly, unmarried aristocratic woman. In order to retain her reputation, Margaret deduces, this eminent lady was forced to repudiate Margaret at her birth. At the end of "Under the Rose," Margaret, now ostensibly her mother's servant but virtually an adopted child, determines to lead a life of resignation and renunciation, keeping her mother's secret but thereby also fully retaining her own autonomy.

Judging from Christina Rossetti's response to him, her brother was dismayed by the "unpleasant-sided subject" of this poem, but more especially by the fact that it came from a *woman's* pen. Rossetti's reaction to Dante's critique of "Under the Rose" is as illuminating as anything she wrote about her own art, or, indeed, about any other author's work. Not only does it reveal her perceptions of the relationship between art and the commonly accepted sexual roles of men and women, but it also makes explicit her understanding of the relations between poetry and the personal experience of the author. Although she begins the passage with the

self-effacing rhetoric typical of her, she concludes on a strongly assertive
note. To Dante Gabriel she writes,

> *U. the R.* herewith . . . I meekly return to you, pruned and rewritten
> to order. As regards the unpleasant-sided subject I freely admit it: and
> if you think the performance coarse or what-not, pray eject it . . .
> though I thought *U. the R.* might read its own lesson, but very likely
> I misjudge. But do you know, even if we throw *U. the R.* overboard,
> and whilst I endorse your opinion of the unavoidable and indeed
> much-to-be-desired unreality of women's work on many social mat-
> ters, I yet incline to include within female range such an attempt as
> this: where the certainly possible circumstances are merely indicated
> as it were in skeleton, where the subordinate characters perform (and
> no more) their accessory parts, where the field is occupied by a single
> female figure whose internal portrait is set forth in her own words.
> Moreover the sketch only gives the girl's own deductions, feelings,
> semiresolutions; granted such premises as hers, and right or wrong
> it seems to me she might easily arrive at such conclusions: and whilst
> it may truly be urged that unless white could be black and Heaven
> Hell my experience (thank God) precludes me from hers, I yet don't
> see why "the Poet mind" should be less able to construct her from
> its own inner consciousness than a hundred other unknown quan-
> tities.[21]

The keynote of this passage appears in its final sentence, where her description of "the Poet mind" is reminiscent of Keats's ideals of the chame-
leon poet and of "negative capability." But Rossetti's full commentary is
fascinating in several respects. For one thing, her rhetorical strategy is
cunning; more significantly, the strategy contributes to our understanding
of Christina Rossetti's patterns of behavior in life as well as the values that
inexorably support those patterns. Her apparent indifference to the publication of this poem is genuine and reflects her relentless quest for autonomy and self-sufficiency. This quest at last resulted in her virtually
complete withdrawal from active life, as well as her reliance upon "the
Poet mind"—the creative imagination that *generates* experience—to sustain her, to enrich her, and to serve as both a buffer and a mechanism for
mediation between her and the external world that threatened always to
encroach upon her independence.

Like her friend A. C. Swinburne in the second half of his career, Christina Rossetti became an ascetic aesthete, whose spheres of experience,

both secular and religious, were largely internal and imaginative. Both modes of experience were grounded, however, in external—socially and historically "real"—institutions, those of artistic tradition and the church. Her creative impulse oscillated between two ideal passions, whose respective objects were man and God. Both passions were intense and involved suffering, but the experience of them made her always accessible to exquisite, ethereal sensations of the spirit and emotions, sensations akin to the "wakeful anguish of the soul" memorialized by Keats. For Rossetti, only thralldom to art and to religion could generate ideal experiences of this sort that transform and transcend experience in the "real" world. Because of the capacities of the "Poet mind," Christina Rossetti could (unlike Keats) happily renounce life in the world for the superior life of the imagination. Such a life, of course, allows for the sublimation of physical ills and the manipulation of moral values, while ensuring freedom from censure, oppression, and responsibility. The religious aesthete, in life, enjoys the "paradise within" while preparing for the more permanent Paradise of the afterlife. For Christina Rossetti art and prayer became the primary modes, not merely of self-expression, but of *existence*. Rather than attempting to mirror reality, they subsumed it.

Much of Rossetti's poetry, therefore, abjures both didacticism and sincerity, actively resisting autobiographical readings. Many of her poems are self-reflexive, directing our interest to a fictive personality (as in "Under the Rose" and "Maude Clare"); to the process of creation; to specific literary works and general literary traditions that provide the enabling conditions for her own work; or to the created artifact itself, rather than to any external reality or extrinsic concerns. Such poems sometimes appropriately reveal her ability to be playful and ironically detached, to parody the kinds of issues her poetry raises. Such is the case in a poem like "Winter: My Secret." In it the speaker confesses to wearing masks:

> I tell my secret? No indeed, not I.
>
> .   .   .   .
>
> I cannot ope to everyone who taps.
> And let the draughts come whistling thro' my hall;
> Come bounding and surrounding me,
> Come buffeting, astounding me,
> Nipping and clipping thro' my wraps and all.
> I wear my mask for warmth.
>
> (*Poems*, 1:47)

And we are taunted in the last stanza:

> Perhaps some languid summer day,
> When drowsy birds sing less and less,
> And golden fruit is ripening to excess,
> If there's not too much sun or too much cloud,
> And the warm wind is neither still nor loud,
> Perhaps my secret I may say,
> Or you may guess. (47)

We find the clue to understanding this enigmatic poem in its self-parodic tone. The extraordinary fact here is that the work builds a thoroughly engaging relationship between the speaker and reader out of nothing substantial. No events transpire or are described, and even the "secret" has no extrinsic reference. The reader's curiosity and affection for the speaker are generated entirely by means of a fictive enigma that compels our interest. The poem thus becomes a commentary upon itself, upon the "secret" power of art. It also becomes, on an admittedly small scale, an exemplification of artistic perfection, a self-sufficing artifact. That such may be its design is indicated by the clear allusions, in the first three lines of the last stanza, to Keats's odes "To a Nightingale" and "To Autumn," both of which are concerned with acts of poetic creativity and the acceptance of created beauty (whether imaginative or natural) for its own sake.

Like many of Rossetti's poems, "Winter: My Secret" skillfully indulges in linguistic, formal, and metaphorical play. Such works by her are often unsettling because of their self-conscious experimentation and their aesthetic as well as substantive challenges to convention. Yet, unlike "Winter: My Secret," these works frequently close in conventionally settled ways—with the thematic, dramatic, or psychological tensions resolved. Closure, however, very often embodies a literal resignation of the rebelliousness of language, themes, and characterization within the works, a giving over of the potential evoked in the poems for destabilizing the conventional world (of language, social expectations, literary conventions) in which the poems are usually set.

The much-discussed dualisms, contraries, and oppositions in Rossetti's poems open up a space for decoding the world as we know it or expect it to be, and for encoding a new world, or a new apprehension of the old world's genuine truths or possibilities for change. But this potential is often abruptly truncated in the end by a deliberate reintroduction of the conventional world and expectations associated with it. Such a pattern of development enables varied and opposed reader-responses, including relief that conventional "order" or reality is restored; disappointment that a promised new order remains unrealized; or a synthesis of both of these responses, in which emotional, psychological, and aesthetic dissatisfactions evoked by the conclusion refocus reader attention on the generative space that the poem has made visible. The pattern even of Rossetti's nondevotional poems is thus eschatological: by drawing attention to the open-endedness of language, of literary traditions, of social or amatory possibility, she thrusts the reader into a new world that is at first disorienting. But he or she is finally delivered back into the old world that was briefly deconstructed or subverted. Some of Rossetti's best-known and most ambitious poems, including *Goblin Market*, *Monna Innominata*, and "The Lowest Room" operate in this way, as does her early novella, *Maude*. Even the larger structure of her volumes of poetry usually reflects this dialectical mindset, which insistently evokes a concern with purely aesthetic matters by means of the tensions it generates. The counterpoint between the "secular" and devotional poems in her three major volumes of verse (published in 1862, 1866, and 1881), for instance, effectively directs a reader's attention to the distance between the adventurous and the conventional, and finally to the issues of aesthetic modes and motives—of beauty and rhetoric—that displace other potential critical issues, such as thematics, biography, or history.

Even a wholly undisguised ideal of self-sufficing and self-reflexive artistry is clear in a number of Christina Rossetti's poems, though sometimes that ideal is equated with a more conventional ideal of beauty, as it is in "A Summer Wish":

> Live all thy sweet life thro',
>   Sweet Rose, dew-sprent,
> Drop down thine evening dew
> To gather it anew
> When day is bright:
>   I fancy thou wast meant
> Chiefly to give delight.
>
> Sing in the silent sky,
>   Glad soaring bird,
> Sing out thy notes on high
> To sunbeam straying by
> Or passing cloud;
>   Heedless if thou art heard
> Sing thy full song aloud.

Oh that it were with me
    As with the flower;
Blooming on its own tree
For butterfly and bee
Its summer morns:
    That I might bloom mine hour
A rose in spite of thorns.

Oh that my work were done
    As birds that soar
Rejoicing in the sun:
That when my time is run
And daylight too,
    I so might rest once more
Cool with refreshing dew.
                    (*Poems*, 1:42–43)

The symbols in this poem are open ended, of course, but the work might easily be seen to advocate the value of beauty created "chiefly to give delight," and its language insists on the exuberance, the "rejoicing," that accompanies the act of (poetic) creation: "Heedless if thou art heard / Sing thy full song aloud."

"A Summer Wish" also manifests a pervasive characteristic in Rossetti's poetry, both secular and religious: her use of what Ruskin in her own day designated "the pathetic fallacy." The projection by a speaker of a state of mind and emotion upon what would normally be seen as external, objective, and nonfeeling is clearly a solipsistic poetic strategy that reconstitutes "the world" and empirical conceptions of it. (Ruskin saw the practice as originating with the Romantics.) In this way intellectual and emotional responses displace "the world" and regenerate it as artifact or aesthetic object, "a thing of beauty." Ruskin described poets who in this way anthropomorphically impute life to the object-world as "Reflective or Perceptive." In that category he included Wordsworth, Keats, and Tennyson, poets whose work was necessarily limited by its very modes of generation and operation. As Harold Bloom has observed, Ruskin's "Perceptive" poets were later termed "Aesthetic" poets by Walter Pater. They comprise "not a second order but the only poets possible in the universe of death, the Romantic world" in which Rossetti lived.[22] Pater's description of aesthetic poets appeared first in his 1868 review, "Poems by William Morris," and became famous when published as part of the conclusion to *The Renaissance*.

Analysis of the body of Christina Rossetti's poetry in its proper literary-historical contexts demonstrates that, like Morris's work, hers embodies important characteristics of "aesthetic poetry," as Pater describes them, and it does so precisely by means of the dominant tensions upon which it is constructed: between beauty and death; between love of man and love of God; between the ephemeral and the eternal; between the sensory and the transcendent. It "projects above the realities of its time a world in which the forms of things are transfigured. Of that world [it] takes possession, and sublimates beyond it another still fainter and more spectral, which is, literally an artificial or 'earthly paradise.' It is a finer ideal, extracted from what in relation to any actual world is already an ideal" (Sambrook, 105).

What of course distinguishes Rossetti's work from that of Morris and other "aesthetic" poets is that her "finer ideal" is extrapolated largely from Christian texts and doctrine, especially from Neoplatonic reifications of Christian orthodoxy. Indeed, Plato's most distinctive characteristic according to Pater is equally Rossetti's: an "aptitude for things visible, with the gift of words, empowers [her] to express, as if for the eyes, what except to the eye of the mind is strictly invisible, what an acquired asceticism induces [her] to rank above, and sometimes, in terms of harshest dualism, opposite to, the sensible world."[23] For Pater, Plato is "a seer who has a sort of sensuous love of the unseen."

Rossetti's amatory poetry, also like that of "aesthetic" poets, often returns in setting, or merely in theme, to a "profound medievalism," in which "religion shades into sensuous love, and sensuous love into religion." Dominated by a frequently dreamlike atmosphere, poems from "The Convent Threshold," "Three Nuns," and *The Prince's Progress* to "An Old World Thicket," "Paradise," and *Monna Innominata* seem to operate largely in "a Kingdom of reverie": "Of religion this poetry learns the art of directing towards an imaginary object sentiments whose natural direction is towards objects of sense. Hence a love defined by the absence of the beloved, choosing to be without hope, protesting against all lower uses of love, barren, extravagant, antinomian. It is the love which is incompatible with marriage" (Sambrook, 106–7). In the great bulk of the poems, too, there appears "the continual suggestion, pensive or passionate, of the shortness of life . . . the sense of death and the desire of beauty; the desire of beauty quickened by the sense of death." Rossetti's poetry can sometimes even appear to assume "artistic beauty of form to be an end in itself" (Sambrook, 113).

In these Paterian terms, then, we can perceive aestheticism as a fundamental impulse in a large number of Rossetti's works. Her poetry does, of course, embody several major "thematic" concerns. These include the agonizing conflicts between erotic passion and love of God; the manifold beauties of nature; the need to renounce earthly love and all the world's vanities to await death and salvation. Yet these concerns are often subordinated to her interest in attaining an ideally beautiful world—a beatific paradise—or, equally often, to the process of generating such a world in beautiful poetry (or, self-reflexively, to beauty's multifarious powers and its historical precedents). Thus Rossetti is manifestly self-conscious about form in her poems, about the literary origins of her subject matter, and about language, the processes and effects of signification in reconstituting reality. As we shall see, however, such reconstitutions often operate on more than an aesthetic and self-referential level. They can also serve to present a critique of social reality, literary tradition, or the ideologies inherent in both.

THANKS to Rebecca Crump's systematic presentation of Christina Rossetti's poetry and the processes of its creation, we now can better understand the nature and effects of her aesthetic self-consciousness. We can also test our critical assumptions about Rossetti, and, seeing how they fail, begin to construct new ones. As the reward for our efforts, we may well revise our traditional image of Rossetti as a repressed, unfulfilled, patient Victorian woman who turned in despair from human love to the devout, chaste, and chastening love of Christ. This role she may well have filled. But beyond it she persistently and as a comprehensive vocation played out the role of artist, and her art in every sense sustained her. Her art—like that of Keats and, from formalist and aestheticist perspectives, that of the troubadours, Dante, the Petrarchans, and the early Tennyson, all of whom she deliberately assimilated—reflects the ideal of self-sustaining redemptive beauty. Ultimately, the interaction of the traditions that enthralled her resulted in the Keatsian tempering of a Dantean mysticism in which human and divine love merge and become fulfilled in art. These Romantic literary mythologies, I would argue, incorporated but transcended Christina Rossetti's merely personal experiences of love and religion. That her purely aesthetic sensibilities superseded even these mythologies allowed her to become one of the most enduring Victorian poets.

CHAPTER 2.

THE POETICS OF

"CONCISENESS"

W E can properly understand Christina Rossetti's artistic values and procedures only when they are placed within the relevant contexts of their development and implementation. Such contextualization also enables enhanced perceptions of the "meaning," relative canonical value, and reception history of her work. Reconstructing the aesthetic, social, and religious ideologies of Rossetti's immediate environment, out of which her poetics emerged, clarifies the interaction in her poetry among Pre-Raphaelite, Ruskinian, and aestheticist impulses. These impulses uniquely accommodated the High Anglican values with which she grew up and which increased in importance to her as she aged.

PRE-RAPHAELITE AND RUSKINIAN AESTHETICS

In an 1886 essay William Sharp, the devoted friend of Dante Rossetti and an intimate of the whole Rossetti family, made a statement that most present-day students of the Pre-Raphaelites would find startling. Four years after Dante Rossetti's death he compared the popularity of Christina Rossetti's poetry with that of her ostensibly more famous brother: "The youngest of the Rossetti family has, as a poet, a much wider reputation and a much larger circle of readers than even her brother Gabriel, for in England, and much more markedly in America, the name of Christina Rossetti is known intimately where perhaps that of the author of the *House of Life* is but a name and nothing more."[1] Although we might be skeptical that various prejudices molded Sharp's opinion, evidence suggests that it was widely shared. Two years later a writer in *Harper's New Monthly Magazine* insisted that "Christina Rossetti's deeply spiritual poems are known even more widely than those of her more famous brother."[2] Clearly at work in these evaluations is an implied distinction between popularity and notoriety. For most readers Christina Rossetti's poems were more accessible than those of her brother, but her work was also and distinctively more compatible with the fundamental aesthetic (as well as moral) values of its audience. As Sharp further noted, "she has all the delicacy and strength of her brother's touch, [but] she is free from the frequent obscurity or convolution of style characteristic of Dante Gabriel Rossetti in his weakest moments."[3]

Despite its stylistic divergence from her brother's poetry, Christina Rossetti's work was not anomalous among either generation of Pre-Raphaelites. Even Swinburne, whose antiorthodoxy and iconoclasm seem to conflict most profoundly with Rossetti's values, enthusiastically hailed her as the "Jael who led our hosts to victory." Throughout her poetry and much of her prose Christina Rossetti demonstrated true and deep affinities with Pre-Raphaelite aesthetic values. A careful examination of her poetry significantly increases our understanding of Pre-Raphaelitism as a major phenomenon of Victorian cultural change, one that is radically innovative but still deeply rooted in tradition. As much as her brother, Swinburne, or Morris, and certainly to a greater extent than figures more peripheral to the Pre-Raphaelite circle, Christina Rossetti produced works that appear to be dominated by the same aesthetic consciousness and literary values that make Pre-Raphaelitism the central but variegated movement which unintentionally spawned the aestheticism of the 1880s and 1890s.[4] Pre-Raphaelitism, in fact, influenced aesthetic thought in a way that made the movement central to the transition from the sentimental moral idealism of the Victorian mainstream to the variously nihilistic, skeptical, and ironic value systems that dominate modern poetry.

That most Victorians perceived Christina Rossetti as unequivocally Pre-Raphaelite in her poetic affinities becomes clear when we read through the contemporary reviews of her three major volumes of poetry, along with those of the *New Poems* and the collected *Poetical Works* edited by William Michael Rossetti and published after her death. The reviewers— men and women, English and American—focused on a variety of characteristics that dominate her poems and that they perceived as uniquely Pre-Raphaelite. These include her close attention to detail and her "pictorial" modes of representation; the medieval atmosphere and settings that appear repeatedly in her poems; her appreciation of the world's physical beauty and its expression in lush images; the intensity of her poems, which seems inseparable from their "sincerity"; her preoccupation with love and her experimental approaches to it as a dominant topos; and even her religious devotion, which at least two critics described as "aesthetic mysticism." With the important exception of devout religiosity, these characteristics of Rossetti's poetry are still considered major components of Pre-Raphaelitism.

In 1866 *The Nation* printed a review of Christina Rossetti's first two volumes of poetry. It begins, "any American reader who for the last two or three years has occasionally seen and admired the stray poems attributed to Miss Rossetti, being asked to describe them by one word, would have pronounced them Pre-Raphaelite."[5] Some thirty years later another American reviewer reprinted "When I Am Dead, My Dearest" and, in order to emphasize "the spiritual relationship of the author to the poets of the group sometimes styled 'Pre-Raphaelite,'" pointed out the resemblance between Rossetti's poem and Swinburne's "Rococo."[6] An anonymous commentator in *Book Buyer* asserted during the same year that Christina Rossetti's "poetic vision had all the glow and delicacy of invention which animates the canvas of the English pre-Raphaelite."[7] And with the greater self-consciousness of an historical critic, Edmund Gosse, writing the year before Christina Rossetti's death, carefully examined her relations to the other Pre-Raphaelite poets. He cited the seven poems she contributed to *The Germ* in 1850 and acknowledged the order in which the first well-reviewed Pre-Raphaelite volumes were published: by her, by Morris, by Swinburne, and finally by Dante Gabriel Rossetti. He then concluded:

> It is with these poets that Miss Rossetti takes her historical position, and their vigor and ambition had a various influence upon her style. On this side there can be no doubt that association with men so learned and eager, so daring in experiment, so well equipped in scholarship, gave her an instant and positive advantage. By nature she would seem to be of a cloistered and sequestered temper, and her genius was lifted on this wave of friendship to heights which it would not have dreamed of attempting alone.[8]

As we know, Dante Rossetti's influence *was* indeed crucial in inducing Christina to publish her volumes of poetry with some regularity. Beyond this knowledge, it is useful for the historical critic interested in patterns of cultural change to determine with some precision what aesthetic values and moral perceptions the brethren had in common; the extent to which these were seen by their contemporaries as commonplace or genuinely innovative; and finally the degree to which the brethren's reliance upon such values and perceptions, as they found them in literary models, shaped their own work and molded patterns of artistic practice that diverged from the mainstream, opening up new directions in art for their contemporaries and successors.

In *The Pre-Raphaelite Imagination* John Dixon Hunt has begun the large task of making such determinations. His catalog of the general "modes" of Pre-Raphaelite imagination quite properly includes

> First, the enthusiasm for what was seen as the picturesque and in-spiratory Middle Ages, to which most Pre-Raphaelites looked for subject matter and even technical knowledge. Second, growing out of these mediaeval interests, their introspection and the fashion in which they chose to communicate their meditations and the shadowy depths of the psyche. Third, their celebration of the noumenous; the search for a dialect of symbolism subtle enough to convey their ap-prehension of a meaningful world beyond exterior description and rational habits of mind. Fourth, an account of one specific symbol invoked by almost all of the Pre-Raphaelites—the famous image of a woman with large, staring eyes and masses of heavy hair. . . . Fifth, their attempt, often uneasy and hesitant, to accommodate themselves to a modern world of photography and scientific definition by means of realistic description, frequently of subject matter ignored by most other Victorians. There are, naturally, connections between these five topics, but they seem to represent distinct and important elements in the complex fabric of Pre-Raphaelitism.[9]

Significantly, Hunt concludes this catalog of elements by stressing that "all were imitated by the first Pre-Raphaelite brothers and are equally integral parts of the imagination of the 1890's."[10] Throughout his study, which carefully examines the evolution of the Pre-Raphaelitism of 1848 into the aestheticism of the nineties, Hunt focuses his attention primarily on the work of the painters in the first brotherhood and then on Swinburne, Morris, and Dante Rossetti among the poets of the second; he thus leaves Christina Rossetti to be perceived as a shadowy figure on the outskirts of Pre-Raphaelitism.[11] Most other modern commentators on the movement also usually evade any discussion of the relations between Pre-Raphaelit-ism and the aesthetics that inform Christina Rossetti's poetry. At least one of the most helpful modern critics of Pre-Raphaelitism, Cecil Lang, feels compelled to ignore consideration of her work under the general rubric of "Pre-Raphaelitism" when he is using it strictly as a critical, rather than an historical, term. Within his "descriptive definition" of Pre-Raphaelite writing as " 'visualized poetry of fantasy' or 'fantasy crossed with realism,' " he excludes "nearly all the poetry of Christina Rossetti."[12] Such exclusion is imperative, Lang claims, in the service of "nuances of appreciation" and making "nice discriminations."[13] As we shall see in later chapters, such discriminations do indeed need to be made in order fully to understand how Rossetti's poetry serves, ultimately, as a critique of the values of her era very different in focus and ideology from the critique supplied by her brother Dante, or by Morris and Swinburne. Yet, as is already clear, Rossetti's own contemporaries, when viewing the literature of their age *critically*, very often made no "nice discriminations" between the central aesthetic of her work and that which shapes the poetry of the other Pre-Raphaelites.

Victorian reviewers were sometimes distressed and sometimes delighted to see a new "school" of poets on the scene, as they discussed the accumulating volumes of Pre-Raphaelite verse during the 1860s, 1870s, and 1880s. Different critics emphasized different characteristics of the poets' works, but, as we have seen, most of them perceived in Christina Rossetti's poetry a special combination of traits that seemed uniquely Pre-Raphaelite. Reviewers did, for instance, discuss her poetry's "painterly" qualities, which in some cases enabled them to see continuity rather than disjunction between the work of the first brotherhood in the visual arts and that of the second in poetry. Richard La Gallienne, writing in *The Academy* (1891), insisted upon the "rich material symbolism" that pervades Christina Rossetti's verse. It has, he noted, "that 'decorative' quality, as of cloth of gold stiff with sumptuous needle-work design, which is a constant effect in the painter's poetry."[14] J. R. Dennet, in *The Nation* (1866), observed the extent to which, like that of the other Pre-Raphaelites, Christina Rossetti's poetry was "picturesque": "It was her practice to dwell elaborately upon details."[15] And in the same year the *Athenaeum*'s anonymous reviewer of *The Prince's Progress and Other Poems* argued that Rossetti redeemed her work only "by painting scenes which, though touched by the light of imagination, are yet as vividly true as if they were photographs of familiar objects."[16]

This critic also emphasized the medievalism that was, and still is, seen as essential to the Pre-Raphaelite artistic vision. His emphasis is implicit in his focus upon the stasis of the "pictures" Christina Rossetti "offers to us":

She does not unveil to us the face of humanity until the flush of human impulse has died away. We do not see the conflict of the heart, but the sequel of that conflict. Hence, there is in some of her best pictures the air of the cathedral rather than that of the world without. Her saints and heroes have not the stir and dust of life about them;

but they smile to us in a repose almost mournful, like effigies from a stained window or the sculptured forms of knight and dame in the coloured light of the aisle.[17]

Alice Law, in a eulogistic essay written for the *Westminster Review* the year after Christina Rossetti's death, also strongly insisted upon the importance of medievalism to the Pre-Raphaelites. She took care to point out that "it is this prevailing mediaeval Pre-Raphaelite attitude which so markedly separates Miss Rossetti's—as also her brother's—poetry from that of all her predecessors and contemporaries."[18] She explains:

The keynote of much of Miss Rossetti's word-music is its aesthetic mysticism and rich melancholy. [These qualities are] associated, . . . as in the works of her brother and other Pre-Raphaelites, with the deep mediaeval colouring, and quaint bejewelled setting of an old thirteenth- or fourteenth-century manuscript. The women of Miss Rossetti's pages have much in common with the long-tried Griseldas or ante-Renaissance type, with the slow fading Isabella of Boccaccio or the olive-wreathed, flame-robed virgins of the *Divine Comedy*.[19]

The Pre-Raphaelites' attention to picturesque detail, the medievalist atmosphere and settings, the pervasive melancholy of their works, and their awareness of their art's primarily Christian literary and pictorial origins—all are described in Law's commentary as also the fundamental characteristics of Christina Rossetti's poetry. In designating "aesthetic mysticism" as the composite final effect of these traits, Law unintentionally raised the issue that is ultimately central to any full understanding of Christina Rossetti's position in the Pre-Raphaelite movement, as well as to all accurate perceptions of the place Pre-Raphaelitism holds in the development of Victorian artistic culture away from its predominantly moralizing function toward the culture of aestheticism. This issue is religion.

Since her own era, Christina Rossetti's devout Christianity has often been seen as a characteristic that divides her from the other, avowedly non-Christian, members of the Pre-Raphaelite circle. This belief persists despite the distinctly religious "atmosphere" of much of the work produced by both generations of Pre-Raphaelites: its use of biblical images and typology; of religious figural language; and, more especially and pervasively, of medievalist backgrounds and settings that were seen by their early audiences to have clearly devotional, if not dangerously "Romanist," associations. When discussing Pre-Raphaelitism as an historical movement, we must remember that the first brotherhood was inspired largely by the sacramental aesthetic articulated by Ruskin in volume 2 of *Modern Painters*, and that—regardless of their personal religious beliefs—the artistic practices of the poets in the second brotherhood in many ways extended the artistic precepts of the first brotherhood.[20] Both generations produced works that rely upon the careful presentation of natural detail in order to convey transcendental Truth—hence, perceptions of their "aesthetic mysticism."[21] What Herbert Sussman has observed to be true for the painters of the first brotherhood holds also for the poets of the second. Their procedure is everywhere largely figural—or symbolist, to use language appropriate to current perceptions that their work does as much to foreshadow modern artistic and literary developments as to imitate medieval ones.[22] More clearly and concisely than any other commentator, Sussman explains the system of values crucial in understanding the central precepts of Pre-Raphaelite art as they derive from Ruskin's sacramental vision of the world.[23]

> Ruskin developed an aesthetic in which the facts of nature, of history, even of contemporary life can become through the intensity of their representation radiant with transcendent meaning. Within this view, realism and symbolism are not opposed but interdependent. In theory, at least, . . . the more accurately each minute fact of the phenomenal world is reproduced, the more forcefully the spiritual significance will shine through. Such an aesthetic depends upon faith in a sacramental universe. . . . To the religious scientist, the physical world is itself a form of language, a book written by God that men must decipher. To . . . Ruskin, the more clearly the artist can reproduce this language by creating the illusion of confronting the phenomenon directly, the more forcefully the content of this natural language will emerge. For the early Ruskin, the highest example of such an art is, of course, the work of Turner. The fusion of mimetic and religious criteria in Ruskin's defense of Turner's "Truth" provides the background for the sense of sacred mission informing the Brotherhood's own adherence to scientific realism and also helps explain Ruskin's comparison of the Brotherhood to the stylistically opposite work of Turner in his "Pre-Raphaelitism" pamphlet of 1851. (*Fact*, 4–5)

During the year before Ruskin's pamphlet was published, seven poems by Christina Rossetti appeared in *The Germ*.[24] The brethren's apparent receptivity to her work suggests that they perceived no radical disjunction between the "sacramental" values her poems displayed and their own aesthetic principles. Indeed, if Sussman's statement of the brotherhood aesthetic is correct, and if all the brethren had accepted Ruskin's aesthetics with his own soul-felt sincerity, there would have been no discrepancy. After all, Dante Rossetti was perennially fascinated by religious typology and iconography; James Collinson, Christina's sometime fiancé, was, as it turned out, inalterably Roman Catholic; Holman Hunt was as obsessively devout as Christina herself; art theorists like John Tupper who wrote for *The Germ* shared her own and Ruskin's sacramental vision of the world; and all of the brethren were devoted Ruskinians, regardless of their religious dispositions.[25]

Like the brethren, Christina read Ruskin with interest.[26] A great number of Rossetti's devotional poems, and many of her "secular" love poems as well, appear to be grounded in Ruskin's theories of typical and vital beauty. In volume 2 of *Modern Painters* Ruskin defines "beauty" theocentrically as "either the record of conscience, written in things external, or . . . the symbolizing of Divine attributes in matter, of . . . the felicity of living things, or . . . the perfect fulfillment of their duties and functions. In all cases it is something Divine; either the approving voice of God, the glorious symbol of Him, the evidence of His kind presence, or the obedience to His will by him induced and supported" (*WJR*, 4:210). Typical Beauty is "the symbolizing of divine attributes in matter" and, as George Landow makes clear, it "most directly partakes of the Holy."[27] A number of precise correspondences exist between Ruskin's ideas of beauty in its relation to the divine and those of Christina Rossetti.

In a passage originally intended for the second volume of *Modern Painters*, Ruskin revealed the experiential origins of his conception of the beautiful.[28] One July evening, observing a storm in the Alps, in an epiphanic moment he became aware of "the real meaning of the word Beautiful." The mountains, like "mighty pyramids[,] stood calmly in the very heart of the high heaven," while "the ponderous storm writhed and moaned beneath them." At that moment he came to understand that all things in nature which are "the type of God's attributes" are capable of turning "the human soul from gazing upon itself" and fixing the spirit "on the types of that which is to be its food for eternity;—this and this only is in the pure and right sense of the word B E A U T I F U L" (*WJR*, 4:364–65).

This is a common pattern of experience in Rossetti's poetry, as it is in biographical reminiscences that punctuate her prose writings.[29] Compare, for instance, this passage from *The Face of the Deep*: "Once, years ago in Normandy after a day of flooding rain, I beheld the clouds roll up and depart and the auspicious sky reappear. Once in crossing the Splügen I beheld that moving of the mists which gives back to sight a vanished world. Those veils of heaven and earth removed, beauty came to light. What will it be to see this same visible heaven itself removed and unimaginable beauty brought to light in glory and terror! auspicious to the elect, by aliens unendurable" (*Face*, 217).

Basic to Rossetti's view of all human perceptions, as to Ruskin's, is the belief that "All the world over, visible things typify things invisible" (*SF*, 244). She explains more fully that "common things continually at hand, wind or windfall or budding bough, acquire a sacred association, and cross our path under aspects at once familiar and transfigured, and preach to our spirits while they serve our bodies" (*SF*, 203). Rossetti's conclusions to her investigation of the relations among Nature, God, and human perception, which runs throughout *Seek and Find*, serve almost as a summary of the central tenet of Ruskin's moral and sacramental theory of art in *Modern Painters*, volumes 1 and 2. "To exercise natural perception," Rossetti maintains, "becomes a reproach to us, if along with it we exercise not spiritual perception. Objects of sight may and should quicken us to apprehend objects of faith, things temporal suggesting things eternal" (*SF*, 180).

Rossetti also reveals an implied acceptance of Victorian beliefs—variously articulated by Carlyle, Tennyson, Browning, Keble, Isaac Williams, and others—in the poet as prophet. But Ruskin, too, repeatedly returns to this essential doctrine of his theocentric aesthetic (even in works written during his long years of religious crisis); he repeats it not only in a larger number of different contexts but also more emphatically and in more diversified language than any of his contemporaries except perhaps Browning.[30]

Ruskin expressed his perceptions of the poet as prophet most forcefully between 1846 and 1856.[31] It was during these and the next five years that Christina Rossetti was most keenly interested in his work, his relations with the Pre-Raphaelite Brotherhood, and especially his patronage of her brother. (Ruskin was reading and evaluating her early poems in 1861.)[32] As Landow observes, Ruskin "takes quite seriously and quite literally the idea that to imagine deeply is to prophesy, and that to be an artist and poet is to be a prophet; and he can do this because his theory of the allegorical imagination derives from a theological tradition which holds that such a mode is necessary to accommodate divine truths to the human condition."[33] In volume 2 of *Modern Painters* Ruskin explains that the power of prophecy is the "very essence" of imagination (*WJR*, 4:225). Its "first and noblest use is, to enable us to bring sensibly to our sight the things which are recorded as belonging to our future state, or as invisibly surround us in this." Ultimately then for Ruskin, the penetrating, prophetic imagination of the artist works for the salvation of his or her audience.[34] Only the noblest men and women, of course, have such powers of artistic prophecy: the greatest are those who embody in their works the "greatest number of the greatest ideas" (*WJR*, 5:66). The gifts of such an artist cannot be acquired, however: "the greatness . . . is, in the most conclusive sense, determined for him at his birth" (*WJR*, 5:68). Though modest in her expression of the same doctrines, Rossetti does, nonetheless, quietly insist upon them: "Natural gifts are laid as stepping-stones to supernatural: the nobler any man is by birthright, if keen of insight, lofty of instinctive aim, wide of grasp, deep of penetration, the more is he able and is he bound to discern in the visible universe tokens of the love and presence and foreshadowings of the will of God" (*SF*, 180). Rossetti is not referring exclusively to poets or artists, but such figures would certainly be included among the "nobler" men she describes.

The language Rossetti uses here reminds us inescapably of the hierarchical and evolutionary metaphors that form the substructure of Tennyson's *In Memoriam*. Once again, however, we are forced to recall the extent to which hierarchical and historically typological modes of perception were pervasive among the Victorians. They are, in fact, crucial to Ruskin's commentary on Typical Beauty in *Modern Painters*, and they dominate Christina Rossetti's concluding remarks in *Seek and Find*. In volume 2 of *Modern Painters* Ruskin explains how proportion, as one aspect of Typical Beauty, is a principle fundamental to both the physical and the moral worlds. Sensitivity to proportion results in perceptions that are analogical, typological, and hierarchical. Ultimately, all things are thus sequentially unified, forming

> links in chains, and steps in ascents, and stages in journeys; and this, in matter, is the unity of communicable forces in their continuance from one thing to another; and it is the passing upwards and downwards of beneficient [*sic*] effects among all things, the melody of sounds, the continuity of lines, and the orderly succession of motions and times; and in spiritual creatures it is their own constant building up, by true knowledge and continuous reasoning, to higher perfec-

tion, and the singleness and straightforwardness of their tendencies to more complete communion with God. (*WJR*, 4:94–95)

Concerned with the achievement of unity with both God and Nature as a means to redemption, Rossetti moves toward her conclusion to *Seek and Find* by citing a passage from Romans that would equally well have served Ruskin's general purpose: "Nor will the contemplation of any creature, whether higher or lower than man in the scale of creation, avail us anything, unless by help of it according to its proper endowment and capacity we discern Jesus, in Whom 'dwelleth all the fulness of Godhead bodily' (Col. ii. 9): 'For the invisible things of Him from the creation of the world are clearly seen, being understood by the things that are made, even His eternal power and Godhead' (Rom. i. 20)" (*SF*, 326). Rossetti's and Ruskin's concern with hierarchical accessions and with emblematic correspondences between the material and spiritual worlds reveals the underlying preoccupation of both writers with the necessary orderliness of all art in which true beauty inheres. Ruskin repeatedly emphasizes the "orderliness of beauty or its dependence upon order."[35] His six "orderly" aspects of Typical Beauty frequently appear as themes, formal characteristics, or significant aspects of the emotional texture of Rossetti's verse. They include infinity (or incomprehensibility of the divine), unity, repose, symmetry, purity, and moderation (Ruskin's equivalent of the Tractarian value of "Reserve").

In addition to the clear parallels between Ruskin's ideas of Typical Beauty and Christina Rossetti's implicit as well as explicit aesthetic values, striking correspondences to his concept of Vital Beauty also emerge in her work. As Landow succinctly explains it, "Vital Beauty . . . is the beauty of living things, and it is concerned not with form [as Typical Beauty is] but expression—with the expression of the happiness and energy of life, and, in a different manner, with the representation of moral truths by living things." Landow properly emphasizes that "this second form of Vital Beauty is closely related to Ruskin's religious world-view, since these beautiful truths exist as part of a divinely ordained great chain of being in which each living creature plays a role as agent and as living emblem of divine intention." Full comprehension of Vital Beauty as it is embodied in living creatures depends principally upon "sympathy," the ability imaginatively to identify with the object of our interest or scrutiny.[36]

Rossetti's extraordinary capacity for sympathetic identification with her subjects and personae is manifest throughout her poetry, as is her common procedure of drawing moral or theological lessons from the experience of such sympathy. Her devotional poem "Consider the Lilies of the Field" (from *Some Feasts and Fasts*) is exemplary:

> Flowers preach to us if we will hear:—
> The rose saith in the dewy morn:
> I am not fair;
> Yet all my loveliness is born
> Upon a thorn.
> The poppy saith amid the corn:
> Let but my scarlet head appear
> And I am held in scorn;
> Yet juice of subtle virtue lies
> Within my cup of curious dyes.
> The lilies say: Behold how we
> Preach without words of purity.
> The violets whisper from the shade
> Which their own leaves have made:
> Men scent out fragrance on the air,
> Yet take no heed
> Of humble lessons we would read.
>
> But not alone the fairest flowers:
> The merest grass
> Along the roadside where we pass,
> Lichen and moss and sturdy weed,
> Tell of his love who sends the dew,
> The rain and sunshine too,
> To nourish one small seed.
>
>   (*Poems*, 1:76)

Employing the empathetic imaginative powers of the "Poet mind," Rossetti here demonstrates a Blakean capacity for observation and identification. Such sympathetic identification and a resulting awareness of "divine intention" is also characteristic of her nondevotional poetry, in which the moral precepts or teleological epiphanies are often expressed obliquely rather than directly, through symbol, allegory, or implication.[37] Rossetti's sympathetic imagination, often subject to retrospective interpretation through her typological and analogical habits of mind, appears most directly, however, in her devotional prose works.

Two passages from *Time Flies: A Reading Diary* typify her Ruskinian perceptions of Vital Beauty. In her entry for 30 March, Rossetti recalls an experience with a "pill millipede" that occurred one holiday at Penkill Castle. Surprised to discover the insect on her bedroom floor, she explains good-humoredly that "toward my co-tenant I felt a sort of good will not inconsistent with an impulse to eject it through the window." Having picked it up, she finds a "swarm" of baby millipedes in her hand. "Surprised, but resolute," she puts the family outside, but finds serious meaning in the episode. "Pondering over this trifle," she concludes, "it seems to me a parable setting forth visibly and vividly the incalculable element in all our actions. I thought to pick up one millipede and behold! I was transporting a numerous family." Thus, "if . . . we cannot estimate the full bearing of action, how shall we hope to estimate the full extent of influence?" Rossetti describes a similarly emblematic experience with nature in the entry for 26 June. It involves an encounter between a spider and his shadow witnessed at Meads: "They jerked, zigzagged, advanced, retreated, he and his shadow posturing in ungainly indissoluble harmony. He seemed exasperated, fascinated, desperately endeavouring and utterly helpless." She understands, of course, that the spider is terrified by his black "double" and vainly attempts to flee it. The interpretation of this simple "Parable of Nature," however, is sophisticated: "To me this self-haunted spider appears a figure of each obstinate impenitent sinner, who having outlived enjoyment remains isolated irretrievably with his own horrible loathsome self." And, "if thus in time, how throughout eternity?"[38]

Ruskin's ideas of Typical and Vital Beauty—worked out with greater systematization and in greater detail than Rossetti's—clearly provide a ground for understanding her habits of mind and her artistic practice in both prose and poetry. So do Tractarian poetics, as George B. Tennyson has correctly insisted (*VDP*, 198–213). But it is crucial to recall that Ruskin's aesthetic theories were deeply affected (if not instigated) by the Tractarian influences to which he was subject as an undergraduate at Oxford.[39] Just as the structures of poems and prose works by Rossetti (including *Time Flies*) often imitate the pattern of Keble's *The Christian Year*, so the systematic and detailed descriptions of plants appropriate to given occasions in *Called to Be Saints* mimic Ruskin's own descriptive botany throughout the first two volumes of *Modern Painters*. *Seek and Find* vaunts an even more characteristically Ruskinian organization, sequentially observing and providing emblematic analyses of the elements or the general categories of natural phenomena. In her book Rossetti sets out to articulate the various "truths" of nature. Ultimately, she and Ruskin (along with the Tractarians) attempt, with varying degrees of self-consciousness, to extend and redirect the general Romantic project of coming to spiritual terms with their sensory responses to the external world, its beauty in potential and its realized beauty, as well as its (ostensibly) failed or corrupt beauty. This project, of course, had its source for western writers in Plato, but more directly for the Romantics, for Ruskin, Rossetti, and the Tractarians, in medieval religious and aesthetic thought. Its culmination in the nineteenth century appeared, after the mediation of the Pre-Raphaelites, in the avant-garde work of Hopkins, Pater, Wilde, and the aesthetes.

ROSSETTI'S AVANT-GARDE POETICS

In examining Christina Rossetti's religious "divergence from the Pre-Raphaelite type," Edmund Gosse begins where most modern critics end when they attempt to deal with the issue. Such critics follow the pattern established by W. J. Courthope, who in 1872 wrote a lengthy and historically significant essay entitled "The Latest Development in Literary Poetry: Swinburne, Rossetti, Morris." Christina Rossetti, whose first two volumes of poetry had by this time been long in print, is conspicuous here by her absence. Courthope excludes her from his treatment of this school of "literary poets" because in describing the common characteristics of Swinburne, Rossetti, and Morris he focuses upon their "antipathy to society," the "atmosphere of . . . materialistic feeling [that] pervades the poetry of all three," their "atheism," their use of love as a theme with an "esoteric signification," and the poetic representation of beloved women not so much in the tradition of "the sainted lady of Dante," but rather "as the models of the painter's studio."[40] Courthope altogether ignores discussion of verbal play, the play with literary and iconographic traditions, and the experimental, often radical poetics that characterize Pre-Raphaelite poetry, especially that of Swinburne and Christina Rossetti.

Courthope's description of Pre-Raphaelite poetry excludes the work of Christina Rossetti because of his emphasis on the brethren's clearly subversive or antiorthodox traits. He perceives them as a disquieting avant-garde. Although, as we shall see, social subversiveness (but of different kinds) is a characteristic common to both Christina Rossetti's verse and that of the other poets, even an emphasis upon the less superficial and more essential traits of Pre-Raphaelitism I have already discussed would have compelled Courthope to number Christina Rossetti, along with Swinburne, Morris, and Dante Gabriel Rossetti, among these new "literary" poets.[41] Beyond the caustic social criticism Courthope apparently ignored in Christina Rossetti's work, many of its formal characteristics and moral arguments can be perceived—and indeed were perceived by some of her contemporaries—as a manifestation of new, avant-garde tendencies arising in Victorian poetry during the second half of the century.

The distinctive characteristics of Pre-Raphaelite poetry were, as I have shown, clearly described by their contemporaries and have been further cataloged by modern students of the movement.[42] More important, however, than any mere listing of the components of Pre-Raphaelitism, at least to the student of nineteenth-century cultural change, is developing an awareness of the special and highly self-conscious ways in which the Pre-Raphaelites simultaneously looked backward and forward in the framework of literary history. They revived aesthetic precepts they perceived as common to medieval and Romantic modes of imaginative expression. In revising these, they prefigured subsequent (aestheticist and modernist) modes that built upon and emerged from the revisionist poems the Pre-Raphaelites themselves generated. The Rossettis, Morris, and Swinburne thus constitute an avant-garde not primarily because they intentionally subverted contemporary values, but rather because their subversiveness resulted from a compulsion to disregard the topical so that they might pursue a transcendent order of beauty and experience which was figured in the phenomenal world and recorded in medieval and Romantic literature, but which resisted the constraints and limitations that any predominant concern with the immediate and the topical imposed.

What finally distinguishes the Pre-Raphaelite poets—as an avant-garde rebelling through revisionist reworkings of particular traditions in the artistic and literary past—from their contemporaries, is the timelessness of their work. Their obsession with mutability largely enforces upon them a withdrawal from active life and from the moral, social, political, and "modernist" psychological issues with which the work of their literary contemporaries was preoccupied. These issues were central, for instance, to the "novels with a purpose" of the day; to the poetry of alienation written by Arnold, Browning, and Tennyson, who often used settings from the past to facilitate commentaries upon present-day issues; and, of course, to the even more irrepressibly topical prose works of Ruskin, Carlyle, Arnold, and—in the moral and religious spheres—Newman. Although almost all of the major works written by these canonical writers have the power to transcend their topical subject matter, they frequently originated from contemporaneous concerns and events in a way that work by the Pre-Raphaelites does not appear to have done.

In a surprising number of ways the poetry of Christina Rossetti, unlike the work of these writers, fits the avant-garde pattern that generally characterizes Pre-Raphaelite art and poetry and that the aesthetes, beginning with Pater and extending through Yeats, seized upon as providing an essential background to and basis for their own work.[43] As we shall see in chapters 4 and 5, however, Rossetti's poetry does, even through its avant-garde strategy of withdrawal, obliquely provide a critique of the false values and false premises of topical work by her contemporaries. Moreover, the religious element of Rossetti's poetry, rather than conflicting with its avant-garde tendencies, uniquely contributes to them. Herbert Sussman quite correctly argues that "paradoxically it was the Ruskinian aim of reviving sacred art and restoring the high moral position of the artist that thrust the [Pre-Raphaelite] Brotherhood, within the cultural situation of mid-Victorian England, into modernist strategies and an avant-garde artistic role." Sussman further maintains that "it is the continuation of these avant-garde methods and of an avant-garde position, rather than similarities of style and subject matter" that constitutes "the essential link" between the two generations of Pre-Raphaelites.[44] It was, of course, Christina and Dante Gabriel—as poets of the first brotherhood and as exemplars of avant-garde aesthetic values and poetic procedures—who provided models for Morris, Swinburne, and the more peripheral second-generation poets. Perceptions of the link between the sacramental, Ruskinian aims of the first brotherhood and the ostensibly aestheticist predispositions of members of the second brotherhood are reinforced when we recall that, before their conversion to art by Rossetti, both William Morris and Edward Burne-Jones had intended to become priests.

If we keep clearly in mind the paradoxical relations between the revivalist, sacramental, and medievalist concerns of the Pre-Raphaelites on the one hand, and their innovative, avant-garde stylistic and formal procedures on the other, we can more fully understand the extent to which the work of Christina Rossetti is truly Pre-Raphaelite. Not only does her verse have in common with other Pre-Raphaelite poetry the characteristics cited by her contemporary reviewers, but it also pursues formal and stylistic novelty, as is particularly clear to modern readers of poems like *Goblin Market*.[45] Indeed, one crucial paradox of Pre-Raphaelitism—its use of tradition to create an art novel for its time—is as visible in the styles the poets experiment with and the poetic forms they employ as in their subject matter.[46] While introducing new, symbolist stylistic techniques and reversing or countering their readers' expectations through the use of extremely intense imagery or diffuse syntax, the Pre-Raphaelite poets also assiduously attempt to revive archaic literary forms such as the ballad and the sonnet sequence.

Such procedural dichotomies are, of course, conspicuous in the work of Christina Rossetti as well as in the poems of Morris, Swinburne, and her brother.[47] Her sonnet sequences, *Monna Innominata* and *Later Life*, and her numerous ballads exist in tension with her formally novel children's poems and works like *Goblin Market*. Her intertextual use of traditional forms is often revisionist and self-reflexive as well. The extremely self-conscious artistry of her sonnets, for instance, suggests that she, like her brother, believed that the very form of the love sonnet had, as its tradition developed, acquired an aura, an ambience, and a symbolic value that might be used perceptibly to redirect and even subvert the values traditionally associated with it. In her experiments with form, however, Christina Rossetti surpasses her brother and approaches the radical innovativeness of Swinburne.[48] In practice both of these Pre-Raphaelite poets might be seen to foreshadow a precept basic to the aestheticist poets of the 1890s and first expressed in radical form by Walter Pater in 1873. In his essay "The School of Georgione," Pater asserts a vital tenet of art for art's sake: "That the mere matter of a poem, for instance, its subject, namely, its given incidents or situation . . . should be nothing without the form, the spirit, of the handling, that this form, this mode of handling should become an end in itself, should penetrate every part of the matter: this is what all art constantly strives after, and achieves in different degrees."[49]

In 1893, the year before Christina Rossetti died, Edmund Gosse made a critical pronouncement that reflects the aestheticist vogue of admiration for the purely formal accomplishments of her poetry. By that time Gosse's exalted regard for her was shared by many prominent poets and critics, among them A. C. Swinburne, Gerard Manley Hopkins, Richard La Gallienne, Oscar Wilde, Arthur Symons, Lionel Johnson, and Theodore Watts-Dunton. Gosse described Rossetti as a writer "severely true to herself, an artist of conscientiousness as high as her skill is exquisite. . . . [She is] one of the most perfect poets of the age,—not one of the most powerful, of course, nor one of the most epoch-making, but . . . one of the most perfect." Gosse insists that she is "a writer to whom we may not unreasonably expect that students of English literature in the twenty-fourth century may look back as the critics of Alexandria did toward Sappho and toward Erinna."[50] Almost two decades later, Ford Madox Ford went so far as to canonize Christina Rossetti at the expense not only of her brother, but also of Arnold, Tennyson, and the Brownings. Ford concluded definitively, "Christina Rossetti seems to us to be the most valuable poet that the Victorian Age produced."[51]

Such commentaries by Gosse and Ford demonstrate the advancement of Christina Rossetti's reputation since her first systematic sallies as a poet into the public sphere. By 1859, with the help of Dante Rossetti, she had begun quietly searching for a commercial press to publish a volume of her poems. One of Dante Rossetti's first steps was to submit them to John Ruskin for evaluation. Ruskin's stodgy response is still notorious, but it is of special interest because, as we have seen, the aesthetic modes of Christina Rossetti's verse are largely Romantic and typological: precisely Ruskinian, in fact. In November 1859 Ruskin wrote back to Dante Rossetti that his sister's poems

> are full of beauty and power. But no publisher—I am deeply grieved to know this—would take them, so full are they of quaintness and other offences. Irregular measure (introduced to my great regret in its chief willfulness by Coleridge) is the calamity of modern poetry. The *Iliad*, the *Divina Commedia*, the *Aeneid*, the whole of Spenser, Milton, Keats are written without taking a single license or violating the common ear for metre; your sister should exercise herself in the severest commonplace of metre until she can write as the public likes. Then if she puts in her observation and passion all will become precious. But she must have the Form first.[52]

That Ruskin did not find the aesthetic underpinnings of Rossetti's verse familiar is both startling and intriguing, although his typically condescending attitude toward women may well have prevented him from looking beneath the surfaces of her poems. Further, apart from *Goblin Market*, we cannot know which poems he was given to read.[53] Similarly, Ruskin's rigid, traditional standards of poetic excellence did not allow him to appreciate the formal perfection of Rossetti's poetry that Gosse, Swinburne, Hopkins, and Wilde, for instance, so greatly admired. Nor is it surprising that the flexibility and pluralism of post-structuralist directions in critical discourse nearly one hundred years after their time have begun to reinvigorate an interest in the formal experimentations, the semiotic play, and the prosodic sophistication of Rossetti's poetry. The trend was begun (albeit grudgingly) by Stuart Curran with his 1971 acknowledgment of Rossetti as "an introspective and serious craftsman." Curran especially admired her "willingness to grapple with form" and "her most consistently remarkable poetic attribute," her "facility in rhyming and fitting thought into poetic form without a trace of awkwardness."[54] Only since 1979, however, has intensive formal and prosodic analysis of Rossetti's poetry begun to enhance our perceptions of her technical virtuosity. Crump's edition of her poems and Jerome McGann's description of Rossetti as "a great craftswoman" have led the way (*NER*, 240).

Subsequent commentators have disclosed and analyzed with special clarity Rossetti's careful use of anaphora, the density of her language, the typically "dialogic form" of her lyrics, and her highly sophisticated metrics, including the use of "restricted phrasal emphasis, long vowel sounds, heavy caesuras, tolling regularity of beat" and "displaced beats."[55] To these techniques must be added her calculated uses of abnormal syntax, frequent punning, deliberately archaic verbal and pronominal forms, intentional anticlimax, verbal repetition as musical (and thematic) leitmotiv, paradox, oxymoron, dialectical progressions, and rhetorical questioning. The "perfect surfaces" of her poems, so often acknowledged by critics, result from these techniques, but so do perfect thematic, psychological, and literary-historical or parodic "depths."

Most technical analysis of Rossetti's poetry has been conducted in specific thematic contexts and in the service of broader arguments about the ideological bases of her poetry (McGann), about the relative position of her work in the Victorian canon (Wilde and Rees), or about her position as a mediator of the Christian Victorian woman's resignation to mutability, unfulfillment, and the need for patient endurance (Rosenblum, Mermin, Blake, and Gilbert). Technical analysis of her poems outside of such thematic contexts, however, can yield important conclusions about her frequent prosodic strategies, their aesthetic grounds, their origins, purposes, and formal effects. The primacy of artistry and the subordination of theme in Rossetti's poetry should already be clear from chapter 1. The technical analysis of three neglected but representative poems that follows leads to corollary conclusions. "Autumn" is a short lyric about the transience of love; "Songs in a Cornfield" is a 117-line dialogic poem on the same subject; and "An Old World Thicket" is a long descriptive poem whose significant, largely epistemological focus is the relations between the self and the external world. All three poems embody Rossetti's typical formal and prosodic "irregularities" and experimentations, so admired by Gosse and disparaged by Ruskin.

Rossetti wrote numerous seasonal poems, including two entitled "Autumn," one in 1853 and one in 1858. Although both are prosodically experimental, the earlier poem not only shows closer attention to her ideal of poetic "conciseness," but it also demonstrates more effort at "filing and polishing," as she described her work to revise poems for *The Prince's Progress.*[56]

> Care flieth,
> Hope and Fear together:
> Love dieth
> In the Autumn weather.
>
> For a friend
> Even Care is pleasant:
> When Fear doth end
> Hope is no more present:
> Autumn silences the turtle-dove:—
> In blank Autumn who could speak of love?
>
> (*Works*, 310)

Readers of this poem may immediately observe the work's dominant irony—that its deeply serious theme, the death of love, seems counteracted by the lightness of its rhymes and meter. But that apparent theme is also belied by the poem's close on the accentually stressed, masculine rhyme-word "love." The bottom-heaviness of the two-stanza shape reinforces the effect, as does the irregular metrical alteration between trochaic and iambic feet: the metrical flights of the first stanza of this poem about mutability are slowed almost to stasis by the increased line lengths of stanza two and the comparative metrical regularity of the final couplet. Transience is artistically transformed into permanence, as is so frequently the case in Rossetti's verse. Complementarily, the archaisms "flieth," "dieth," and "doth" deliberately ground the poem historically, in effect undercutting the present tense of the poem but also extending its assertions backward in time, thus making them timeless or perpetual.

"Autumn" forcefully realizes Rossetti's ideal of conciseness. The absence of background information (about the speaker and his or her situation), as well as the lack of any logical and causal connections or explanations, invites projection and deduction as a primary mode of reader response. But the high level of prosodic and lexical control demands a focus on the universal rather than the personal, on the "silences" and "blanks" of love that finally celebrate its inexorable power rather than resignedly lamenting its inevitable death. That is, partly by means of the concluding couplet's weight, a simultaneously formal and thematic paradox emerges. The poem itself gives "silences" and "blank" love a new and poignant voice as well as a clear and visible form. The articulated absence generates a powerful presence, reviving the cares, hopes, and fears of love's past springs—its sources and seasons. *Not* to speak of love is impossible, as the form and the words of the poem demonstrate, thus answering its closing rhetorical question. The rhyme of the concluding couplet constitutes a deceptive act of closure. The speaker's (and poem's) refusal to be blank and silent suggests that Care, Hope, Fear, and Love itself exist in a perpetually autumnal state of dissolution, but because Fear of losing Love (the inspiration for art) never ends, Hope of its continuance or recovery is always present.

Like "Autumn," "Songs in a Cornfield" discusses transient love, but this later poem displays Rossetti's extraordinary virtues as a craftswoman even more strikingly than "Autumn," and indeed as fully as any other poem she composed, including *Goblin Market*. Its metrical complexities so impressed Sir G. A. Macfarren that he set the poem to music as a *cantata* during Rossetti's lifetime (*Works*, 484). From one of Christina's letters to Dante Rossetti during the preparation of *The Prince's Progress and Other Poems*, we learn that both he and Swinburne admired the poem. In this letter Rossetti claims "Songs in a Cornfield," finally, as "one of my own favorites." Presumably, therefore, it faithfully embodies her highest aesthetic values. It is also one of the very heavily revised poems of her 1866 volume.[57] The work was initially composed in 1864 and presents a cycle of unanswered love "calls." But for publication the second of the original "songs" in the poem was excised and replaced (with what in the published version appears as Rachel's song), and the final twelve lines of the original work were deleted altogether, not only making the conclusion more powerfully climactic but also making the entire poem self-reflexive.

"Songs in a Cornfield," like so many of Rossetti's poems (including "Three Nuns," *Goblin Market*, and "A Triad"), is wholly "dialogic" in Mikhail Bakhtin's sense of the word. Not only is the poem comprised of an interaction among the voices of four singers who sing three songs (only one in unison) and an objective narrative voice, but the very language and meter of these voices are heterogeneous and nonhegemonic. The poem presents multiple perspectives on mutable love. A further interaction—among resonances of appropriated texts from Tennyson, Keats, and Swinburne—along with a subtle interchange among complementary emblem systems accomplishes a destabilizing effect. That effect is replicated in the poem's metrical gymnastics and echoes the poem's themes of loss and abandonment.

The triadic and symmetrical structure of this poem begins with a description of Marian's sorrowful questions about her unreturning lover. It concludes with a speculative fantasy of his return after her death; the final stanza ironically employs the same rhyme words as the first stanza. After the narrative introduction to Marian's plight, May, Rachel, and Lettice sing a monitory song about devotion to "a false false love." The middle section of the poem (ll. 57–85), as these reapers "rest from toil," recounts Rachel's "second strain," an emblematic and potentially mythological lament at the departure of the "sunny," "wise," and "good" swallow. (Rachel's song is reminiscent of both the concluding stanza of Keats's "To Autumn" and Swinburne's "Itylus," which was published the same year as *The Prince's Progress*.) Next "listless Marian" sings, "like one who hopes and grieves," an elegiac song for the dead (herself? her beloved?). The final brief stanza envisions the return of the beloved, who will "not find her at all, / He may tear his curling hair / Beat his breast and call." His spectral appearance provides another questioning voice, disoriented and disappointed, which will remain unanswered.

In the themes and in the prosody of this poem there is no security, only discontinuity, dislocation, disorientation, displacement, and anomie, as we see from the first stanza:

> A song in a cornfield
>   Where corn begins to fall,
> Where reapers are reaping,
>   Reaping one, reaping all.
> Sing pretty Lettice,
>   Sing Rachel, sing May;
> Only Marian cannot sing
> While her sweetheart's away.
>   (*Poems*, 1:126)

The first line clearly echoes the poem's title, but with the destabilizing substitution of singleness for plurality, isolation for prospective choral unity. This effect is reinforced immediately by the irregularity of the iambic trimeter line, and later by the absence of any continuity or complementariness among the three songs as well as by the contradictory fact that Marian finally *does* sing. In the second, historically retrospective stanza, an irregular, breathless, jog-trot rhythm underscores Marian's sense of desperation, an effect that is only exacerbated when the narrative voice settles into aphoristic imperatives, parallel structures, and regular meter: "Let him haste to joy / Lest he lag for sorrow."

A ground of certainty does emerge in the triune song of May, Rachel, and Lettice, with its use of anaphora and refrain, its predictable meter, dependable rhymes, and its perfect symmetry. The three maidens confidently recommend taking "'wheat to your bosom, / But not a false false love.'" The alternating iambic trimeter and tetrameter lines describing nature's and the reapers' repose at noon seem similarly comforting, with their alternating masculine rhymes and lulling sibilants. But the mood changes abruptly with Rachel's song of the swallow.

> "There goes the swallow—
> Could we but follow!
>   Hasty swallow stay,
>   Point us out the way;
> Look back swallow, turn back swallow, stop swallow.
>
> "There went the swallow—
> Too late to follow:
>   Lost our note of way,
>   Lost our chance today;
> Good bye swallow, sunny swallow, wise swallow.
>
> "After the swallow
> All sweet things follow:
>   All go their way,
>   Only we must stay,
> Must not follow; good bye swallow, good swallow."
>
>   (*Poems*, 1:128)

The substance of Rachel's song recalls the violence and ruin that characterize Procne and Philomela's story; here, moreover, even after Procne's metamorphosis as an immortal bird and potential guide to transcendence, the swallow is unreachable. The swallow's role as an emblem of loss and inevitability is onomatopoeically drawn out by the hollow internal rhymes and the extended line lengths at the end of each stanza, and by the nearly spondaic finality of the bird's name itself, which is preceded by an irregular, often spondaic five-foot meter.

The stanzaic and metrical pattern is different and disorienting once again in Marian's song, with its masculine rhyming quatrains and truncated last lines.

> "Deeper than the hail can smite,
> Deeper than the frost can bite,
> Deep asleep thro' day and night,
>   Our delight.

"Now thy sleep no pang can break,
No tomorrow bid thee wake,
Not our sobs who sit and ache
    For thy sake.

"Is it dark or light below?
Oh but is it cold like snow?
Dost thou feel the green things grow
    Fast or slow?

"Is it warm or cold beneath,
Oh but is it cold like death?
Cold like death, without a breath,
    Cold like death?"
                    (*Poems*, 1:128–29)

The play with meter and with anaphora here is masterful. With the beginning and end rhymes of the first stanza and its regular iambs, Rossetti introduces a chant that culminates with the echoed syntactical patterning of the third and fourth stanzas and the conclusiveness of radical repetitions in the fourth. The harsh anomie of "cold like death" is echoed in the two final lines of the poem ("He may tear his curling hair, / Beat his breast and call"). These come as a sharp interruption of the lulling anaphora (expressed once again in multiple sibilants) of the last stanza's first six lines—three sets of syntactically identical conditional statements. The poem's fundamentally dialogic mode of discourse ironically emphasizes the absence of communication between lovers and among maiden friends. The reader's sensitivity to their isolation from one another because of conflicting values, expectations, and desires culminates with the poem's final, infinitely self-echoing monosyllable, "call."

Unlike "Autumn" and "Songs in a Cornfield," but like most of Rossetti's devotional poems, "An Old World Thicket" is comparatively regular in form and meter. Its innovation lies, rather, in the subtlety and ingeniousness of its larger structure. It is a colorful poem, dense with striking images that accumulate symbolic weight and typological resonances only with the last three stanzas, whose Christian iconography is unmistakable; in them a "patriarchal ram" leads "meek mild" sheep "Journeying together toward the sunlit west." By this point "heavenly harmony" has been restored to the speaker's previously anguished spirit.

"An Old World Thicket" is a thirty-six stanza, elegiac poem of epistemological and teleological exploration. Like Wordsworth's "Intimations Ode," this work traces the dialectical interaction between the stunning beauty of external nature and the "rage," "despair," and "weariness" of the solipsistic and suicidal speaker who, after stanza eleven, attempts in vain to close out nature's "jubilee." Very early in the poem she describes the visual and auditory spectacle of the ubiquitous forest birds:

> Such birds they seemed as challenged each desire;
>   Like spots of azure heaven upon the wing,
>   Like downy emeralds that alight and sing,
>   Like actual coals on fire,
>   Like anything they seemed, and everything.
>
> Such mirth they made, such warblings and such chat,
>   With tongue of music in a well-tuned beak,
>   They seemed to speak more wisdom than we speak,
>   To make our music flat
>   And all our subtlest reasonings wild or weak.
>
> Their meat was nought but flowers like butterflies,
>   With berries coral-coloured or like gold;
>   Their drink was only dew, which blossoms hold
>   Deep where the honey lies;
>   Their wings and tails were lit by sparkling eyes.
>   (*Poems*, 2:124)

But the "sweetness of [such] beauty" only moves the speaker "to despair." Although unable to blind herself to nature's beauty or to silence its symphony, she does succeed in projecting upon all its music her internal "sound of lamentation." The poem's peripeteia occurs finally in stanza twenty-nine, when abruptly "Without, within me, music seemed to be." The focus of the central half of this work (stanzas twelve through twenty-eight), unlike Wordsworth's "Ode," is thus upon the speaker's internal, purgatorial cacophony, described in stanzas fifteen and sixteen:

> Such universal sound of lamentation
>   I heard and felt, fain not to feel or hear;
>   Nought else there seemed but anguish far and near;
>   Nought else but all creation
>   Moaning and groaning wrung by pain or fear,

Shuddering in the misery of its doom:
My heart then rose a rebel against light,
Scouring all earth and heaven and depth and height,
Ingathering wrath and gloom,
Ingathering wrath to wrath and night to night.
(*Poems*, 2:125–26)

The illumination eventually achieved is expressed mutedly and only in symbolic or typological, rather than didactic and directly philosophical, terms. "An Old World Thicket" closes on the image of the "homeward flock" at peace, "journeying well,"

And bleating, one or other, many or few,
Journeying together toward the sunlit west;
Mild face by face, and woolly breast by breast,
Patient, sun-brightened too,
Still journeying toward the sunset and their rest.
(*Poems*, 2:128)

Although it closes with a focus on Christian typology, the poem is deliberately intertextual with its pervasively embedded verbal and thematic echoes of Keats, Wordsworth, and Tennyson. But as with all of Rossetti's revisionist poems, the author appropriates the language and themes of her precursors only to redirect them and provide a retrospective commentary upon the values their poems project.[58] Rossetti's poem begins in a secular, Keatsian vein, echoing the "Ode to a Nightingale"— "Awake or sleeping (for I know not which) / I was or was not mazed within a wood." It adopts and adapts lush Keatsian and early Tennysonian hedonistic image patterns. (Stanza ten reminds us of "The Palace of Art" as inescapably as stanza fourteen invokes "The Lotos-Eaters.") But Rossetti concludes her poem by rejecting the vocabularies and the secular epiphanies of Keats and early Tennyson, as well as the pantheistic revelations of Wordsworth, in favor of a quietly symbolic, traditionally Christian apocalypse; she leads her precursors, as it were, out of the wilderness of Romantic speculation.

Rossetti's traditional Christian solution to the Romantic and Victorian literary problem of alienation from nature and to the more characteristically Victorian problem of despair at life's meaninglessness is accomplished in formally unremarkable, iambic pentameter, five-line stanzas that contain a fourth tetrameter line. The stanzas use four different a-b rhyme schemes that alternate irregularly. Just as the thirty-six stanza structure of the complete poem suggests trinitarian concerns, however, so the use of combinations of five in the meter and stanzaic form may reflect Rossetti's play with medieval numerology, in which five is perceived as a "perfect" number (Christ's wounds) or the "quintessence." Further, if the poem's title and the speaker's situation ultimately present a revisionist perspective on Eden and refer to man's postlapsarian loss of direction, this poem's pentastiches may be seen to allude formally to Israel's (mankind's) initial recovery of direction by the end of the Pentateuch. That Christina Rossetti indulged in such formal puns is apparent in many poems, most notably in the fourteen-sonnet *Monna Innominata*, which she designated a "sonnet of sonnets."

Locally and generally the structure of this poem, with its central image patterns of sound and sight, is dialectical rather than dialogic. From the opening words ("Awake or sleeping"), contraries—and oxymorons—proliferate. These include oppositions between despair and hope, meaningless natural phenomena and meaningful symbol, external and internal, birth and death, sun and moon, hope and fear, silence and sound, mourning and jubilee, depth and height, peace and strife, light and darkness, strength and weakness. But just as inner and outer music are harmonized after stanza twenty-eight, and as the visual becomes visionary at "glorious" sunset, so all dialectical oppositions are implicitly synthesized. The movement of the poem as a whole is from the external to the internal, but finally to the eternal that incorporates—and reconciles—both.

A Wordsworthian marriage of mind and nature thus occurs by the end of the poem, where imagery of the golden sunset symbolizes not only the unity of the external world, but also the unificaton of the internal with the external:

> Each twig was tipped with gold, each leaf was edged
> And veined with gold from the gold-flooded west;
> Each mother-bird, and mate-bird, and unfledged
>   Nestling, and curious nest,
> Displayed a gilded moss or beak or breast.
>
> *(Poems,* 2:128)

Clearly in Rossetti's poem, however, it is not the mind that is "A thousand times more beautiful" than the earth "on which it dwells." Rather, from the start of the poem "right-minded" nature serves as a potential revelation of teleology and of nature's "fabric more divine." The challenge for the speaker is not only to recognize but also to synthesize nature's glory. The epistemological process that must occur, then, is not one of projection but one of "awakening" from the sleep of self to the divine and teleologically assured synthetic and synesthetic interaction—expressed in musical, visual, and marital imagery—of all natural phenomena, including the mind of man. Indeed, the pattern here is more reminiscent of Coleridge's "Frost at Midnight" than the last lines of the *Prelude*, book 14. Stanzas twenty-nine through thirty-two of Rossetti's poem read,

> Without, within me, music seemed to be;
>   Something not music, yet most musical,
> Silence and sound in heavenly harmony;
>   At length a pattering fall
> Of feet, a bell, and bleatings, broke through all.
>
> Then I looked up. The wood lay in a glow
>   From golden sunset and from ruddy sky;
> The sun had stooped to earth though once so high;
>   Had stooped to earth, in slow
> Warm dying loveliness brought near and low.
>
> Each water drop made answer to the light,
>   Lit up a spark and showed the sun his face;
> Soft purple shadows paved the grassy space
>   And crept from height to height,
> From height to loftier height crept up apace.
>
> While opposite the sun a gazing moon
>   Put on his glory for her coronet,
> Kindling her luminous coldness to its noon,
>   As his great splendour set;
> One only star made up her train as yet.
>   (*Poems*, 2:127–28)

Just as the poem echoes, redirects, and "marries" earlier, Romantic texts, so the objects and elements of nature in these stanzas and the one that follows mirror, echo, redirect, and marry one another in muted apocalypse. The divine text of nature becomes a paradigm not only for the text of this poem but also for the cumulative texts of all (Romantic) poets seeking revelaton of ultimate realities. Similarly, the "text" (lesson) of this poem is echoed in the prosody of its stanzas, which are dense with intro-

active end rhymes, internal rhymes, assonance, and consonance. The poem's multifarious oppositions are undercut and unified finally by the musical harmonies in which they are expressed.

"An Old World Thicket" is a subtle showpiece of Rossetti's characteristic technical procedures (and her thematic concerns), but it is also an embodiment of her fundamentally Ruskinian aesthetics, in which Typical and Vital Beauty interact. This work, like many of her poems, illustrates the basis of Rossetti's aesthetic thought in the convergence of Ruskinian art theory, Tractarian and medievalist poetics, and the typological habits of mind basic to all of these. Any detailed analysis of the apparent theoretical grounds of Christina Rossetti's aesthetics and poetic practice might well begin by observing the ways in which the two dominant metaphors (music and golden sunlight) in "An Old World Thicket" evoke the central tenets of Ruskinian aesthetics, as well as the typological mindset underlying those aesthetics and much mid-Victorian thought on poetry, painting, and theology.

Early in *Seek and Find*, in a context obviously appropriate to analysis of the thematic structure of "An Old World Thicket," Rossetti discusses the ordinarily deficient visual capacities of man, which can be improved only with the help of the "eyes" of faith:

> Faith accepts, love contemplates and is nourished by, every word, act, type, of God. The Sun, to our unaided senses the summit of His visible creation, is pre-eminently the symbol of God Himself: of God the giver, cherisher, cheerer of life; the luminary of all perceptive beings; the attractive centre of our system. The Sun, worshipped under many names and by divers nations, is truly no more than our fellow-creature in the worship and praise of our common Creator; yet as His symbol it none the less conveys to us a great assurance of hope. (*SF*, 34)

Not only does this passage serve as an obvious gloss on Rossetti's poem, but it also reveals her characteristic concern with symbolic or typological correspondences between phenomena, on the one hand, and "moral" (or theological) interpretation of them, on the other. This concern is ubiquitous in Rossetti's poetry and prose, and although it is too pervasively Victorian to derive exclusively from any single writer or text, her readings in Ruskin certainly would have provided a clear-minded, authoritative theoretical grounding for her lifelong poetic practice.

AESTHETICISM

Despite the Ruskinian aesthetic values that Christina Rossetti clearly shared with the members of the first brotherhood, commentators on her volumes of poetry published during the most productive years of Morris, Swinburne, and her brother had to strain somewhat, as modern critics do, to understand how the religious dimension of her poetry is fully compatible with the nonreligious, purely aesthetic values of the second generation of Pre-Raphaelite poets. Yet such values do obtrude in her poetry, and her reviewers clearly intuited some authentic compatibility between them and her religious devotion, struggle as some of these critics must to articulate it.

J. R. Dennet, for instance, was less than clear-minded about possible relationships between the orthodox religious element of Rossetti's verse and the more general values of the Pre-Raphaelites, but he did perceive that their "sensuousness" and Christina Rossetti's own is somehow reconciled in her poetry with religious devotion. After pronouncing her poems unequivocally Pre-Raphaelite, he observed that

> her pieces [are] full of that phase of religious feeling which contemplates, not without sentimentality, God made man, which, we may almost say, agonizes at the feet of a Saviour who suffers and yearns, who is bleeding and aching with fleshly wounds. To have attributed to Pre-Raphaelitism such qualities as these would, perhaps, have been to give it a definition rude or incorrect. But whether right or wrong . . . it was not a mistake to fix upon these as the distinguishing features of Miss Rossetti's poetry, and if with these we name a pervading sensuousness, we have the list of its essential characteristics complete.[59]

As Herbert Sussman and many other critics have pointed out, precisely this apparent paradox of sensuous spirituality is central to the Pre-Raphaelites, sensory phenomena being looked upon by them and by Ruskin as figures of transcendent Truth.

Unlike Dennet, Alice Law, writing during the heyday of aestheticism, discerned no conflict between Rossetti's religiosity and the work of the other Pre-Raphaelites, primarily because she perceived medievalism as the essential feature of Pre-Raphaelite art and poetry. Aware that the central movement of Rossetti's poems is repeatedly from sensuality and *eros* to spirituality and *agapē*, Law was confident that the same modulation of one type of passion into another, higher type was characteristic of Pre-Raphaelitism, and, of course, of the medieval writers the Pre-Raphaelites admired and imitated. Law was apparently untroubled by the issue of orthodoxy, as she described "how Miss Rossetti, like her medieval prototype, sought and found consolation for the unsatisfied yearnings of the heart in devout prostration of the spirit, and the up-lifting of the soul to God. As in the Pre-Raphaelite heroine, the earthly love became transfigured by the heavenly; the overflowing of human emotion found an outlet in religious ecstasy."[60]

Like Law, an anonymous reviewer for *The Critic* in 1895 found unproblematical the transposition of earthly, sensuous passion to a spiritual plane, a movement that occurs repeatedly in Christina Rossetti's poetry. Comparing Dante Gabriel Rossetti's work with that of his sister, this critic explains that "their characters as artists are singularly alike. Both think in sensuous, concrete images. . . . Both are strongly attracted by moral ideas, which, with rare exceptions, are used by the brother as poetic material, but which finally become dominant in the sister, though to the weakening of her art. Sensuousness is the key-note in the poetry of both. . . . The 'Rossetti virus' is a peculiar mingling of sense and soul in a sort of mystical aestheticism."[61] It is striking that this reviewer should have hit upon the same terms, in describing the Rossettis' "mystical aestheticism," that Alice Law used to describe the unique character of such poetry. The coincidence is understandable, however, because the simultaneously concrete and spiritual, aesthetic and mystical, effects of much Pre-Raphaelite poetry result largely from the poets' use of phenomenal reality as a vehicle for their quest after the ideal. The typological mindset and procedures that they most often employ in this quest are rooted in religious tradition and in medieval literature. Each generation of Pre-Raphaelites either pervasively or sporadically imitated such literature with a high degree of self-consciousness.

Writing two years before Alice Law and the American reviewer of *The Critic*, Edmund Gosse discussed more fully than either of them the problem that Christina Rossetti's religious devotion seems to pose for those who wish to perceive her as wholly Pre-Raphaelite. He acknowledged that "critics have taken for granted that she was a satellite, and have been puzzled to notice her divergences from the type." Candidly, he further explains,

> of these divergences the most striking is the religious one. Neither Gabriel Rossetti, nor Mr. Swinburne, nor Morris has shown any decided interest in, the tenets of Protestantism. Now Miss Christina

Rossetti's poetry is not merely Christian and Protestant, it is Anglican; not her divine works only, but her secular also, bear the stamp of uniformity with the doctrines of the Church of England. What is very interesting in her poetry is the union of this fixed religious faith with a hold upon physical beauty and the richer parts of nature which allies her with her brother and their younger friends. She does not shrink from strong delineation of the pleasures of life even when she is denouncing them.⁶²

Gosse did not ultimately see Rossetti's devout Anglicanism as an element that set her apart from the other Pre-Raphaelites. Rather, he perceived it as a "very interesting" aspect of the work she accomplished in her true "historical position" as a Pre-Raphaelite. His language suggests his belief that her poetry's religiosity visibly adds a dimension to Pre-Raphaelitism that illuminates that movement's pervasive aesthetic.

A crucial system of values in Christina Rossetti's aesthetics—derived from the tradition of courtly love, as well as Petrarchan and Dantean poetry—was absent from Tractarian poetics and sublimated in Ruskin. The importance of this tradition to Rossetti resulted in the apparent bifurcation of her creative energies and the division of her works into the traditional "secular" and "devotional" categories. Yet every careful reader of her poetry must observe that the two categories very often overlap or modulate into one another, as is especially clear in works like *Goblin Market* (with its overt patterns of Christian symbolism), "Three Nuns," "The Convent Threshold," "Twice," and *Monna Innominata*. Such poems suggest that the "division" between the two spheres of Rossetti's creative activity are reconciled in a holistic aesthetic that comes out of her grounding in medieval poetry and medieval theology.⁶³ Unlike Gerard Manley Hopkins, who shared his imagistic conventions exclusively with the movement Jerome Bump has identified as "religious medievalism," Christina Rossetti derived her poetic practice also from the "rival" variety of medievalism: what Bump describes as "the secular religion of courtly love."⁶⁴ Clearly, however, among the writers who were the foremost practitioners in verse of the courtly love ethos (Petrarch and Dante, for instance), the secular—especially the erotic—and the religious interpenetrate, often becoming metaphors for one another. This is commonly the case in Rossetti's ostensibly secular poetry concerned with obstacled or unfulfillable love.

Ultimately, Christina Rossetti's medievalist combination of *eros* and *agapē*, of the phenomenal and the ideal, of the sensual and the spiritual, became central to the art of the aesthetes in the 1880s and 1890s. Along with Pater and her brother, she must be seen finally as an unwitting mediator between Ruskinian and decadent aesthetics. As Graham Hough reminded readers forty years ago, "the attempt to find a connection between art and religious experience is a major preoccupation of the later nineteenth century. . . . [Dante] Rossetti's poetry is filled with Christian imagery; Pater is obsessed with the conflict between pagan and Christian religious ideals, and many of the aesthetes of the nineties found that the worship of beauty could be satisfactorily consummated only within the Catholic Church. A French critic in the nineties wrote a book on *Ruskin et la religion de la Beauté*."[65]

As we have seen, for Ruskin the perception of the beautiful is contingent upon the perception of the divine. Such perception transforms our consciousness of the world around us, as well as our desires, motives, goals. That is, the "radiance" that results from perceptions of divine immanence is shed (as in "An Old World Thicket") upon all perceived phenomena and informs all experience. Similarly, for Christina Rossetti "Love" (which Ruskin does not discuss in the context of aesthetics) is an overwhelming attraction to what is perceived as the beautiful (or ideal). Not surprisingly, in "The Key" to *Called to Be Saints* Rossetti is effusive in using the terminology of aesthetics to describe the saints (men translated to the realm of the ideal) she will discuss in her book:

> How beautiful are the arms which have embraced Christ, the hands which have touched Christ, the eyes which have gazed upon Christ, the lips which have spoken with Christ, the feet which have followed Christ. How beautiful are the hands which have worked the works of Christ, the feet which treading in his footsteps have gone about doing good, the lips which have spread abroad His Name, the lives which have been counted loss for Him. How beautiful upon the mountains were the feet of them who brought glad tidings . . . how beautiful was the wisdom of those unlearned and ignorant men, whose very opponents felt they had been with Jesus.[66]

In many of her "secular" poems, obstacled earthly love is often transposed into divine love, *eros* into *agapē* (as it is in Petrarch, Dante, and many of their troubadour precursors) without requiring alterations in language and image patterns. ("Twice" and *Monna Innominata* are typical of these.) Many of Rossetti's love poems, however, serve to expose misguided, that is, transient earthly ideals of love; in doing so, they savor love's absence, love's decay, or its demise; often they express the laments of love's deluded victims. In every case the focus is upon earthly love's inadequacy and the impossibility of achieving genuine fulfillment through it, as Rossetti suggests in "The Heart Knoweth Its Own Bitterness": "How can we say 'enough' on earth— / 'Enough' with such a craving heart?" Only religion provides dependable idealities. "O Jesus, quicken me. . . . / O Jesus, rise in me. . . . / O Jesus, drink of me."

Because the aesthetes, too, found ultimate satisfaction only in idealities, it is no surprise that, as John Dixon Hunt has observed, Rossetti's "piety and moral fervour were no obstacle to [their] appreciation [of her]."[67] Indeed, John Heath Stubbs has quite properly insisted that Pater, "the real philosopher of the later Aesthetic Movement [in England]," held much in common with Christina Rossetti's and with Ruskin's "aesthetic Hellenism [and] a religiosity whose source must be looked for in the 'ritualist' tendency which had followed up the Oxford Movement, and which had affinities, also, with the aesthetic Catholicism of Chateaubriand."[68] Pater's 1868 review, "Poems by William Morris," located the source of Morris's poetry (and by extension much Pre-Raphaelite poetry) in the second of two major strains of the medieval spirit, those of "mystic religion" and "mystic passion." These correspond, of course, to Jerome Bump's "rival" varieties of medievalism. Like Morris's early work, much of Christina Rossetti's poetry of disappointed love originates in this medievalist strain of "mystic passion," where the "strong suggestion" of "a choice between Christ and a rival lover" often emerges, and where "religion shades into sensuous love, and sensuous love into religion" (Sambrook, 106). As we have seen, Pater described the Provençal sources of Morris's poetic topoi in terms that apply equally well to much of Christina Rossetti's love poetry: "Earthly love . . . becomes a prolonged somnambulism. Of religion it learns the art of directing towards an imaginary object sentiments whose natural direction is towards the objects of sense. Hence a love defined by the absence of the beloved, choosing to be without hope, protesting against all lower uses of love, barren, extravagant, antinomian" (Sambrook, 106–7).

For Christina Rossetti, even more than for Morris, the imaginative energies of the artist must be directed to capturing all "higher" uses of love in order to awaken perceptions in the reader of that which is truly beautiful and therefore ideal. With Rossetti, as with Ruskin and the aesthetes, the perception of beauty does result in "love," that is, an irrepressible desire for the ineffable and unattainable, for the divine spiritual essence of material beauty. Ultimately, therefore, the effects of *ascesis* and *aesthesis* become identical and interchangeable in discourse. Pater and his followers perceived the beautiful as divine; Ruskin and Rossetti perceived only the Divine, finally, as beautiful.

In Rossetti's poetry the union of the sensual and the spiritual, the quest to attain an ideal of transcendent love and beauty, and the frequently medievalist atmosphere appealed to the aesthetes. But other components of her work powerfully attracted them as well. They admired the formal sophistication of her poems; her use of commonplace details for symbolist purposes, often to achieve noumenal effects; the lushness of her imagery; the melancholy moods of many of her poems whose focus is on mutability and death; and the literary self-consciousness—one might even say the parodic quality—of many of her poems.

Rossetti's aestheticist critics believed that in her poetry she had made the full dimensions of her matter inextricably dependent upon the forms and styles she employed and therefore ultimately ineffable outside of the poems themselves. This belief is clear in Alice Law's opening comments on Rossetti's poetry. "Like some magic web," she explains, "it seems woven of a substance so elusive, intangible, and of such an almost gossamer tenuity as defies handling, and constitutes at once the critic's ecstasy, wonder, and despair." Law attempts to be precise on this point. When she first read Rossetti's poems, the beauty of them, she insists, "danced ever before me, but, like the phantom of her own *Fata Morgana*, it eluded capture. The absence of all harsher and more rugged qualities, of all topical didacticism, of rigid philosophical system on which we can lay hold, their seeming artless, yet aesthetic and finished perfection, all these combine to give the poems an air of elevated inaccessibility which renders critical approach difficult." In the following paragraph Law modulates, appropriately, into fully Paterian rhythms and diction in order to describe her responses to Rossetti's poetry. The influence of Pater's conclusion to *The Renaissance* is unmistakable here: "We are all at times conscious of the passing of certain swift and fugitive emotions which only a very gifted minority among us is qualified to express. Miss Rossetti is one of these; she has . . . condensed into word-crystals the mind's melancholy vapours, its evanescent clouds of dream, that indescribable 'nothingness' which eluding our clumsier mental grasp floats tantalisingly about us, but threatens to melt imperceptibly at a touch."[69]

Striking in these passages is the extent to which Law, like many other critics of Rossetti in the 1890s, was sensitive almost exclusively to the aestheticist effects of her poetry. Similarly significant to the historical critic is the fact that after Rossetti's death the writers most eager to champion her work were aesthetes themselves or had very clear affinities with the aesthetic movement and its central figures. They included Arthur Symons, Edmund Gosse, William Sharp, Richard La Gallienne, and Oscar Wilde, in addition to Alice Law.

These writers, and other more modern commentators as well, focus special attention upon two aestheticist characteristics in Christina Rossetti's work beyond its artistic polish, its "finished perfection." Both are, clearly, extensions of other traits peculiar to Pre-Raphaelitism. The first characteristic is Rossetti's sometimes almost monotonous attention to the commonplace, which has obvious connections with the Ruskinian and Pre-Raphaelite concern for a truthful representation of natural detail. And the second characteristic—the Keatsian, melancholy gloom that dominates a great number of her poems—is often also the pervasive mood of her brother's poetry, as well as that of works by Swinburne and Morris, although these two younger poets energized their despondency in various ways.

Christina Rossetti's preoccupation with the details of quotidian experience is often apparent in the images, settings, and events of her poems, but it is far more pervasive in her prose writings: her letters, her devotional commentaries, and her single collection of short stories with the appropriately prosaic title, *Commonplace and Other Stories* (1870). John Dixon Hunt has quite properly observed that the stories in this volume foreshadow the "'vocabulary' of urban description[,] . . . the accompanying chorus of grief and pain," and the "essentially unheroic" emphasis upon "commonplace circumstances" that dominate the fiction of the 1890s in England and are usually seen to originate from late nineteenth-century French realism, with its *symboliste* qualities. Indeed, as Hunt mentions, the reviewer of *Commonplace* for the *Sunday Times* (12 June 1870) compared Rossetti's work to modern French fiction. Hunt himself sees significant resemblances between her stories and such aestheticist fiction as Arthur Moore's "Second Thoughts," Ella D'Arcy's *Monochromes*, and the anonymous "Three Stories" of *The Yellow Book*, volume 2.[70] Yet the emphasis on realistic details in Rossetti's fiction, while portending such fiction of the 1890s, clearly looks backward as well, growing out of the figural tendencies and the essentially typological mentality that link Christina Rossetti's literary values to the aesthetics of the first Pre-Raphaelite Brotherhood and the first two volumes of Ruskin's *Modern Painters*. The central images and minor details in Rossetti's stories are thoroughly pedestrian and realistic, as are the settings of many historicist and literary paintings by members of the first brotherhood. It was, in fact, precisely the realistic representation, the "reduction" of sacred history to the level of quotidian detail and mundane experience, that invited such attacks upon early works by Pre-Raphaelite artists as the now-notorious critique by Dickens of John Everett Millais's *Christ in the House of His Parents*. Without the benefit of Millais's obviously exalted subject matter, Christina Rossetti typically assumes, in the background of her stories, the potentially transcendental value of even the most ordinary images and events.

Rossetti's attention to the prosaic details of life, however, looks backward not only to its sources in Ruskin and the aesthetics of the first Pre-Raphaelite brethren, but also, and even more fundamentally, as we shall see, to the hermeneutics of medieval Christian theology. Yet in admiring and perhaps even imitating Rossetti's performance in *Commonplace* and her manifestly symbolist poems, aestheticist writers of the nineties seemed to ignore the ultimately sacramental purpose behind her ostensibly aestheticist practices. As is already clear, her intent was not to be an aesthete, but rather, in a minor key, to be a prophet.

Rossetti's aestheticist critics were able to underplay the seriousness of her Christian values, perhaps, because they so greatly admired her symbolist uses of the commonplace details of life and her lush, Keatsian depiction of melancholy states of mind. The intense representation of such moods is insistent in nearly all her work, as is her preoccupation with death. (See, for instance, "Rest," "The Dead Bride," "When I Am Dead, My Dearest," "The Dream," "Wife to Husband," "Night and Death," "Death's Chill Between," "The Last Answer," and "Sweet Death.") Both traits result from her extremely heightened sensitivity to mutability. Although salvation, as a reward for suffering endured in life and as a release from life's multifarious pains, is unquestionably Christina Rossetti's own ultimate goal and that of many poetic personae she creates, it is never a certainty. Indeed, her anxiety over the extreme uncertainty of salvation inspires the despondent moods of her poetry and complicates the efforts of renunciation that characters in her poems either spontaneously make or that they learn to value after episodes of misguided self-indulgence.

Typical in her works is an emotional and psychological pattern that begins with optimistic expectations but modulates into melancholy pessimism. We see this pattern even in her devotional writings. The opening of her first commentary on "Nights and Days" in *Seek and Find* is telling. Rossetti begins by insisting that we must view the diurnal round, that inescapable reminder of mutability, from a wholly optimistic Christian perspective: "There is something full of hope, noble and very consolatory in this sequence of evening and morning, night ending in day, not day in night; night introducing to the opportunities and capabilities of day, not day hastening downwards to the recess and obliteration of night" (*SF*, 68). The emergence of day out of night symbolizes resurrection: "We behold, as in a lovely figure, the death-stricken life which we lead in this world's twilight, passing out of itself into the immortal life of heaven's noon; that noon attained, our probationary course is fulfilled and finished" (*SF*, 68). Rossetti's probing mind is, however, hardly satisfied with such simple Christian optimism. She goes on to qualify, and in effect, to retract it:

> Nevertheless, because this world is fraught with the confusion and ruin, with the disjointedness (so to say), the disproportion, the reversals of blessings into curses and life into death brought about by the Fall, it is no marvel that while "evening and morning" compose the entire day of our hopes, morning and evening make up the recurrent days of our duty; labour before repose, watchful effort before sleep. . . . Still, although we must do with our might whatsoever our hand findeth to do, because we are hastening to that grave where there is neither work, nor device, nor knowledge, nor wisdom (Eccles. ix. 10), there is yet a certain fretting anxiety which may beset us in our daily round of duty, but which has no promise of blessing. (*SF*, 69)

Rossetti's poems, devotional and nondevotional alike, most often through their melancholy tone reflect the "fretting anxiety" caused by her hypersensitivity to mutability, a term that, when applied to her work, comprehends her preoccupation with "the confusion and ruin, . . . the disjointedness, . . . the reversals of blessings into curses and life into death brought about by the Fall."

A passage cited earlier from Walter Pater's essay, "On Aesthetic Poetry," is, ironically, relevant to any consideration of the appeal Christina Rossetti's melancholy concern with mutability and death had for the writers of the 1890s. In its "pagan spirit," he asserts, "aesthetic poetry" is characterized by "the continual suggestion, pensive or passionate, of the shortness of life. This is contrasted with the bloom of the world, and gives new seduction to it—the sense of death and the desire of beauty: the desire of beauty quickened by the sense of death" (Sambrook, 113). Pater finds this "complexion of sentiment . . . at its height" in Dante Gabriel Rossetti, but it is also and repeatedly apparent in his sister's poetry. In "Wife to Husband," for instance, we see precisely the kind of contrast between death and "the bloom of the world" that Pater describes. In this poem a dying wife compares her own dolorous fate to the specifically sensual pleasures that will remain for her widower:

> I must drift across the sea,
> I must sink into the snow,
> I must die.
>
> You can bask in the sun,
> You can drink wine, and eat:
> Good bye.
>
> *(Poems,* 1:57)

Rossetti presents an even more emphatic contrast between death and worldly beauty in "Sound Sleep." All around the central figure of the poem, who is dead and awaiting resurrection, "wild flowers are creeping," and

> There the wind is heaping, heaping
> Sweetest sweets of Summer's keeping,
> By the corn fields ripe for reaping.
>
> *(Poems,* 1:57)

Such juxtapositions of death and the beauties of the world that impel desire are, in fact, ubiquitous in Rossetti's works and often account for the lush melancholy, the Keatsian gloom that overshadows but enriches them.

According to John Dixon Hunt, it was this aspect of Rossetti's poetry "which seems to have had the most influence upon the nineties." It was what "Dante Gabriel referred [to] when he described his sister as 'seated by the grave of buried hope.'" As Hunt further explains, "like her brother and like Pater, . . . she saw the transience and the vanity of all earthly things. Part of her poetry surmounts this and celebrates the divine security of immortal life. . . . But another part of her poetry seems too fascinated with . . . earthly corruption to be able to seek the consolations of immortality."[71] The attraction this latter characteristic of her work held for the aesthetes is apparent from many of the admiring statements reviewers of the nineties made about her poetry. Arthur Symons acknowledged that "Rossetti's genius is essentially sombre, or it writes itself on a dark background of gloom. The thought of death has a constant fascination for her, almost such a fascination as it had for Leopardi or Baudelaire." The comparisons with Leopardi and Baudelaire, for those with the traditional view of Rossetti, are startling. Symons saw even in her religious poems (some of which he described as "magnificent" and "splendid") a corollary to her preoccupation with death: the "recurring burden of a lament over the vanity of things, the swiftness of the way to death, the faithlessness of affection, the relentless pressure of years."[72]

As Pater revealed, however, such concerns with mutability are irresistible to the aestheticist sensibility when they are presented alongside an unusual awareness of what William Morris called "the beauty of life." Edmund Gosse commented upon precisely this feature of Rossetti's poetry when he remarked that "her habitual tone is one of melancholy reverie, the pathos of which is strangely intensified by her appreciation of beauty and pleasure."[73] And these comments by Richard La Gallienne reflect the same perception: "The note of loss and the peculiar sad cadence of the music, even though the song be of happy things, is [a] distinctive characteristic of Miss Rossetti's singing. It wells through all, like the sadness of the spring. Her songs of love are nearly always of love's loss; of its joy she sings with a passionate throat, but it is joy seen through the mirror of a wild regret."[74] La Gallienne's responses to Rossetti's "tragic" note, like the remarks of Gosse, focus upon the frequently observed Keatsian qualities of her verse: the juxtaposition in it of images of beauty taken from nature and preoccupations with love, mutability, loss, and death.

Aesthetes in the 1890s were clearly attracted by these characteristics of Christina Rossetti's poetry, along with its other typically Pre-Raphaelite components: its realistic—sometimes lush and sometimes austere—pictorial descriptions of nature; its commonplace details; its concern with the psychology of passion; its medievalism; and its pursuit of stylistic and formal innovations. Especially appealing to such writers as a very significant aspect of these last traits was Rossetti's literary self-consciousness, a quality that inescapably accompanies any intensive concern with style and form and that implicitly insists upon the autonomy of art, whose value in the world is absolute.

Recent studies of Rossetti have begun to expose the full extent to which her art depends upon literary models. Despite the ostensibly personal and sincere voice that speaks from many of her lyrics of disappointed love as well as from almost all of her devotional poetry, her work is as genuinely intertextual in its extrapolation of particular models as any poetry written by Swinburne or Morris or her brother. This is not to say that what she wrote was mostly derivative or merely imitative, but rather that its inspiration, forms, techniques, and sanction often came from eclectic literary, religious, and philosophical sources that she, like any important poet, adapted in order to express her own special preoccupations. These clearly included the whole range of typical Pre-Raphaelite concerns, which she presents from an especially intense sacramental angle of vision. While treating such traditional topics as erotic and spiritual love, mutability, the quest for salvation, and the beauty of nature, however, Rossetti self-consciously imitated and revised tradition or diverged from it in an avant-garde pursuit of appropriate, if not ideal, forms and prosodic modes. Thus her concerns (and her poetry) are at once traditional and radically innovative, sincere and artificial, self-effacing and self-promoting, self-expressive and parodic. Because of these features of her poetry Rossetti stands out (perhaps in greater relief than any of her contemporaries) as a pivotal figure in some of the most important cultural transitions that took place between 1850 and 1900. Moving freely between aesthetic and moral value systems that derive syncretically from medieval, Romantic, and contemporary literary and religious culture, she is able to forge and to sustain her individuality, to reinforce and retain her artistic, as well as her personal, integrity.

If we perceive Rossetti's art as multivalent—as a vehicle of self-expression, aesthetic exploration, spiritual sustenance, and self-recovery through cultural synthesis—we can best approach her poetry from a variety of critical perspectives in turn. This procedure must begin, however, with analysis of the culture of ideas and the specific literary texts out of which her unique sensibilities, her aesthetic values and procedures, her emotional predispositions and religious faith, evolved. It concludes with a determination of the new cultural directions to which her poetry points.

CHAPTER 3.

"WITH HEAVENLY ART":
PRE-RAPHAELITISM,
AESTHETICISM, AND
ROSSETTI'S
DEVOTIONALIST
IDEOLOGY

IN a footnote to his essay, "The Religious Poetry of Christina Rossetti," Jerome McGann has observed that "it is a commonplace of Rossetti criticism that her poetry is the best expression we have of the ideas and attitudes of Tractarianism." He objects, however, that "this is a most misleading view (though not entirely wrong); one might rather turn to a work such as John Keble's *The Christian Year* for an epitome of Tractarian ideology. Rossetti's evangelical sympathies kept her Protestantism resolute" (*RP*, 143). In opposition to McGann's view, George Tennyson not only "seconds" Raymond Chapman's "long overdue case for seeing Christina Rossetti as directly and fully a product of the Oxford Movement," but he further insists that she is "the true inheritor of the Tractarian devotional mode in poetry" (*VDP*, 198). McGann's objection to this position (a position that Jerome Bump also supports) derives from his perception that the premillenarianist concept of Soul Sleep (or psychopannychism) is "the single most important enabling principle in Rossetti's religious poetry. . . . No other idea contributed so much to the concrete and specific character of her work" (*RP*, 135).[1] McGann can argue this case because he focuses his discussion of Rossetti's religious poetry on the pervasiveness in her work of a "special employment of the traditional topos of the dream vision. Several of Rossetti's poems set forth paradisal visions, and in each case these proceed from a condition in which the soul, laid asleep, as it were, in the body is permitted to glimpse the millenial world. In fact, the logic of Rossetti's verse only allows her access to that world through the dream visions that are themselves only enabled by the concept (and the resultant poetic reality) of Soul Sleep" (*RP*, 35).

Tennyson's and McGann's positions are not mutually exclusive (as McGann's first parenthesis suggests). What makes them compatible, ironically, is what each critic emphasizes—from his own ideological vantage— as Rossetti's very particular historical circumstances. It was precisely Rossetti's unique historical situation that allowed her to mediate between the characteristic Pre-Raphaelite emphasis on aestheticist idealities (especially as presented in dreams or waking visions) and a High Anglican ideology that absorbs not only a degree of evangelicalism, but also the influence of John Keble, Isaac Williams, and even John Henry Newman. Rossetti's aesthetic values were, like Ruskin's, Romantic, transcendental, and even Platonic, but they were also sacramental and, unlike Ruskin's, sacramental in radically conservative, often Tractarian ways.

PRE-RAPHAELITE AESTHETICS AND PRE-RAPHAELITE SACRAMENTALISM

As we have seen, late nineteenth-century reviewers frequently observed that Christina Rossetti's devout religiosity distinguished her from the other Pre-Raphaelites. Such commentators appear to have forgotten the early, ostensibly sacramental work of the first members of the brotherhood, who were not only painters, but also poets and self-proclaimed art theorists as well. The emphasis of reviewers like W. J. Courthope upon the "literariness," the "common antipathy to society," and the aestheticism— "the atmosphere of . . . materialistic feeling [that] pervades the poetry"— is not surprising in light of the work published by Morris, Swinburne, and Dante Gabriel Rossetti after 1858.[2]

After all, as David Riede has demonstrated, when Dante Rossetti prepared his *Poems* of 1870 for publication, the most extensive and "the most important revisions were designed to eliminate any impression of religious faith in his book."[3] In 1847 Rossetti had forwarded a number of these poems, later heavily revised, to William Bell Scott as a group entitled *Songs of the Art Catholic*. (Some, including "My Sister's Sleep" and "The Blessed Damozel," were published under the Pre-Raphaelite imprimatur in *The Germ*.) The success of Rossetti's alterations to these early drafts and the revised poems' resulting compatibility with the work of Swinburne and Morris is affirmed by Courthope's typical assertion that all three poets either "quietly avow" or "passionately profess" atheism, "not as the supplanter of superstition, but as the rival of Christianity."[4]

Such a conclusion is distant indeed from Ruskin's insistence, during his 1853 Edinburgh lectures, that the Pre-Raphaelites were in the process of rehabilitating contemporary art, restoring it to the heights of spirituality and truth that characterized painting during the late medieval period and the early Renaissance. With the single exception of work by the Pre-Raphaelite Brotherhood (P.R.B.), he asserted,

> the great and broad fact which distinguishes modern art from old art . . . [is] that all ancient art was *religious*, and all modern art is *pro-fane*. . . . That is to say, religion was its first object; private luxury or pleasure its second. . . . [For] all modern art . . . private luxury or pleasure is its first object; religion its second. . . . Anything which makes religion its second object, makes religion *no* object. God . . . will *not* put up with . . . a second place. . . . He who makes religion his first object, makes it his whole object: he has no other work in the world than God's work. (*WJR*, 12:135)

The clear implication of Ruskin's remarks is that, in pursuing absolute truth to nature and to historical details, the Pre-Raphaelite painters were God's apostles. Two years earlier, before meeting any of the brethren, Ruskin had written his first letter concerning Pre-Raphaelitism to the *Times*.[5] Like many early viewers of works by members of the P.R.B., he went so far as to suspect them of "Romanist and Tractarian tendencies." Had Ruskin read the second number of *The Germ* (February 1850), his suspicions might have been reinforced by certain ambiguities in F. G. Stephens's brief essay, "The Purpose and Tendency of Early Italian Art." Searching for models that the P.R.B., as a new and aspiring school of "historical painters," might follow, Stephens found precedent only in the early Italian painters who possessed "a feeling which, exaggerated and its object mistaken by them, though still held holy and pure, was the cause of the retirement of many of their greatest men from the world to the monastery." Of course, Stephens insisted (the example of James Collinson was not yet available to him), "the modern artist does not retire to monasteries, or practice discipline; but he may show his participation in the same high feeling by a firm attachment to truth in every point of representation. . . . By a determination to represent the thing and the whole of the thing, by training himself to the deepest observation of its fact and detail, enabling himself to reproduce, as far as possible, nature herself, the painter will best evince his share of faith" (Sambrook, 58).

In such passages, readers like Ruskin might well see as much of a leaning toward "old" religious belief and modes of expression (in the Tractarian vein) as toward the new and diametrically opposed, historical perspectives on religious understanding inaugurated by the Higher Criticism. Whichever view of Pre-Raphaelitism a reader or viewer adopted, the inalterable fact remained that most early P.R.B. pictures were occupied with what William Michael Rossetti termed "Christian Art Design" or the "sacred picture."[6]

The transition from the sacramentalism of Pre-Raphaelite painting, poetry, and aesthetic theory during the period 1848–53 to the aestheticism of the second generation of Pre-Raphaelite poets hinges upon the avant-garde techniques and habits of mind adopted by both generations. As Herbert Sussman has observed, the early brotherhood "effort to restore . . . the authentic tradition in sacred art" required "a rejection of the artistic tradition offered by established institutions." But, "once the religious motivations dissolved, the sense of opposition remained, to be passed on through Rossetti to Morris, Swinburne, and the aesthetic movement" (*Fact*, 55). With these historical matters clear, then, Christina Rossetti can be seen not only as the "Jael who led [the Pre-Raphaelite] hosts to Victory" with the recognition accorded her 1862 volume of poems, but also as the poet who, in the pervasive Tractarian tendencies of her poetry, remained true to the topoi, the habits of mind, and the ostensibly sacramental aesthetics of first-generation Pre-Raphaelitism.

As we have already seen, of course, Rossetti's work has much in common with the later poetry of her brother, Morris, and Swinburne. Yet—in addition to its careful attention to the details of nature, its highly sensory images used to accomplish noumenal effects, and its preoccupation with betrayed or disappointed love—her poetry's use of symbolism and typology, its medievalism, its employment of dream visions, and its preoccupation with suffering and with visionary idealities as a relief from suffering allow readers to perceive her poetry as simultaneously Pre-Raphaelite and Tractarian. Through analysis of Rossetti's devotional poetry, we can, in fact, begin to understand some previously underemphasized connections between Pre-Raphaelite and Tractarian aesthetics.

PRE-RAPHAELITISM AND TRACTARIANISM

If we include her juvenilia, Christina Rossetti wrote about five hundred specifically devotional poems, that is to say, about half of her total poetic production. But a large number of her nondevotional poems also have clearly religious subjects or subtexts. As McGann has noted, in reality nearly all of Rossetti's poems are, in the broadest sense, religious (*RP*, 137). Many of these poems—especially those connected specifically with liturgical rituals or religious occasions, those depicting dialogues with Christ, and those based on biblical texts—would seem to have little in common with the typical topoi, stylistic techniques, or thematic concerns of Pre-Raphaelite poetry. But a great number do, in one way or another, embody recognizable Pre-Raphaelite characteristics alongside those that Rossetti borrowed from Tractarianism. Before exploring the Pre-Raphaelite qualities of Rossetti's devotional poems, it will be helpful to review and expand upon the already established ways in which these works reflect the influence of the Tractarian poets, especially John Keble and Isaac Williams. Beyond this, analysis of the aesthetic precepts behind Tractarian poetry will allow a fuller understanding of the elements even second-generation Pre-Raphaelite poetry has in common with the productions of the Tractarians.

The resemblances between Rossetti's poetry and Tractarian religious values have been convincingly enumerated and to some extent elaborated by Raymond Chapman, George B. Tennyson, and, in less detail, Georgina Battiscombe. Chapman observes Tractarian influence in the sacramental emphasis of those poems by Rossetti that literally or metaphorically employ motifs of baptism, communion, and marriage; and those that stress the value of virginity, the need for obedience, or the inevitability of guilt and the desirability of penitence. He remarks upon her concern with the self as individual, citing Newman's insistence that "God beholds [us] individually." Further, Chapman suggests a direct connection between Tractarianism and Rossetti's "attraction to the conventual life"; her veneration of St. Augustine; her interest in good works and social reform; her insistence upon self-sacrifice, self-denial, and self-abnegation; her uses of typological symbolism; and even her strong sense of heaven as a reality, a sense that is counterpointed by a Puseyite quest for "total union with Christ."[7] Tennyson similarly determines that Rossetti's uses of typology, nature imagery, and liturgical forms are characteristically Tractarian, as are her poems based upon the Church calendar, those inspired by acts of prayer, those that yearn for oneness with God, and, finally, those that demonstrate the viability of poetry itself—as a mode of artistic discourse—in "seeking deity" (*VDP*, 200–203).

Such direct connections between Rossetti's art and Tractarianism become more convincing in light of the significant "hard" evidence that she was attracted to works by members of the Oxford Movement. Such evidence includes her elegiac sonnet on Newman (*Works*, 280); her possession of his *Dream of Gerontius*; and her hand-illustrated and underlined copy of *The Christian Year* by Keble.[8] Though, according to William Michael Rossetti, Christina "thought *nothing* of Keble as a poet" (Bell, 335), she clearly did admire the work of Isaac Williams, whom she quoted (on the value of auricular confession) to Dante Rossetti in a letter of 1881 (*FL*, 103), mentioned admiringly in her preface to *Seek and Find*, and remarked upon repeatedly in her letters. Also crucial in this connection is Rossetti's religious tutelage at the hands of the Revs. William Dodsworth and W. J. E. Bennett, along with Canon Burrows, all of whom had close relations with Pusey and the Tractarian movement.

Yet Rossetti's art serves as a vehicle for mediating between the system of religious values taught her in part by these men, on the one hand, and the aesthetic and social values of Pre-Raphaelitism, on the other. For her, it seems, Tractarianism and Pre-Raphaelitism constituted separate but compatible, indeed deeply related, ideologies. Within each of her published volumes until 1893, for instance, she insisted upon juxtaposing her "Pre-Raphaelite" poems—often concerned with some version or situation of erotic love—with her "devotional" poetry. In 1893, perhaps in response to the special popularity of her specifically devotional poems as well as from a desire to order them all within a coherent structure, she collected her devotional pieces as *Verses*.[9] Her lifelong habit of placing the Pre-Raphaelite poems alongside the devotional works, however, tells us a good deal about her own (and indeed her publisher Macmillan's) awareness of a reading public that would see the two kinds of verse as mutually reinforcing rather than mutually exclusive. This audience she clearly differentiated—even by her choice of a publisher—from one that possessed what might be described as an exclusively devotionalist ideology. These latter readers would be responsive uniquely to her volumes of devotional and biblical commentary in prose and poetry published by the Society for Promoting Christian Knowledge (SPCK); they would be especially sympathetic to the exegetical as well as the sacramental and liturgical concerns, backgrounds, and procedures of such work.

However, the former audience, which bought her volumes of poetry in gradually increasing numbers from 1862 to 1904, would ostensibly have perceived the ways in which her nondevotional poems served as corollary works to the devotional pieces. A number of elements are common to both groups of poems, and indeed to Pre-Raphaelite and Tractarian poetry in general. Some would be immediately apparent to all readers, while others require discussion to demonstrate the full scope and significance of their connection in the two "schools" of verse.

Readily admissible as a common characteristic of both is the highly self-conscious revival of sonnet sequences. Isaac Williams's *The Altar* (1847), for instance, is a series of over two hundred sonnets dealing comprehensively with "all aspects of 'the Great Christian Sacrifice,' as the subtitle of the volume puts it, beginning with Gethsemane and ending with the descent of the Holy Spirit on Pentecost, in other words, the events from Holy Week to Whitsunday as reflected in the Mass" (*VDP*, 168). The plan of this volume reminds us not only of Wordsworth's ecclesiastical sonnets, but, in more strictly formal terms, of Dante Rossetti's *House of Life*, as well as Christina Rossetti's *Monna Innominata* and *Later Life*.

Similarly, the interest in medieval topoi and literary forms, along with attempts to create a medieval atmosphere in their works, is an undeniable feature common to the Pre-Raphaelites and Tractarian poets.[10] The culmination of the "medievalizing tendency that links the Oxford Movement to the Gothic Revival" is, as George B. Tennyson notes, Isaac Williams's *The Cathedral, or the Catholic and Apostolic Church in England* (1838) (*VDP*, 155). In this thick volume, Williams has elaborately "undertaken to do nothing less than write poems for all of the features of a vast Gothic cathedral, taking the reader through four main aspects of the structure, the exterior, the nave, the choir, and finally the pillars and windows. . . . Each section of Williams's church is so divided and subdivided in terms of its symbolic significances that he is able to extract an almost endless variety of religious topics from the intricacies of the plan" (*VDP*, 156–59). Williams's medievalist tendencies in this volume are reminiscent not only of the subject matter and literary backgrounds of Morris's *Defence* volume and Swinburne's numerous medievalist poems (including "Laus Veneris," *Tristram of Lyonesse*, and *The Tale of Balen*), but his book also suggests a pattern for the organizing architectural metaphor of the *House of Life* sonnets, many of which seem "medieval" in their invocation of Dantean and Petrarchan backgrounds, and in their use of allegory and typology.[11] Beyond this, as we have seen, almost every early commentator on Pre-Raphaelite verse observed that its medievalism was a definitive feature.

An insistence upon other elements common in special ways to Pre-

Raphaelite as well as Tractarian poetry and aesthetics will seem more controversial. Such elements include: a detailed focus upon sacramentally resonant, often symbolic and typological nature images; a concern with palpably realized emotional suffering and with death, often producing poems that stress mutability, that expose a Romantic quest for permanence, or that become fundamentally elegiac in tone; and, finally, an interest in beauty itself as a poem's subject matter—arrived at diversely by means of a focus on ritual or (implicitly) on literary precursors and paradigms, or on the connections between art and faith generally defined. Taking each of these common topoi separately and analyzing representative poems by Christina Rossetti for each, we can explore more fully than heretofore the connections between the aesthetic values of Pre-Raphaelitism and those of Tractarian poetry.

THE clearest and most comprehensive statement of Tractarian views of nature appears in Keble's Tract 89 (1840). This tract is the counterpart, one might say, of several Pre-Raphaelite commentaries appearing in *The Germ* that insist upon the principle, in historical as well as landscape art, of absolute fidelity to the details of nature, the Pre-Raphaelite doctrine that most inclined Ruskin to the brotherhood's defense. Entitled "On the Mysticism Attributed to the Early Fathers of the Church," Keble's essay treats the central Tractarian concepts of Analogy and Reserve, but also, "taken as a whole, the Tract is the most thoroughgoing defense of . . . the symbolic mode of seeing the world that can be found after the Renaissance" (*VDP*, 53). This is especially true of the last third of the tract, "Mysticism as applied to the Works of Nature, and generally to the external World."[12] In the essay Keble defines the analogical interpretation of Nature as "the way of regarding external things, either as fraught with imaginative associations, or as parabolic lessons of conduct, or as symbolic language in which God speaks to us of a world out of sight: which three might, perhaps, be not quite inaptly entitled, the Poetical, the Moral, and the Mystical phases or aspects of this visible world."[13] Newman clarifies this definition of Analogy, describing it as "the Sacramental system; that is, the doctrine that material phenomena are both the types and the instruments of real things unseen."[14]

Images of nature operate pervasively in such an analogical fashion in a great number of Pre-Raphaelite paintings by members of the original brotherhood. But it is less clear that they function this way in poems by the "atheistic" Rossetti, Morris, and Swinburne, though they clearly do in the works of Christina Rossetti. Yet significant early poems by these men do quite deliberately present nature images that invite analogical and typological religious interpretation, although to some modern readers it may seem that the authors purposely undercut the possibility of such interpretation.[15]

Morris by no means stresses minutely detailed nature images in his early poems, but he does include potentially typological details that have ambiguously sacramental resonances: the image of Launcelot awakening at the close of "King Arthur's Tomb" with "hands bleeding from the stone," for instance; the cruciform position of Margaret at the conclusion of "The Wind"; and the pervasive flood imagery in "The Haystack in the Floods." Similarly, in *The Earthly Paradise*, passages open to analogical interpretation punctuate the narrative, as does the lyric that introduces the "November" section. Here the careless "dreamer" describes his midnight moonlit vision of an allegorized November:

> The changeless seal of change it seemed to be,
> Fair death of things that, living once, were fair;
> Bright sign of loneliness for me,
> Strange image of the dread eternity.[16]

Also fraught with symbolic, potentially Christian images is Swinburne's 1857 poem, "Queen Yseult," in which Tristram's mother, Blancheflour, dies in childbirth. She is described as "Very beautiful and dead / In the lilies white and red." Tristram is subsequently discovered "Lain among the lilies bare."[17] Poems by Dante Rossetti, too, parade potentially sacramental images (even after his extensive antireligious revisions): "The Blessed Damozel," with that figure's "three lilies in her hand" and seven stars in her hair; "The Woodspurge," whose central image is of the flower's "three cups in one"; and "The Honeysuckle," plucked where "the hedge on high is quick with thorn." Though "thinn'd" by the "thorns and wind," the prize flower still seems "sweet and fair" to the speaker.

Although such works do not go nearly so far in their analogical and typological uses of nature imagery as do Christina Rossetti's works or poems by Keble and Williams, they do clearly open a space for Christian interpretation to any reader who comes to the poems predisposed to such a mode of reading. On the surface they appear to pose, at least in part, as sacramental artifacts. Although she is discussing Pre-Raphaelite painting rather than verse, Carol Christ assesses with admirable precision the way nature images sometimes function in Pre-Raphaelite poetry as well:

The detailed representation of even the smallest objects . . . makes each one a possible focus of contemplation[,] thus [implying] a symbolic view of the world, in which each object can become instinct with meaning. By thus singling out each object, the Pre-Raphaelites build into their painting stylistically the impetus to a sacramental view of reality. . . . Such portrayal reflects an assumption about the way man perceives. Faced with a world of natural objects instinct with symbolic meaning, man can understand that meaning by intensity of contemplation.[18]

Such intense contemplation of images in nature often results in the religious epiphanies or analogical interpretations of the world that characterize many of Christina Rossetti's devotional poems. "Consider the Lilies of the Field" (1853) and "Thou knowest . . . thou oughtest therefore" (before 1893) are two of Rossetti's transparently analogical, but representative, devotional poems that thematically depend wholly on "reading" natural objects. Both are short works, but in striking ways they reflect Keble's beliefs about the proper employment of nature images in poetry.

Before looking at these poems, it is helpful to recall the contexts and origins of Keble's theories, which apply so well to Rossetti's devotional verse. Those theories depend very heavily on the work of Wordsworth and Coleridge, so much so that Keble dedicated his *Lectures on Poetry* to Wordsworth, the "true philosopher and inspired poet, who by the special gift and calling of Almighty God, whether he sang of man or of nature, failed not to lift up men's hearts to holy things." In Keble's view, Wordsworth was "a chief minister, not only of sweetest poetry, but also of high and sacred truth."[19] In these lectures, so thoroughly grounded in Wordsworthian aesthetics, Keble distinguishes two kinds of nature poets: those who through Analogy seek after God's veiled truths; and those who turn to nature primarily as a respite from care and worry. Christina Rossetti's work, including "Lilies of the Field," clearly places her in the first category, where "Nature is the paradigmatic example of God's speaking" to man "by Analogy, yet . . . with Reserve" (*VDP*, 67).

"Lilies of the Field" begins with its conclusion; that is, after the speaker has intensely contemplated nature and come to understand that "Flowers preach to us if we will hear," the bulk of the twenty-four-line poem is taken up with their lessons to us:

The rose saith in the dewy morn:
I am most fair;
Yet all my loveliness is born
Upon a thorn.
The poppy saith amid the corn:
Let but my scarlet head appear
And I am held in scorn;
Yet juice of subtle virtue lies
Within my cup of curious dyes.
The lilies say: Behold how we
Preach without words of purity.
The violets whisper from the shade
Which their own leaves have made:
Men scent our fragrance on the air,
Yet take no heed
Of humble lessons we would read.
(Poems, 1:76)

Like so many of Rossetti's poems, this one's first stanza seems to vaunt its own simplicity. In that sense the work insists upon its own Reserve, imitating God's Reserve in veiling Himself behind the symbolic surfaces of nature. Yet, also like the world of nature it describes, this devotional piece has what Rossetti elsewhere describes as "hidden meanings" in addition to its obvious lesson (*Face*, 19). As is often the case with Rossetti's work, these meanings are communicated artfully, through deliberate punning and syntactical play. In line three above, for instance, "born" is a pun suggesting both generation and endurance in the face of life's suffering ("thorns"). The poppy's placement "amid the corn" (the grain of our daily bread) insists upon the need for relief from the quotidian, relief that comes in the form of a sacramental "cup of curious dyes" (an elaborate pun). The lilies next become emblematic not only of Christ's sacrifice, but, more importantly in this context, of the entire world of nature as well as the poem that re-presents its images and thus paradoxically preaches "without words." The lilies' "whispering" humility reinforces the doctrine of Reserve, as does the very dialogical structure of the poem, which translates striking visual images into speech, thereby effacing the flowers' potentially ostentatious beauty that would first attract attention to them. Similarly, the deliberately unpolished, simple form of the work (with its irregular rhymes and irregular iambic meter), along with the overt lesson of the poem, serve to devalue *its* potential as an aesthetic object. To realize such potential requires intense contemplation on the part of the reader, corollary to the speaker's intense contemplation of nature. Such contemplation yields the poem's final lesson:

> The merest grass
> Along the roadside where we pass,
> Lichen and moss and sturdy weed
> Tell of His love who sends the dew,
> The rain and sunshine too,
> To nourish one small seed.
>
> (*Poems*, 1:76)

"Thou knowest . . . thou oughtest therefore" is a later poem than "Lilies of the Field," and one of Rossetti's *Songs for Strangers and Pilgrims*. Like "An Old World Thicket," it is an epiphanic poem, a Petrarchan sonnet in which revelation occurs with the volta. Up to the sestet the speaker is downcast by the passage overhead of a "dazzling cloud," made to feel "how low I was." Just as the grief-stricken speaker in Dante Rossetti's "The Woodspurge" focuses his attention upon that flower with its "cup of three," the persona here focuses upon the "comforting" grass beneath her, which "bows" as the wind blows over it, bending "In homage at a message from the sky." What nature "preaches" to the highly self-conscious speaker is the paradox of strength in weakness and the need for patience:

> As the grass did and prospered, so will I;
> Tho' knowing little, doing what I know,
> And strong in patient weakness till the end.
>
> (*Poems*, 2:320)

By the last line the speaker thus learns, through the application of Analogy, to imitate the self-effacement of the grass and to adopt Reserve in place of the pride that generates envy of the dazzling cloud at the sonnet's beginning. This poem demonstrates that policy, using simple, unembellished images and largely monosyllabic diction to express emotion quietly.

Thus, like "Lilies of the Field," "Thou knowest . . . thou oughtest therefore" simultaneously embodies a Pre-Raphaelite attention to the details of external nature and an attention to the fundamental precepts of Tractarian aesthetics, especially as they are expressed by Keble. Rossetti's sonnet even contains verbal echoes of Keble's poem for the fourth Sunday in Advent from *The Christian Year*, which also espouses patience and humility:

But patience! there may come a time
    When these dull ears shall scan aright
Strains that outring Earth's drowsy chime,
    As Heaven outshines the taper's light.

These eyes, that dazzled now and weak,
    At glancing motes in sunshine wink,
Shall see the King's full glory break,
    Nor from the blissful vision shrink.

Rossetti's poetry, like Keble's, is in clear ways designed to illustrate the analogical mode of perception and, thus, like nature be a "handmaiden to divine truth . . . [and] reinforce Christian truth . . . not originate her own" (*VDP*, 100–101). The great bulk of Rossetti's devotional poems that focus on images from nature operate in this fashion, as do many of her works not specifically designated as devotional.[20]

As characteristic of Pre-Raphaelitism as its careful, often analogical and typological use of details from nature to present some higher Truth, is its fundamentally elegiac quality. This is especially the case in poems by both Rossettis, Morris, and Swinburne, as critics have long emphasized. These poems concern themselves with emotional and psychological suffering, often caused by an obsession with mutability and death that results in a Romantic quest for permanence. The conclusion of such a quest is frequently envisioned either as absolute relief from suffering or as union with a dead or unattainable beloved in some ideal afterlife that suggests Keats's notion of an existence in which all the pleasures of this life are repeated "in a finer tone." Exemplary poems of this kind are well known and include Dante Rossetti's "The Blessed Damozel," "The Portrait," the "Willowwood" sonnets from *The House of Life*, and "The Stream's Secret"; Morris's "Sir Peter Harpdon's End," "Concerning Geffray Teste Noir," and even "The Blue Closet." In Swinburne's work, as in Christina Rossetti's, the pattern is pervasive, though his emphasis is most frequently upon relief from suffering through death; his ideal afterlife is depicted as a totally peaceful reintegration with the objects of nature in a mode of pantheistic revitalization. Among such poems are "The Triumph of Time," "The Garden of Proserpine," "Ave Atque Vale," and "The Lake of Gaube." (Crucial passages in *Tristram of Lyonesse* also reflect this pattern.)

Almost ubiquitous in Christina Rossetti's devotional poems, too, is the expression of intense suffering and the depiction of beatitude in an ideal "flowering land of love" as a relief from life's suffering and a reward for enduring it. Rossetti wrote more poems treating this constellation of concerns than works dealing with any other single religious topos. All her verse that discusses mutability, suffering, or death and presents paradisal visions has clear and specific relations to Tractarian aesthetic theory and Tractarian poetry, as well as to the broader traditions of Christian eschatology. In any final estimate, however, the dominance of dreams and visions as modes of perception, and the repeated insistence upon the depiction of Paradise as a fully *aesthetic* ideal (where union with the beloved and fulfillment will occur) distinguish these very numerous poems as largely Pre-Raphaelite and aestheticist in subject, tone, and handling, despite their connections with Tractarianism.

Tractarian theories of poetry, especially Keble's and Newman's, are fundamentally expressive. These theories, like those poets' analogical uses of nature imagery, can be traced to Wordsworth. For Newman, according to Alba Warren, poetry can provide "a solace for the mind broken by the sufferings and disappointments of actual life; and [it] becomes, moreover, the utterance of the inward emotion of a right moral feeling, seeking a purity and a truth which this world will not give."[21] But as George B. Tennyson has explained, "the inner emotion that is purged is not so much pity and terror as a yearning for something beyond" (*VDP*, 38). That yearning is the theological analogue, we might say, of Wordsworth's "something evermore about to be." For Keble, too, "poetry has its source in a powerful emotion natural to all men, an emotion that rises up to seek expression and in expression finds relief. That emotion is religious: it is the desire to know God." Poetry thus becomes a catharsis for the artist or in Keble's own phrasing, a "divine medicine" providing release (*VDP*, 58–60). In short, it gives palpable form to a craving, a yearning, a *sehnsucht* described in most Pre-Raphaelite poetry as erotic in nature. The failure to satisfy what Christina Rossetti repeatedly designates as the "craving heart" results during life in intense suffering, and in the fear of an inability ever to attain fulfillment (redemption), and this fear generates self-loathing of a sort common to English religious poetry from Donne to Hopkins.

Rossetti's "craving" for fulfillment is often expressed in the conventional "spousal" imagery of religious verse, the speaker described as a bride and Christ as the Bridegroom. It is also expressed—reciprocally, from the perspective of each—in appetitive images: "I thirst for thee, full font and flood" ("I Know You Not," *Works*, 243); "The longing of my heart cries out to Thee, / The hungering thirsting longing of my heart" ("The gold of that land is good," *Poems*, 2:187); "Jesus, drink of me"

("Shut Out," *Poems*, 1:56); "Stretch forth thy hand to succour me" ("For a Mercy Received," *Works*, 235). This profound and unappeasable desire for Christ, the ideal lover, is the essential cause, but also at times the consequence, of the disdain Rossetti's poems predictably express for all forms of earthly success or gratification. Such soul-longing results in severe suffering (on occasion presented in images of Christ's agony, with which a poem's speaker identifies). This suffering can sometimes give way to visions of fulfillment in all-embracing love and a condition of beatitude in Paradise.[22] Or, as is more often the case, the yearning appears spontaneously to generate, as in a fantasy, aesthetic images of Paradise, presenting in highly concrete sensory detail attained ideals of beauty and love. The premises behind such movements in Rossetti's devotional poetry are clarified in her *Gifts and Graces* poem under the epigraph, "Subject to like Passions as we are." Discussing "whoso hath pangs of utterless desire," she explains:

> Anguish is anguish, yet potential bliss,
> Pangs of desire are birth-throes of delight;
> Those citizens felt such who walk in white,
> And meet, but no more sunder, with a kiss;
> Who fathom still unfathomed mysteries,
> And love, adore, rejoice, with all their might.
> (*Poems*, 2:250–51)

The "anguish" repeatedly articulated in the devotional poems, like Keats's "wakeful anguish of the soul," thus becomes a beneficent sensation because it leads to new levels of self-awareness and self-completion.[23] Yet for Rossetti, these are achieved not by immersing oneself in the experience of this world, as Keats requires of us in his "Ode on Melancholy," but by a solipsistic process of mental projection into the realm of the ideal. Suffering, however, is often the prerequisite for such a projection, as is the anguished culmination of suffering in death. At the end of sonnet 26 of *Later Life*, for instance, Death is invoked as a mysterious, "veiled" gateway, an avenue out of life, which is "dead for all its breath,"

> . . . full of numbness and of balk,
> Of haltingness and baffled short-coming,
> Of promise unfulfilled.
> (*Poems*, 2:149)

In one of the *Songs for Strangers and Pilgrims*, we are instructed to "Bear up in anguish" for "ease will yet be sweet" (*Works*, 140). More specifically in "I Look for the Lord," life's losses, frustrations, and disappointments are exposed as the cause of such anguish:

> Our wealth has wasted all away,
>   Our pleasures have found wings;
>
> .   .   .   .
>
> Our love is dead, or sleeps, or else
>   Is hidden from our eyes;
>
> .   .   .   .
>
> Our house is left us desolate. . . .
>   (*Works*, 151)

And the speaker implores the Lord to

> Lead us where pleasures evermore
> And wealth indeed are placed,
> And home on an eternal shore,
> And love that cannot waste.
>   (*Works*, 151–52)

In Rossetti's devotional poems, as in most Pre-Raphaelite love poetry, speakers are usually martyrs who suffer "horrible pain . . . struggle and doubt." Death is, however, the resting place in preparation for "joy in the end," a state of Soul Sleep in which the martyr will not "wake to her anguish again."

In Keble, too, we find a concern with suffering, but it is often generalized, even projected upon Nature, which, as a clear result of original sin, emits "groans" and experiences "travail pains" so that it seems to "mourn" ("Fourth Sunday in Advent"). Such descriptions sometimes lend Keble's verse, as George B. Tennyson observes, a sad and elegiac character common as well in Rossetti's frequent verses on life's travail (*VDP*, 99). One of Rossetti's fullest descriptions of the causes for suffering in life (analogous to stanza three of Keats's "Ode to a Nightingale") appears in a poem from *Christ Our All in All*, "Thy Friend and thy Father's Friend forget not":

> Earth is half spent and rotting at the core,
>   Here hollow death's heads mock us with a grin,
>   Here heartiest laughter leaves us tired and sore.
>   Men heap up pleasures and enlarge desire,
>   Outlive desire, and famished evermore
> Consume themselves within the undying fire.
>   (*Poems*, 2:202–3)

Such lines are presented predictably in Rossetti's poetry from the elegiac perspective of one who has abandoned the world, whose potential in it is dead, and who hopes only to "Make mine anguish efficacious" while waiting for death, watching for the Judgment, and hoping for eventual fulfillment in Paradise. Fears of inadequacy to achieve these goals, however, sometimes result in the deepest suffering of all—self-loathing, an experience of self that is antithetical to, but just as solipsistic as, the imaginative renderings of the paradisal ideal that appear far more often in her work.

The sense of unworthiness also appears in Keble's poetry, but only rarely and without the intensity of Rossetti's depiction.[24] Her expressions of inadequacy more often resemble the painful captivity in particular perceptions and mental states characteristic of her brother's poetry or that of Hopkins in the dreadful sonnets.[25] A number of Christina Rossetti's devotional poems explore aspects of the "tormented mind tormenting yet." In sonnet 4 of *Later Life* the speaker compares herself to the "Thief in Paradise," incapable of pursuing the ways of and to the Lord, sinful and inadequate to overcome those sufferings on life's path that are obstacles to salvation:

> So tired am I, so weary of today,
>   So unrefreshed from foregone weariness,
>   So overburdened by foreseen distress,
> So lagging and so stumbling on my way,
> I scarce can rouse myself to watch or pray.
>   (*Poems*, 2:139–40)

The especially strategic use of anaphora, internal rhymes, and sibilants in these lines succeeds so well that the reader is virtually mesmerized, verbally compelled to identify with the speaker's condition. Indeed Rossetti's poems of despair and self-torment are some of the most effective devotional works she wrote.

The speaker in "The Thread of Life" laments her total isolation from God and mankind, even her "inner solitude," and asks, "who from thy self-chain shall set thee free"; thus "am I mine own prison." The second sonnet of the triad concludes with a version of chiasmic play that renders the absolute quality of her captivity in self: "I am not what I have nor what I do; / But what I was I am, I am even I" (*Poems*, 2:122–23). Equally powerful but more graphic are the self-descriptions in "For thine Own Sake, O My God":

Wearied I loathe myself, I loathe my sinning,
My stains, my festering sores, my misery:
Thou the Beginning . . . didst foresee
Me miserable, me sinful, ruined me.
                                    (*Poems*, 2:189)

Similarly, in "An exceeding bitter cry" (from *Christ Our All in All*), the speaker is desolated by self "contempt and pangs and haunting fears" of inadequacy (*Works*, 218). Elsewhere, she exclaims, "I to myself am bitterness" or laments that "Steeped in this rotten world I fear to rot" (*Poems*, 2:199). And in "Who Shall Deliver Me?" she prays for strength "to bear myself; / That heaviest weight of all to bear." Having locked "All others . . . outside myself," she asks rhetorically, "who shall wall / Self from myself, most loathed of all?" (*Poems*, 1:226).

The alternative to such despair and self-deprecation is the "hope deferred" of salvation and union with Christ the beloved Bridegroom in an idealized afterlife. The frequency of this topic in Rossetti's devotional works would seem to minimize the significance of the antithetical strain of solipsism in her poetry. This latter strain, as we have seen, focuses not only on self-imprisonment and self-loathing, but also on the inevitability of loss, betrayal, disappointment, physical pain ("festering sores"), and psychological anguish. And it pervades her love poetry as thoroughly as her devotional verse. In response to such suffering, her works—prose commentaries as well as poetry—espouse the necessity of resignation and patient endurance.

The wakeful anguish reinforced by such a negative, sometimes morbid, perspective on life was clearly a source of creative inspiration for Rossetti, as it was for her brother Dante Gabriel and for Swinburne; it provided a subject matter upon which infinite variations could be played. Moreover, it satisfied—in a way that no other worldview could—the spiritual demands and obligations of the religious ideology that she had adhered to from her earliest years. It also fulfilled her special psychological and emotional needs. At the same time it provided the perfect entryway into the structure of feminine values and virtues that most middle-class Victorian women were prevailed upon to inhabit.[26] Clearly these could be successfully manipulated to take full advantage of both Pre-Raphaelite and Tractarian patterns of artistic expression.

Such assertions of the interpenetration of artistry and ideology find clear support in one of Rossetti's unpublished letters. On 3 January 1888, she wrote to Caroline Gemmer (pseudonymn, Gerda Fay), an intimate friend for nearly twenty-five years, appropriately wishing her a "happy new year." Despite the ostensibly obligatory quality of this salutation, Rossetti immediately takes up the issue of happiness in earnest. At fifty-eight she could without equivocation sum up her position on this issue so crucial to the central topoi of her poetry and her prose works. "Happiness," she explains,

> is in our power even when continual pleasure is out of the question. In *will* at least. I am that contented "droner" who accounts her assigned groove the best. Here [in this groove] I can, if I choose, please God: and what more could I do elsewhere? Besides in justice I am bound to avow that even my (small) limited amount of self-knowledge certifies me that some of my actual trials are exquisitely adapted to my weak points. Do you know I suspect I find a *grinding groove* less galling than you do? I feel at home among anxieties and depression; and as the bulk of even my human heart is now in the other world, double shame would it be to me if the remainder had no tendency at all to betake itself thither.[27]

NOT only Rossetti's heart, but also her mind and her pen venture, as it were prematurely, to the "other world" of total fulfillment in love of Christ, the community of saints, and the purely aesthetic beauties of a paradisal ideal. Gazing upon *Beata Beatrix*, her brother's famous portrait of Elizabeth Siddal completed after Siddal's death, the viewer steeped in Christina Rossetti's devotional poetry is likely to see in it an attitude far more characteristic of speakers in Rossetti's poems than of her sister-in-law. In dozens of poems Rossetti repeatedly depicts an aesthetic heaven whose atmosphere is powerfully reminiscent of the idealities sought after or fully presented in much Pre-Raphaelite painting and poetry, including that of her brother.[28] In doing so, however, she also radically extends a fundamental precept of Keble's poetics, first articulated in his eighty-page review essay on Lockhart's *Life of Scott* (1838). Speaking of what he later defined as one form of Reserve, God's deliberate "hiddenness" from mankind, Keble insisted that art, including poetry, is mimetic, but "the thing to be imitated or expressed is some subject of desire or regret, or some other imaginative feeling, the direct indulgence of which is impeded."[29] In her numerous poems describing Paradise, Rossetti takes what began for Keble as a qualified Aristotelian doctrine in decidedly Platonic—and Pre-Raphaelite—directions.

The emphasis upon dreams and dream visions as (often escapist) mental constructs in Pre-Raphaelite poetry has long been accepted as one of its most salient features.[30] And as Margaret Lourie has recently pointed out, "the problem for modern critics . . . is not to dissociate dreams from the Pre-Raphaelites, who rather fancied themselves as residents of dreamland anyway, but to determine what it has typically meant for critics to call these poets dreamers."[31] Christina Rossetti would certainly never have perceived or deliberately represented *herself* as a resident of dreamland, although a number of her poetic personae are inhabitants. She strongly felt the painfully concrete realities of the quotidian world and sensed with equal power the reality of the nonmaterial transcendent world upon which her religious belief and the "historical" events and texts that supported such belief were based. Readers who do not accept at face value Rossetti's own religious self-representations, however, can see her paradisal poems in a way that either of her brothers, for instance, might have, or as Jerome McGann describes them: they are "poetic idealizations" or fantasies—like those that so often dominate the works of the other Pre-Raphaelite poets. Such idealizations answer Rossetti's "emotional needs," embodying "images which at once sustain her deepest and most frustrate desires, and which also help to reveal the circumstances which are responsible for experiences of misery and betrayal" (*RP*, 139).

When they are not invoking or describing the power of Christ's love, Rossetti's paradisal poems discuss fulfillment for the longing, craving heart; or they emblematically depict the "new Jerusalem" in highly aesthetic images. Often a single poem will do both, sometimes in such a way that the poem's literary self-consciousness is projected as corollary to the process of formulating religious idealizations; the poem itself fulfills the longing that stimulated its production. In these poems that envision "the times of restitution," the speaker dependably expects that "My God shall fill my longings to the brim" (*Works*, 156). His "Sweet love" is "the one sufficiency / For all the longings that can be" (*Works*, 205). The passion "for one to stir my deep," to "Probe my quick core and sound my depth" will be fully consummated: "I full of Christ and Christ of me" (*Works*, 193). The "Love which fills desire / And can our love requite" suffices and makes "my garden teem with spices" (*Poems*, 1:90).

Rossetti often enhances her depictions of the condition of fulfillment, or even beatitude, by generating idealized descriptions of the environs in which it occurs. These are equally often juxtaposed with images of this world's inadequacies, which the "ecstasy" of Paradise supplants. In Paradise there "cometh not the wind nor rain / Nor sun nor snow," and there "The Trees of Knowledge and of Life" display "leaves and fruit / Fed from an undecaying root" (*Works*, 149). There, too, the angels, all like Dante Rossetti's transfigured Damozel, "Now yearning through" their perfect rest "gaze / Earthwards upon their best-beloved / In all earth's ways." But, by contrast with the inhabitants of Dante Rossetti's heaven, those in his sister's long for their mates without "pain, as used to be their lot" (*Works*, 149). Such contrasts between this world, even in its prelapsarian perfection, and the next also structure an untitled lyric from *Some Feasts and Fasts*:

> Four rivers watered Eden in her bliss,
> But Paradise hath One which perfect is
>   In sweetnesses.
> Eden had gold, but Paradise hath gold
> Like unto glass of splendours manifold
>   Tongue hath not told.
>
> (*Poems*, 2:220)

This poet's tongue, however, insistently tells what she envisions "beyond all death and ills": "Refreshing green for heart and eyes, / The golden streets and gateways pearled" (*Poems*, 2:271). Indeed, much verse in *The New Jerusalem and Its Citizens* is devoted to description of the heavenly beauties in store for all brides of Christ. As McGann suggests, these works present "imaginative transpositions" of natural objects, usually including precious commodities, gems, and metals, which are themselves commonly subject to transposition into artifacts. In "The Holy City, New Jerusalem," Paradise is not only a Keatsian or Spenserian "garden of delight" where "Leaf, flower, and fruit make fair her trees," but it is, more prepossessingly, a city "built of gold, / Of crystal, pearl, and gem," where "song nor gem / Nor fruit nor waters cease" (*Poems*, 2:280). This "glimmeringly radiant" land of the heart's desire proffers hedonistic delights even more powerfully suggestive of decadence. This "land we see not makes mirth and revel," is full of "soft speech and soft replying" and blossoms "sweet beyond . . . knowing." Here "all balm is garnered to ease you," and "all beauty is spread out to please you" (*Poems*, 2:268).

The irony of all these poems is, of course, that they speak the "unutterable," reveal knowledge of the unknowable, envision the unseen. In short, they realize the unattainable. Despite Rossetti's ubiquitous emphasis upon "hope deferred," her poems often palpably create the world they desire. The vividness of her visions undercuts the urgency of her speakers' frequently expressed desire

> . . . to see these things again,
> But not as once in dreams by night;
> To see them with my very sight,
> And touch and handle and attain.
>
> ("Paradise," *Poems*, 1:222)

She erects a heaven of art that is the poetic reflex of her Christian ideology, just as her poetic persona can be the reflex—the "lovely mirror, sister, Bride"—of Christ ("Advent Sunday," *Poems*, 1:212). This aestheticist quality of her poetry becomes all the more striking in light of her admonition against such visionary speculation. In *The Face of the Deep* she insists that "God's perfect Will and not our own desire or imagination is the standard of beatitude" (*Face*, 127).

Yet the inseparability of art from the attainment of ideal mental or visionary states is another feature common to both Pre-Raphaelite poetry and Tractarianism. It allows varied levels of intertextuality, that is, of a deliberate appropriation of significant literary precursors, on the part of each school of poetry. Just as, in Pre-Raphaelite poems such as Dante Gabriel Rossetti's "Love's Last Gift" or "The Burden of Nineveh," art becomes self-sustaining and self-reflexive—the only palpable verification of lived experience as well as emotional and psychological aspiration beyond it—so for the Tractarians and for Christina Rossetti the expression of religious emotions and the attainment of religious ideals is by definition an artistic enterprise.[32] George B. Tennyson describes as "a standard Tractarian position" Newman's insistence that religion is in fact the "truest" poetry (*VDP*, 40). "Revealed Religion," Newman explains, "should be especially poetical—and it is so in fact. . . . It presents us with those ideal forms of excellence in which a poetical mind delights, and with which all grace and harmony are associated. It brings us into a new world."[33] For Newman and Isaac Williams especially, but also for the Tractarians generally, George B. Tennyson properly emphasizes "the joint and mutually reinforcing activity of religion and art. For every explicit Tractarian assertion of the primacy of religion, there is a counterbalancing, implicit approach to religion through art. Aesthetic concepts so tinge the religious one as to make it a nice question which is primary. What is clear is that the one inevitably calls forth the other" (*VDP*, 23). The ultimate logical extension of the Tractarian insistence upon the interpenetration of art and religion is Newman's and Williams's special concept of the Church itself as a work of art (*VDP*, 48).

This equation, as central to Tractarian aesthetics as is the identification of erotic love and art for the Pre-Raphaelites, helps to explain what otherwise might seem a heterogeneous juxtaposition of moral values, aestheticist images, and self-conscious literary allusion, appropriation, or imitation in Christina Rossetti's devotional poems. As we have seen, Rossetti's numerous lyrics envisioning Paradise as a "garden of delight" often dwell on the sensory beauties to be enjoyed there:

> Jerusalem is built of gold,
>   Of crystal, pearl, and gem:
> Oh fair thy lustres manifold,
>   Thou fair Jerusalem!
> Thy citizens who walk in white
> Have nought to do with day or night,
> And drink the river of delight.
>   ("New Jerusalem and Its Citizens,"
>   *Poems*, 2:280)

The "golden streets" of Paradise, its "glassy pools," harps, and "crowns of plenteous stars," along with its inner and outer rings of harmoniously singing saints, are all deployed to describe what is implicitly God's vast artistic design. That design is represented microcosmically in the design of the work of art that describes these sublime aesthetic phenomena as if from the eyepiece of a telescope. At the same time, however, these objects of beauty are coterminous with the moral virtues that they emblematize: Paradise has "All gems . . . for glad variety, / And pearls for pureness radiant glimmeringly, / And gold for grandeur where all good is grand" (*Poems*, 2:281).

Appropriately, Rossetti's heaven of art often appears to find its objective correlative in literary paradigms that are self-consciously echoed or imitated. Much has been written recently, for instance, on Rossetti's debts to Herbert, both technical and thematic.[34] But as we have seen in discussing "An Old World Thicket," Rossetti sometimes also offers revisionist reworkings of motifs from Romantic poetry—especially that of Wordsworth and Keats—in her devotional works. Nor is it surprising that some of her favorite biblical passages emerge from the ornate texts of Solomon's Song of Songs, which "loves and longs":

Doves it hath with music made of moans,
Queens in throngs and damsels in throngs,
High tones and mysterious undertones,
That Song of Songs.
("In the day of his Espousals,"
Poems, 2:318)

The self-conscious literariness of Rossetti's enterprise in her devotional as well as her "secular" poetry is perhaps most clearly demonstrated by her inclusion, among the devotional poems, of virtual parodies of works by her brother and Swinburne. On 13 December 1861 she composed "Within the Veil," whose titular pun is understood as soon as we realize that the poem's subjects are two brides of Christ, one present and one future. Both are genuinely "blessed" damozels whose concerns are not at all with the loves of this world but only with the beauty attainable in the next:

She holds a lily in her hand,
Where long ranks of Angels stand:
A silver lily for her wand.

All her hair falls sweeping down,
Her hair that is a golden brown,
A crown beneath her golden crown.

Blooms a rose-bush at her knee,
Good to smell and good to see:
It bears a rose for her, for me.

Her rose a blossom richly grown,
My rose a bud not fully blown
But sure one day to be my own.
(*Works*, 234)

These simple rhyming tercets mock the greater, though subtle, formal complexities of her brother's "The Blessed Damozel," which already exists on the borderline of parody, with its thematic and imagistic dialogues with Milton, Dante, and Keats, along with its playfully elegiac dialogue between lovers in this world and the next. Similarly, in "Whitsun Monday" Christina Rossetti ironically manipulates Swinburne's typical anapests, his characteristic image patterns (river/sea, tree/fruit, silence/sound), and even the commonplaces of his poetic diction, but she does so for orthodox purposes: that is, to subvert his ostentatious iconoclasm.[35]

Although, as George Tennyson has demonstrated, the Tractarian poets evidence a high level of literary self-consciousness, the Pre-Raphaelite poets operate at a significantly higher level of artistic self-awareness, as even their earliest critics realized. Christina Rossetti's artistic origins and literary debts are diverse and often plain to see in her works. As we know, they range from Herbert to Maturin to Wordsworth, Keats, Coleridge, Tennyson, the Tractarians, and her fellow Pre-Raphaelites. Yet for her, as for her brother Dante Gabriel, the literary precursor who had perhaps the most powerful influence upon the unique nexus of artistry and religious belief in her work was the great Italian whose poetry was her father's obsession until the day he died. As Rossetti herself admitted, for her the "Dantesque vortex" was inescapable. But the Dantean influence was, as we shall see, also wholly compatible with the Tractarian and other literary strains that molded her art.

CHAPTER 4.

AESTHETICISM

AND THE

THEMATICS OF

RENUNCIATION

great number of Rossetti's poems take erotic or spiritual passions as their thematic focus. The preface to her powerful sequence of love sonnets, the *Monna Innominata*, recalls the proper originary context for such poems. It is "that land and that period which gave simultaneous birth to Catholics, to Albigenses, and to troubadours" (*Poems*, 2:86). In fact, most of her love poems emerge from the same impulses—variously secular and religious—that informed medieval literature. Walter Pater classified the products of such impulses in the traditions of "mystic passion" or "mystic religion." Pater saw these traditions as culminating in courtly love and Arthurian materials, on the one hand, and the poetry of Dante, on the other. In Rossetti's poetry, the two traditions interact compatibly, becoming rich sources of formal literary values and ideology that she can appropriate for her own, uniquely Victorian purposes. Rossetti uses these two traditions synthetically to generate forceful and beautiful poetic artifacts that are monitory (or prophetic). In her work they combine with values derived from Tractarianism, Pre-Raphaelite aesthetics, Saint Augustine, Plato, and Thomas à Kempis. They enable her to convey ideals and describe idealities that implicitly or explicitly repudiate the *value* (as well as the material and erotic *values*) of the world in which they are initially set. These poems are therefore powerfully ideological and find their paradigm in her well-known sonnet, "The World":

> By day she woos me, soft, exceeding fair:
>   But all night as the moon so changeth she;
>   Loathsome and foul with hideous leprosy,
> And subtle serpents gliding in her hair.
> By day she woos me to the outer air,

> Ripe fruits, sweet flowers, and full satiety:
> But thro' the night a beast she grins at me,
> A very monster void of love and prayer.
> By day she stands a lie: by night she stands
>   In all the naked horror of the truth,
> With pushing horns and clawed and clutching hands.
> Is this a friend indeed that I should sell
>   My soul to her, give her my life and youth,
> Till my feet, cloven too, take hold on hell?
>
> (*Works*, 182)

Like many of Rossetti's best poems, this sonnet (from 1854) is deeply intertextual, undertaking a dialogue with generalized literary, religious, and mythical traditions whose forms and ideologies Rossetti transvalues. Formally, "The World" is an intriguing revision of the Petrarchan sonnet. Their continuity insisted upon through anaphora, the first two quatrains and the first tercet function as a unit that describes the temptress; the final tercet presents the question that enables the speaker (and prospectively the reader) to escape the traditional dialectics—of beauty and horror, desire and destruction, seduction and damnation—which the first three sections of the poem articulate. One can elude a personal repetition of the Fall through wholesale renunciation, through nonparticipation in the setting and dialectical field of values where the Fall takes place.

The poem's form echoes its thematic substance, rejecting the strict requirements of the Petrarchan sonnet in which erotic desire (often with the inevitable sequels of seduction and/or self-destruction) has been traditionally expressed. Beyond this formal strategy, however, Rossetti uses a host of traditional images associated with both the Fall and English love sonnets. These include, on the one hand, serpent, fruit, and beast images; and, on the other, images of duplicitous beauty, the fickle moon, and "sweet flowers." These latter images are transposed from their originary Petrarchan contexts of admiration for a beloved. The moral dangers as well as the illusory quality of such images and their uses are exposed through juxtaposition with Satanic reality: the "naked horror" of "pushing horns and clawed and clutching hands."

Here, then, Rossetti's work discloses the spiritual dangers of erotic passion. The thematics of renunciation might be said hypostatically to constitute the ideology of this poem. Such a thematics results not from the combination of particular words, images, or descriptions in the poem, but from all of those, in combination with the work's dialogue with tradition and with the implicit value system of the reader.[1] As in *Goblin Market*, a secular and materialist value system is addressed by use of a concluding commercial metaphor in "The World." But the same value system is also addressed in the poem's rhetorical premises. These present a specifically male self-inquisitor trying to resist an archetypal Eve-figure who is an agent, if not a specter, of Satan. The poem is, thus, designed to operate primarily upon a traditional male audience subject to material and erotic corruption. As historians of the period have repeatedly stressed, Victorian middle-class males—more publicly, visibly, and self-consciously than their progenitors—were confronted on all sides by such temptations to corruption.[2]

Unlike the male speaker in "The World," however, most of Rossetti's characters who confront and often renounce erotic passion are women subject to deception or betrayal by men whose allegiance is implicitly to the material, social, and amatory values of the unregenerate world. Rossetti's finest poems of renunciation, like the *Monna Innominata*, operate dialogically in particular sociohistorical contexts but also and especially in literary contexts. These works depend upon such contexts for their effectiveness and their full "meaning." Before undertaking an exemplary contextual analysis of the *Monna Innominata* it will be helpful to discuss the proper contexts for Rossetti's predominantly secular love poems, along with a taxonomy of these poems, in order to understand how she generated a thematics of renunciation from the array of amatory possibilities—situations, choices, actions—open to Victorian women. Although most of the figures who appear in these poems are not historically localized, the social pressures and moral values that inform their dilemmas and behavior are demonstrably Victorian. Moreover, as Theodor Adorno has argued, such poems' deliberate elision of precise historical settings, their very insistence on their own ahistoricity, indicates the nature of their participation in history.[3] Just as the characters in these poems are compelled to renounce the world that victimizes and stultifies them, the poems themselves reject as unmentionable the specific historical moment in which the situation of women has become, finally, intolerable, compelling total withdrawal from the most important and necessary forms of expected social intercourse.[4]

PRE-RAPHAELITE LOVE

Throughout much Pre-Raphaelite love poetry, a dialectic of desire and renunciation is at work thematically. Whether a depicted passion is visceral or idealized, its object and therefore any fulfillment of desire are almost always unattainable. As a result, the finest poetry of Christina and Dante Rossetti, of Morris and Swinburne, is essentially elegiac: melancholy poetry of intense unsatisfied longing, of unrealized potential, and of loss. The emotional malaise characteristic of Pre-Raphaelite poetic personae prompts most of them eventually to renounce the quest for fulfillment in this world in favor of attaining it in a concretely envisioned afterlife, or in some surrogate form (usually a dream), or in art itself. As I have already observed, the Pre-Raphaelite love poem often becomes a self-conscious emblem of accomplished perfection—of the ideal itself—and of the sense of fulfillment that its contents may, nevertheless, describe as impossible to attain. Art in this way achieves transcendence "outside" the mutable world. Even in the most sensual Pre-Raphaelite poems, such as Swinburne's *Anactoria*, where the poet Sappho speaks, the poetic enterprise assuages the longings of personae who often are themselves artists. Ironically, therefore, this school of poets whom James Buchanan labeled "fleshly" usually depicts desires and pleasures of the flesh only in order ultimately to expose their futility except as passports to a superior and transcendent ideal realm and as inspirations for art, in which the torturous ardors of human passion come most attractively to fruition.

Pre-Raphaelite poetry often thus focuses on the impossibility or transience of promised fulfillment in this world, but also, and as an unexpected corollary, on a speaker's or central character's ultimate sense of inadequacy or unworthiness to achieve a desired fulfillment. It cultivates a tone of languorous melancholy, fully exploiting the elegiac potential of its materials, and is frequently described by contemporary reviewers as "morbid."

In those same reviews, however, we often discover descriptions of Pre-Raphaelite poetry as "aesthetic," because the static meditation of a speaker on desires that cannot be satisfied, on the quest for the unattainable, commonly perpetuates inaction and reinforces the cultivation of melancholy states of mind. Not only in the *Monna Innominata*, but also in many of Dante Rossetti's "elegiac" sonnets and other lyrics—as well as in Morris's Arthurian and Froissartian poems from the *Defence of Guenevere* volume, and pervasively in Swinburne's poetry—we find the poetry of "aesthetic withdrawal."[5] This poetry is fully solipsistic, its speakers or other central figures distant from any possible action to resolve their impassioned mental states. Rather, their inwardness is only enhanced during the psychological events portrayed in the poems. Compelled to dwell on lost possibilities, on memories, on painful and poignant states of feeling, the major characters, like Christina Rossetti's speaker in the *Monna Innominata*, commonly possess "fine" emotional palates. In the tradition that culminates with Keats's "Ode on Melancholy," their souls taste the sadness of Melancholy's might and are "among her cloudy trophies hung."[6] However, unlike Keats's projected Porphyrian hero, who robustly "bursts Joy's grape" before succumbing to Melancholy, the major figures in Pre-Raphaelite poetry renounce all prospects of joy and even any action that would hold Melancholy at bay. Like the plaint of their most sophisticated modern successor, Eliot's J. Alfred Prufrock, their poems linger in the all-consuming chambers of the mind, which, for their creators, becomes a Palace of Art.

While self-consciously resisting the concern with morally impelled, "muscular" action so often echoed and re-echoed by their literary contemporaries, the Pre-Raphaelites also eschewed the fear of solipsism expressed repeatedly by their Romantic progenitors, especially Keats.[7] Keats, in *The Fall of Hyperion*, while condemning his own poetry fervently characterized ideal poets as "physician[s] to all men," not "dreamers weak," or "vision'ries" (lines 161–90). The Pre-Raphaelite "dreamers," in fact, denied the dualism between real and visionary worlds implicit in Keats's description of ideal poetry as well as in his plea for "a life of Sensations rather than Thoughts."[8] As Pater recognized in his 1868 review of William Morris's poems, the Pre-Raphaelites predictably etherealized sensation, displacing it from logical contexts and all normally expected physical relations with objects in the external world. With the Pre-Raphaelites the sensory and even the sensual become idealized, image becomes symbol, and physical experience is superseded by mental states as we are thrust deeply into the self-contained emotional worlds of their varied personae. Very seldom do we have even the implied auditor of Browning's dramatic monologues to give us our bearings, to situate a speaker's perceptions in the phenomenal world. In this respect Pre-Raphaelite poems resemble many from the first two volumes of their much-admired Tennyson (especially "Mariana," "The Lotos-Eaters," "The Palace of Art," and "Oenone"). However, unlike his Pre-Raphaelite emulators, Tennyson, after *In Memoriam*, for the most part rejected predominantly aesthetic poetry.[9]

In Pre-Raphaelite poetry the "real" world, its events and sensations, are dwelt upon but ultimately abstracted. In reading this verse we are ever aware of the mediating mind of a speaker and, sometimes, behind that mind—as in the *Monna Innominata* sonnets—a visionary artist not imitating the external world but distilling emotional and spiritual essences in artifact. The Pre-Raphaelite concern with the quest for beauty has been copiously discussed as it is articulated in the poetry and the prose works of Dante Rossetti, Morris, and Swinburne,[10] but no commentator has observed the full extent to which the ideal and "aesthetic" effects of Christina Rossetti's poetry resemble those of other Pre-Raphaelite poems. Nor have critics discussed the degree to which such effects depend upon the varied efforts of renunciation displayed by the poetic personae the Pre-Raphaelites portray. In the love poetry, and even in the more visceral "passion" poems of all four major Pre-Raphaelites, gestures of renunciation appear to be inevitable, sometimes compulsive. We see them in the major *Defence* poems by Morris, especially "King Arthur's Tomb," "Sir Peter Harpdon's End," and even "The Haystack in the Floods." They pervade Swinburne's work, from "The Triumph of Time" and his Proserpine poems through his epic, *Tristram of Lyonesse*, and such great lyrics as "A Vision of Spring in Winter." The gestures of renunciation that dominate Dante Rossetti's works from "Jenny" and his darker ballads of betrayed love through the *Sonnets from the House of Life* also deeply impinged upon his life. Paradigmatic here is the burial of his manuscript poems with his wife, Elizabeth Siddal, a psychologically complex gesture in which the apparent renunciation of artistic efforts on the subject of love was intended to reflect the death of ideal love. Siddal could emerge as the ideal beloved, as *Beata Beatrix*, only after Rossetti had been forced to renounce her as a real lover. Only in death did she become adequate to the art she helped to nurture, but which superseded the reality of her existence.

The exigencies of renunciation that shape Dante Rossetti's verbal and pictorial art, as well as the poetry of Morris and Swinburne, inhere even more pervasively in Christina Rossetti's poetry. As Arthur Symons observed shortly after her death, "Alike in the love poems and in the religious poems, there is a certain asceticism, passion itself speaking a chastened language, the language, generally, of sorrowful but absolute renunciation. This motive, passion remembered and repressed, condemned to eternal memory and eternal sorrow, is the motive of much of her finest work."[11]

Acts of renunciation in Christina Rossetti's poems, as in major poems by the other Pre-Raphaelites, are aesthetically complex events resulting from a variety of impulses and compulsions. They are sometimes external to the speaker in a poem and can include not only the death of the beloved, whereby renunciation is enforced, but also rejection by the beloved (as in both Rossettis' many poems of betrayal, or in "King Arthur's Tomb" by Morris, or in Swinburne's *Anactoria*). Renunciation can also be forced upon a speaker by sexual inadequacy (as in Swinburne's "Hermaphroditus"), or by the simple unavailability of the beloved (as in Morris's "Peter Harpdon" and "Geffray Teste Noir," as well as Swinburne's *Tristram*). Internal compulsions, too, can require renunciation. Moral compunctions impel it in Dante Rossetti's "Jenny" and Swinburne's "Laus Veneris." Sometimes an extreme sensitivity to the simple fact of mutability—of the sort we see in both sections of *The House of Life*, in poems by Swinburne from "The Triumph of Time" to "A Vision of Spring in Winter," in the final sonnets of Christina Rossetti's *Monna Innominata* and pervasively in her poetry—determines the need to renounce not only the beloved, but also the very desire to live. Such diverse gestures of renunciation account in large part for the retreat from life, the elegiac tone, and the mood of "aesthetic withdrawal" characteristic of Pre-Raphaelite poetry. The resulting melancholy and ethereal final effects that the dialectic of desire and renunciation conveys in this poetry leaves us with the powerful impression of uniform artistic goals, values, and procedures among the Pre-Raphaelite poets.

Just as tracing Christina Rossetti's uses of Dante and Petrarch will illuminate the ways in which the Pre-Raphaelites exploit literary tradition, closely reading her poems of renunciation in the context of her literary and philosophical models can reveal much about a central psychological impulse in Pre-Raphaelite poetry and the aestheticist effects of that impulse. Such exegesis also enables us more fully to understand the emotional and intellectual responses Pre-Raphaelite poetry generates within the reader. These crystallize into a distanced perception of the poem as a thing of beauty which makes use of the sensations and experiences of quotidian reality primarily to withdraw from that reality and create an estranged and static world of art. Perhaps the most useful gloss on the principle animating all the best Pre-Raphaelite verse is, once again, from Keats. In his famous speculative letter to Benjamin Bailey (22 November 1817), he professes: "I have the same Idea of all our Passions as of Love[;] they are all in their sublime, creative of essential Beauty."[12]

PLATO, AUGUSTINE, AND CHRISTINA ROSSETTI

We can readily trace the philosophical backgrounds of Christina Rossetti's Christian idealism and the process of renunciation that serves as the climax to many of her best love poems. These backgrounds, which interact complexly in her art, include the works of three of her favorite authors. Platonic, Augustinian, and Dantean ideals are yoked together in most of her love poems, though they prove only partially compatible.[13] In discussing the *Monna Innominata* (chapter 5), I attempt to demonstrate how Dantean literary ideals and ideals of Christian self-perfection operate. Exegesis of several other renunciatory love poems that implement more ostensibly Platonic or Augustinian ideals of love and transcendence suggest the extent to which Rossetti was able to work artistically in several literary-philosophical traditions at once. She apparently ignored the conflicts among these traditions and conflated their sometimes disparate components in order to generate poems whose focus is always the same, ultimately, as that common to the works of Dante, Plato, and Augustine: the drama of a soul whose quest for an ideal of love, beauty, and spiritual perfection impels an impassioned struggle against the temptations to fulfillment offered by this vain world, which is finally renounced in favor of one that transcends it.

In depicting such dramas, however, Rossetti's concerns with her subject matter are ultimately comprehended within and superseded by aesthetic considerations. Ideals of beauty disclose the "Poet mind" behind the lovers of men and God in her poems. This poet is, finally, a lover of the Beautiful whose artistic activities are sanctioned: 1) by their emulation of God's own operations in His larger Creation; 2) by the poems' exemplary, moralizing function for readers susceptible to the same foibles, temptations, and passionate impulses as the central figures in the poems; and 3) we may well speculate, by their purgative and chastening effect upon Rossetti herself, who is volubly sensitive in her letters and poems to the necessity of resisting the temptations of the world and the passions they inspire. Thus, in many of her poems (including the *Monna Innominata*), art becomes a means of self-instruction, instruction of the reader in worldly vanities, and of revelation, through the poem's beauty and/or perfection, of God's immanence as the Power behind all created beauty.[14]

Very early in *Seek and Find* Rossetti exposes her Christian Platonism, a learned and intuitive philosophy that implicitly reflects the extent to which her aesthetics agrees with and diverges from that of her brother, Swinburne, and Morris. Using as a text Gen. 1:31 ("God saw everything that He had made, and behold, it was very good"), she not only reveals her concept of a comprehensive ideal of Beauty identical with God's being, but also, by extension, she offers a justification (proleptic of Hopkins's Christian aesthetics) for her own continuing artistic productions:

> A work is less noble than its maker: he who makes a good thing is himself better than it: God excels the most of His excellent creatures. Matters of everyday occurrence illustrate our point: an artist may paint a lifelike picture, but he cannot endow it with life like his own; he may carve an admirable statue, but can never compound a breathing fellow man. Wise were those ancients who felt that all forms of beauty could be but partial expressions of beauty's very self: and who by clue of what they saw groped after Him they saw not. Beauty essential is the archetype of imparted beauty; Life essential, of imparted life; Goodness essential, of imparted goodness: but such objects, good, living, beautiful, as we now behold, are not that very Goodness, Life, Beauty, which (please God) we shall one day contemplate in beatific vision. (*SF*, 14)

To understand fully the solipsism of much of Christina Rossetti's poetry—the repeated dwelling on her speakers' mental states—it is crucial to recognize that she perceived apocalypse and salvation as processes of psychic transformation. The goal was "beatific vision" (as in Blake and Dante), for which her special poems that explore psychological depths and mental potential can be seen as a discipline of preparation.

Rossetti placed Plato foremost among those "wise ancients" who "groped after" God as the comprehensive and transcendent ideal of Beauty. Plato had been the subject of her father's five-volume *Amor Platonica*, and Christina herself was such an enthusiastic Platonist that she "lugged down" to Hastings six volumes of his works on her holiday in 1865.[15] Indeed, along with the writings of Dante, Augustine, and Thomas à Kempis, Plato's works provided a cornerstone for the foundation of Christina Rossetti's entire structure of philosophical, theological, and aesthetic principles. The precepts of these writers were assimilated with typological, Tractarian, and Ruskinian modes of perception in the highly concrete images that dominate Rossetti's poetry of ideal passions and mental vision. The uniform process of this assimilation is perhaps best understood using a gloss from Walter Pater. In "The Genius of Plato," first published in the *Contemporary Review* (February 1892), Pater suggestively discussed the "problem" posed by the proliferation of sensory details used by Plato to articulate an ultimately idealistic philosophy.[16] Pater's image of Plato is strikingly similar to the image of Christina Rossetti that emerges from her poems:

> Plato is one for whom the visible world . . . "really exists" because he is by nature and before all things, from first to last, unalterably a lover. In that, precisely, lies the secret of the susceptible and diligent eye, the so sensitive ear. The central interest of his own youth—of his profoundly impressible youth—as happens always with natures of real capacity, gives law and pattern to all that succeeds it. . . . The experience, the discipline, of love, had been that for Plato . . . [in-volving] an exquisite culture of the senses. . . .
>
> Just there, then, is the secret of Plato's intimate concern with, his power over, the sensible world, the apprehensions of the sensuous faculty; he is a lover, a great lover, somewhat after the manner of Dante. For him, as for Dante, in the impassioned glow of his concep-tions, the material and the spiritual are blent and fused together. While, in that fire and heat, what is spiritual attains the definite visibility of a crystal, what is material, on the other hand, will lose its earthiness and impurity. He who in the *Symposium* describes so viv-idly the pathway, the ladder, of love, its joyful ascent toward a more perfect beauty than we have ever yet actually seen, by way of a parallel to the gradual elevation of mind towards perfect knowledge, knew . . . all the ways of lovers.[17]

Although Christina Rossetti may not have had the sexual experiences of love that Pater insists Plato enjoyed, she clearly "knew . . . all the ways of lovers," as is evidenced by her poetry, and as we can infer from her proximity to her brother's affairs and even from her work with "fallen" women. Still, Rossetti's approach to the experience of love, from her earliest poems, required the discipline of renunciation, an agonized rather than "joyful" ascent toward realization of the ideal. (Qualified exceptions to this rule, such as "A Birthday," do appear, of course, but they are rare.) And it is, of course, in the chastening of Platonic process with Christian restraint that the Augustinian backgrounds to her work become relevant.

Lona Packer perceives a parallel between *Goblin Market* and Augustine's *Confessions*, a work she acknowledges as "one of Christina's early favorites" (Packer, 142). In it, as in *Goblin Market*, "fruit . . . appears as the symbolic inducement to sin. . . . The plucking of the forbidden fruit is dramatized and symbolized in the famous pear tree incident. As a young lad, Augus-tine with his comrades steals the ripe pears from the farmer's tree. For Augustine, this irresponsible act of a mischievous boy represents the first free choice of the evil will" (Packer, 142–43). In one commonplace view, then, *Goblin Market* can be looked upon as a poetic drama that, through the use of symbols bearing much weight of Christian tradition, instructs readers in the dangers of succumbing to temptation. Temptation in Rossetti's poem is figured through images extrapolated from Genesis along with renderings of the Fall myth transmitted through centuries of Christian literature, including the highly literary *Confessions* of Saint Augustine.

But beyond this simple and obvious parallel between Rossetti's poem and Augustine's autobiography, there exist a number of methodological similarities between the two, as well as similarities in the very justification for writing; and we can surmise that Augustine's *Confessions* provided one source that Rossetti, as a devout Christian, used to support her continued poetic activity.[18] As early as her writing of *Maude* she recognized the dangers of the poetic vocation for a heroine with strongly religious inclinations. On the one hand, the pursuit of poetic beauty itself could serve as a distraction from higher moral and spiritual endeavors. On the other, success in writing posed a whole constellation of moral problems associated with vanity and ambition. A concern with these obstacles to moral purity and religious devotion appears repeatedly in her poetry. Even in her letters one hears the monitory and self-chastening voice of one tempted by the allure of fame and the attractions of self-reflexive rather than religiously devout works of beauty.[19] However, just as she found in Dante a model of instruction and a pattern of activity that reconciled amatory, literary, and spiritual impulses, Rossetti discovered in Augustine exemplary subject matter for her poetry, as well as a more rigorously philosophical sanction for her vocation as a writer.

That sanction was actually twofold, justifying a life, as well as a poetry, of renunciation. On the most general literal level, Augustine's *Confessions* explains his reasons for renouncing a life of wealth and potential fame for a life devoted to the service of God. But underlying the descriptions of his life of sensual indulgence, worldly ambition, and vain pursuits up to the age of thirty-three is Augustine's explanation of how his career as a rhetorician, a retailer of words, became transformed into his vocation as a writer and minister, a transmitter of God's Word. Augustine's implicit epistemology and his belief in the importance of language in redeeming his fellow man is made clear, in summary, by Marcia Colish, one of the best recent commentators on Augustine:

For Augustine . . . God creates the world and man through His Word, and He takes on humanity in the Word made flesh so that human words may take on Divinity, thereby bringing man and the world back to God. In His redemptive plan, God has already solved for man the problem of His own ineffability. Once joined to God in Christ, human nature is restored in mind and body, and man's faculty of speech is empowered to carry on the work of Incarnation in expressing the Word to the world. For Augustine, redeemed speech becomes a mirror, through which men may know God in this life by faith. And Christian eloquence becomes, both literally and figuratively, a vessel of the Spirit, bearing the Word to mankind, incorporating men into the New Covenant of Christ, and preparing them through its mediation for the face-to-face knowledge of God in the beatific vision.[20]

In practicing her art of "Christian eloquence" Christina Rossetti was, as we saw in chapter 2, playing an Augustinian role as mediator and "prophet."

The profound effect of Augustine's *Confessions* upon Rossetti's perception of her vocation appears (to the reader of her work) in other ways as well.[21] His ultimate dissatisfaction with pleasures of the flesh would certainly have buttressed her renunciatory mentality.[22] And from his discussion of sexuality, Christina may well have learned a good deal about the "ways of lovers" that are repeatedly illustrated in her poems. As Colish observes, Augustine quickly realized that the "cult of his own sensations would not yield happiness, for it at once mingled its insatiable sweetness with suspicion, jealousy, and pain. Still, [he] did not abandon or restrain his sexual exploits. The pain of love, he discovered, has its own subjective attractions; as Augustine loved to love, he also loved to grieve."[23] This pattern of fallen behavior—the description of which requires Augustine to dwell upon the beautiful sensations of the world even after he has renounced them—can be perceived in the background of poems by Rossetti like "An Apple-Gathering," *Goblin Market*, and "Maude Clare." Similarly, in her novitiate novella, *Maude*, Rossetti took up the three moral issues that also preoccupied Augustine in the last stage of his conversion. These include intellectual pride, the desire for worldly fame, and sensuality.[24] Maude's struggles with such impulses results in a psychological agony that can be resolved only with her death. Finally, a model and a theological justification for Rossetti's prose works of biblical exegesis appears in the *Confessions*. In its last three books Augustine—having renounced his career as a rhetorician in favor of a vocation devoted to "bearing the Word to mankind"—undertakes an extensive exegesis of the first chapters of Genesis. Moreover, as Colish observes,

> Scriptural exegesis is undoubtedly one of his favorite occupations, filling as it does the vast bulk of his collected sermons as well as a number of treatises and tracts. It is also one of the interests that he illustrates in the portion of the *Confessions* devoted to his clerical career. The last three books of the *Confessions* are largely given over to a literal and anagogical analysis of the first few chapters of Genesis. This text was evidently one of Augustine's favorites, or at least one that he considered problematic, for he commented on it on three separate occasions. . . . In fact, Augustine's predilection for Genesis has enabled students of his hermeneutical technique to trace his gradual shift from a more to a less figurative type of interpretation. In the books of the *Confessions* devoted to Genesis, Augustine interprets it literally most of the time and is interested in showing that it may have more than one literal sense. He does not neglect to note the commemorative function of language and the role of the Interior Teacher in the study of the Bible.[25]

Much the same kind of wrestling with the conflicts that arise between literal and figurative interpretations of biblical texts appears in the elaborate (and sometimes strained) exegesis of Revelation in Rossetti's *The Face of the Deep*. Revelation engaged her as obsessively as Genesis occupied Augustine, whose hermeneutics Christina Rossetti may well have perceived as a paradigm for her own, not only in *The Face of the Deep*, but also in her other largely exegetical tracts, *Seek and Find* and *Called to Be Saints*. The groundwork for all of these, as well as for her devotional and indeed much of her secular poetry, is Rossetti's irrepressible belief in the power of God's Word and the value of renouncing the nonspiritual satisfactions of this world in favor of imitating Christ by mediating God's Word through her own verbal art.

THE ART OF RENUNCIATION

As a consequence of her inexorably Christian (and ultimately evangelical) attitude toward the uses of language, the body of Christina Rossetti's love poetry takes on a unique shape. In the majority of her works Rossetti, through a gallery of distinctive poetic portraits, explores varied approaches toward the experience of love. But viewed as a group, the poems have a fairly uniform emphasis, and the pattern of experience that dominates the characters in them constitutes a coherent "mythology" of passion. This literary construct usually involves initial desires for fulfillment of passion in this world, which are (or have been) undermined by an experience of betrayal (either by the beloved or by illusory ideals). Renunciation, or at least withdrawal from the active pursuit of love, follows disillusionment; often the speaker craves death, either as an anodyne or as a transposition to an afterlife of absolute Love, in which the beloved is regenerated as an eschatological figure or is replaced by God. Sometimes, too, the art in which the aspiring or frustrated lover is depicted provides a substitute form of fulfillment, supplying aesthetic, rather than sexual or purely spiritual, gratifications.

Two poems provide a useful frame for any systematic discussion of Rossetti's love poetry: "Love," written in 1847, and "Where love is, there comes sorrow," dated by William Michael Rossetti only as "before 1886." Written shortly after her sixteenth birthday, "Love" is an apparently simple poem of five lines, but it clearly exposes the extraordinary scope and significance that the term love held for the young Rossetti:

> Love is all happiness, love is all beauty,
> Love is the crown of flaxen heads and hoary;
> Love is the only everlasting duty;
> And love is chronicled in endless story,
> And kindles endless glory.
>
> (*Works*, 97)

Even this early poem is built upon a set of ambiguities concerning the term love that prefigure the central dialectic of Rossetti's later, numerous love poems. The word "love" here clearly comprehends all orders of it: erotic, filial, and Godly. Moreover, as in the *Monna Innominata*, these orders are not distinct, but in the course of the poem merge with one another and modulate upward. In the first line, the concept that love ubiquitously provides "all happiness" and "all beauty" seems an innocent and simple-minded ideal, except that its metaphoric presence in the second line as "the crown of flaxen heads and hoary" contains resonances of the crown of thorns. These two lines suggest the way in which fallen perceptions and experiences of love are redeemed through the ultimate display of Love: God's for mankind in Christ. Thus—with a continued simplicity reminiscent of Blake's *Songs*—the redemption of this-worldly love results in a perception of it, in line three, as "the only everlasting duty." In line four, moreover, love's position as the preeminent topic for "endless story" not only recalls its tedious repetition in poetry and romance, its embodiment in the literature of the mutable, fallen world, but also suggests that the phenomenon of such literature manifests God's own "endless story," the eternity of Love that comprehends and supersedes such literature. In the last line, truncated for emphasis, we learn that this story "kindles endless glory." But this is an ambiguous statement, reminding us of the vanity of authors in pursuit of fame, but also of the possibility that love literature (as an extension of God's Word) can serve its authors and mankind as a source of redemption. Underlying this brief lyric, then, is a whole galaxy of attitudes toward love, various constellations of which engage Rossetti in her subsequent, exploratory love poems. This body of poems, taken as a whole, fully map that galaxy.

If "Love" wholly exalts the experience and potential of man's passionate impulses, then "Where love is, there comes sorrow" more narrowly emphasizes the ultimate beneficence of experiencing love on earth, despite the suffering such experience inevitably carries with it, for

> Who would not choose a sorrow
> Love's self will cheer tomorrow?
> One day of sorrow,
> Then such a long tomorrow!
> (*Poems*, 2:322)

According to this poem, the impulse to love "only means our good," for it guarantees the capacity for "every sort of bliss" in the afterlife. Again here, a discussion of apparently secular love, or *eros*, opens into a prophecy of eternal, redeemed love, *agapē*. Further, judging from this lyric and from Rossetti's major poems of love (including the *Monna Innominata*), the capacity to enjoy an afterlife of redeemed Love can be adequately expanded in this life only through the suffering wrought by resisting temptations to enjoy erotic earthly fulfillment. Any expectation of such fulfillment is illusory, as *Goblin Market* symbolically shows and as "Three Nuns," "The Convent Threshold," and the *Monna Innominata* demonstrate through their psychodrama.

Most of Rossetti's love poems insist that erotic impulses be simultaneously nurtured and repressed, that we "endure the mood" ("Where love is," line three), along with its inevitably concomitant sorrows, in order eventually to achieve a greater gratification than any attainable on earth.

This thesis is also suggested in a pair of poems Rossetti wrote when she was only fifteen, "Love Attacked" and "Love Defended." In the first lyric the speaker requests relief from the sorrowful fact that love, which is "more sweet than flowers," is also "faster flying." To alleviate the "restless woe" of love, the dead "fools and sages" of the past who now "At length are blest," advise "Indifference" to passion—to be distinguished from conscious renunciation of all possible means for fulfilling it (*Works*, 90). The second poem, however, counters their solution by comparing denial of the impulse to love with denial of the other senses, particularly sight and hearing. The speaker in "Love Defended" insists that despite the "unsightly things" and "awful sounds" to which these senses make us vulnerable,

> . . . the face of heaven and earth
> And the murmur of the main,
> Surely are a recompense
>   For a little pain.
>
> (*Works*, 90)

Similarly,

> . . . though Love may not be free
> Always from a taint of grief,
> If its sting is very sharp,
>   Great is its relief.
>
> (*Works*, 91)

Once again, the experience of passion is intrinsically good insofar as it expands one's capacities for sensation and perception.

But total fulfillment of passion is hardly possible in this world, according to the majority of Rossetti's love poems. These are perhaps best organized into three categories: 1) those that explore the possibility of attaining an implied or explicit ideal of love in this world; 2) those that depict betrayal and disillusionment in love; and 3) those that combine the patterns of the first two categories. Poems in this last group portray a speaker with a clear ideal of love, who endures profound sorrows in pursuit of it, and who finally renounces any possibility of fulfillment in this world for the promise of absolute Love in the afterlife. In some poems of the third category the emphasis is simply on renunciation, the preliminary pursuit of the ideal and its betrayal being implicit or only lightly sketched. Through careful readings of representative poems in each category, we can observe the extent to which the ideal of renunciatory passion that dominates Rossetti's poetry allows her to generate verse that is "aesthetic" in dwelling upon the psychological and physical sensations of insatiable love-longing, while remaining Christian in its emphasis on achieving a transcendental love of God through the experience of such sensations.

Love and the Ideal

Among the most illuminating of Rossetti's poems that explore possibilities of attaining a love-ideal in this world are "A Triad," "Dream-Love," "A Bride Song," and "A Birthday." The first two finally abjure any such possibility, while the second pair, at least on the surface, seem to celebrate a realization of the ideal. On closer inspection, however, we find that "A Bride Song" reflects a state of mind that is conditional. The poem exposes the psychology of an optimist in pursuit of ideal love, and its singer is therefore vulnerable to failure. "A Birthday" retreats in a different manner from any clear delineation of a permanently fulfilled passion in the real world. Moreover, the poem is significantly ambiguous in defining the nature (erotic or spiritual) of the described love.

The power of "A Triad" (1856) is indicated by the opposite responses the poem elicited from Rossetti's contemporaries. At one extreme, Edmund Gosse—who is certainly her most astute early critic—described the sonnet as "marvellous," and in his general review of her work (1893) queried incredulously, "Why has Miss Rossetti allowed this piece, one of the gems of the volume of 1862, to drop out of her collected poems?"[26] At the other extreme, an anonymous reviewer in the *Spectator* sneered, "For voluptuous passion . . . ['A Triad'] could have been written by Dante Gabriel Rossetti."[27] Whereas Gosse values the poem primarily for its aesthetic achievement, the *Spectator*'s reviewer is clearly disturbed by its moral and social implications.[28] Although the sonnet certainly can be viewed as a critique of the facts of love for women in Victorian England, it does not initially invite a reading in its true historical contexts, but rather elides them. The poem portrays three types of female passion—all ultimately inaccessible to true fulfillment, two pursuing delusive pathways to it:

> Three sang of love together: one with lips
>   Crimson, with cheeks and bosom in a glow,
> Flushed to the yellow hair and finger tips;
>   And one there sang who soft and smooth as snow

Bloomed like a tinted hyacinth at a show;
And one was blue with famine after love,
    Who like a harpstring snapped rang harsh and low
The burden of what those were singing of.
One shamed herself in love; one temperately
    Grew gross in soulless love, a sluggish wife;
One famished died for love. Thus two of three
    Took death for love and won him after strife;
One droned in sweetness like a fattened bee:
All on the threshold, yet all short of life.

(*Poems*, 1:29)

Here the parodic use of the Petrarchan sonnet form, synonymous in English poetry with the statement of love ideals, serves to expose and undercut such ideals. One woman is a voluptuary who ambiguously "shamed" herself in love, thus proscribing the possibility of genuine fulfillment. The second, vain and calculating "like a hyacinth at a show," misguided in her goals and values, destroys all potential for genuine love by participating in a "soulless" marriage as "a sluggish wife." The third apparently attempts no gratification of her passionate impulses and "famished died for love." Yet all three are paradoxically "on the threshold" simply by virtue of their all-consuming compulsion to love. Significantly, all "sang of love together." Making up a pathetic but harmonious chorus, the three types of women combine to suggest the various impulses at work in every woman's quest for fulfillment in love. The poem's final phrase, however, suggests that fulfillment would be impossible even to such impulses in combination: not each, but *all* "are short of life." One could infer from this poem that an ideal of fulfillment is attainable but would require a love match in which the woman is able to satisfy her passions without debasing herself as a voluptuary or a dependent. Yet the presence in the sonnet of the woman "blue with famine after love" is monitory. The ambiguous description can be seen not only to characterize a woman in vain pursuit of love, but also to insist that even "after love"—apparently a satisfactory experience—the lover remains unfulfilled (as does Laura in *Goblin Market* after eating the Goblin men's fruits). In short, not just these lovers, but all possible variations upon them, are doomed to be "short of life." Ironically, such lovers turn to "song"—an expression of their frustration and victimization by false ideals—as a surrogate source of fulfillment and harmony in their lives.

Though in most respects—in tone, atmosphere, form, and subject—

"Dream-Love" (1854) is very different from "A Triad," its final thematic point is the same: that no experience of love available in the mutable world is adequate to fulfill the ideal of love our fervent desires compel us to project. Lona Packer describes the work as one of Christina Rossetti's "tenderest love lyrics" and infers that it "expresses . . . the ideality of a girl's first ecstatic response to love" (Packer, 79). That this poem deals in idealities is quite correct, but the vision projected in the poem is not limited by location in a particular visionary's mind. Rather, the poem's ethereal personification of Young Love is mythic and universal. Depicted here is a detached vision of a lover/dreamer, the object of whose dreamed, ideal love remains mysterious.

"Dream-Love" appears in *The Prince's Progress and Other Poems* immediately before "Twice," a poem that presents the dialectic of worldly desire and renunciation in two pairs of specular stanzas. In contrast to the singers in "A Triad" and the speaker in "Twice," "Dream-Love" describes in mythic terms the circumstances of an imaginary, perfect male lover. He can be perfect, however, only because he is wholly unworldly and withdrawn, existing in an erotic dream world. He is fully absorbed into Pater's "kingdom of reverie" where "earthly love" has become "a profound somnambulism" and where love is "defined by the absence of the beloved" (Sambrook, 106–7).

Like many of Rossetti's love poems that focus on the desire to perpetuate passion, despite its arousal in a pathetically transient life and a mutable world, "Dream-Love" is organized seasonally, beginning in "May-time" and concluding as autumn signals the approach of "poppied death." But the poem's thematic direction is subtly rendered by changes in the meaning we are led to derive from its most important symbol, the dove. This symbol frames the poem. The dialectical relationship between mutable reality and a timeless dream world is resolved in this image common to both. On one level a real dove housed in the natural fane where Young Love sleeps, and, on another, a symbol of the ideal love that occupies his dreams, the dove, through the poem's delicate modulations, finally comes to suggest the existence of an eternal love unavailable in this life. Thus, Rossetti exploits the traditional meanings of the symbolic dove, first in its associations with Aphrodite and erotic, "dull sublunary" love, and secondly in its connection with the Holy Ghost and sublime spiritual love. The first stanza of the poem makes clear its symbolic texture and tenor:

> Young Love lies sleeping
> In May-time of the year,
> Among the lilies,
> Lapped in the tender light:
> White lambs come grazing,
> White doves come building there;
> And round about him
> The May-bushes are white.
>
>   (*Poems*, 1:123)

Significantly, Young Love disregards the real world even during nature's traditional time of love, beauty, and innocent rebirth. Built into the lily and lamb symbols here, however, are intimations of death and betrayal. Still, these yield, in the stanza's sixth line, to the doves' ambiguously "building there" in the burgeoning natural world; they are literally building nests for procreation and symbolically building an ideal of love in Young Love's dreams. Throughout the poem the natural world is of equivocal value. In stanza two its moss pillows the dreamer's head, but it also provides a place for his obtrusively absent lover's. Its winds and waters, like the twilight, linger languorously, but the dreamer is oblivious to them. The broad leaves of its trees suggest fulfillment of natural potential, but they "cast shadow / Upon the heavy eyes." Perfect as the real, natural world appears to be here, it contains the seeds of its own destruction, as would love, by extension, in the real world. Ideal, dream love is superior:

> But who shall tell the dream?
> A perfect sunlight
> On rustling forest tips;
> Or perfect moonlight
> Upon a rippling stream;
> Or perfect silence,
> Or song of cherished lips.
>
>   (*Poems*, 1:123)

Indeed, "in waking / The sights are not so fair," and the "song and silence" of the dream "Are not like these below." Young Love enjoys "perfect sleep":

> He sees the beauty
>   Sun hath not looked upon,
> And tastes the fountain
>   Unutterably deep.
> His perfect music
>   Doth hush unto his rest,
> And thro' the pauses
>   The perfect silence calms:
> Oh poor the voices
>   Of earth from east to west,
> And poor earth's stillness
>   Between her stately palms.
>   (*Poems*, 1:124)

Thus, sleeping through the months of nature's passion and fulfillment, Young Love apparently enjoys a parallel experience, but in pure, Platonic or beatific form. Eventually, "Cool shadows deepen / Across the sleeping face" as he drowses "Away to poppied death," and nature's winter comes on. At the end of this staged vision we are required to "close the curtains / Of branched evergreen," an appropriate symbol for this uncondemned Keatsian dreamer, whose enchantment with the ideal has allowed him successfully to withdraw from the real world of nature and the necessarily transient love that would accompany participation in it. "Change," we are told, "cannot touch" either the evergreen or the dreamer "With fading fingers sere." Although nature will sustain her cycles, she will remain "unseen" by the Dream Lover who is now, we assume, permanently transposed to the realm of the ideal. "A dove, may be" will "return to nestle" on the Lover's natural deathbed, a place where life in a dream of Love was indistinguishable from "poppied death."

In "A Bride Song," as in "Dream-Love," Rossetti embeds her indirect descriptions of fulfilling ideal love in idyllic natural surroundings, and once again the movement of the poem is inward, both topographically and psychologically. In the poem's first three stanzas the speaker ostensibly journeys "thro' the vales to my love," according to the refrain that begins each stanza. The "happy small nest of home / Green from basement to roof" that he envisions in stanza one is deep within the vales and distant from the more exterior threats that nature also houses. The home is

> Safe from the spider that weaves
> Her warp and her woof
> In some outermost leaves.
>
> (*Poems*, 1:197)

Yet the natural landscape the bridegroom traverses in pursuit of his bride is otherwise idealized:

> Thro' the vales to my love!
> Where the turf is so soft to the feet
> And the thyme makes it sweet,
> And the stately foxglove
> Hangs silent its exquisite bells;
> And where water wells
> The greenness grows greener,
> And bulrushes stand
> Round a lily to screen her.
>
> (*Poems*, 1:198)

Like nature, the "lily" bride is an ideal of beauty and purity whose symbolic associations with mortality and sacrifice remain unevoked. So perfect is the bridegroom's envisioned beloved that in the poem's final stanza he renounces any need for idyllic nature to house or enhance her. She is sufficient for the bridegroom, and their love would be self-sufficient, were she found:

> Nevertheless, if this land,
> Like a garden to smell and to sight,
> Were turned to a desert of sand;
> Stripped bare of delight,
> All its best gone to worst,
> For my feet no repose,
> No water to comfort my thirst,
> And heaven like a furnace above,—
> The desert would be
> As gushing of water to me,
> The wilderness be as a rose,
> If it led me to thee,
> O my love.
>
> (*Poems*, 1:198)

As he has, until this point, moved physically toward the interior of the vales, the speaker now moves psychologically inward, abandoning the natural world imaginatively to reemphasize the ideal of a self-sufficient love. This movement away from reality, even at its best, to a vision of it at its worst suggests not only the speaker's absolute commitment to his idealized love, but also his sense of desperation in the quest for her, which is still unfulfilled at the end of the poem. The bride of the poem's title is at best a shadowy figure. She is as distant from the lush landscape he passes over and as far from being real as his vision of nature at its "worst." Like the garden turned into a desert, the bride is an entirely conditional creature, an ideal pursued but not realized. In the context of Rossetti's other poems, we are inescapably reminded by "A Bride Song" of *The Prince's Progress*, in which the perfect bride is lost to the dilatory Prince, not because she is an undiscoverable ideal, but because the Prince arrives too late to save her from death. The general point of both poems, which depict a quest after potentially ideal love, is, nonetheless, the same as that of "Dream-Love." Such quests, no matter how inspired or inspiring they may be, cannot ultimately be fulfilled. They must inevitably end in disappointment unless the direction and object of the quest are transposed to a realm outside of the real world—to a dream or a vision, or to an ideal afterlife. And even then, in Rossetti's poems, fulfillment is uncertain. Alternatively, however, passionate impulses may find fulfillment in art.

"A Birthday" is one of Rossetti's most exuberant poems and at the same time, significantly, one of her most "aesthetic." This brief lyric, written in 1857, is dense with beautiful, richly ambiguous images. It is symmetrically structured in two eight-line stanzas. In the first the speaker compares her heart, burgeoning with love, to images of perfect fulfillment from nature: a "singing bird" at home in a "watered shoot"; an "apple tree / Whose boughs are bent with thickset fruit"; a "rainbow shell" paddling in "a halcyon sea." The second stanza moves indoors as the speaker orders preparations for the elaborate ceremonial celebration of "the birthday of my life," because "my love is come to me."

> Raise me a dais of silk and down;
>   Hang it with vair and purple dyes;
> Carve it in doves and pomegranates,
>   And peacocks with a hundred eyes;
> Work it in gold and silver grapes,
>   In leaves and silver fleurs-de-lys;
> Because the birthday of my life
>   Is come, my love is come to me.
>   (*Poems*, 1:36)

Thus, the poem moves in interior directions away from descriptions of the natural world, perhaps because the idealized images of nature that appear in the first stanza carry with them the inevitability of their own disruption. The "singing bird" inhabits a "watered shoot," surrounded by dangerous turbulence. The apple tree with its "thickset fruit" bears weighty resonances of the Fall. The "rainbow shell" paddling in "a halcyon sea" is vulnerable, as a delicate object, to the changing moods of the potentially destructive ocean. These images of natural perfection are momentary and precarious, and the speaker's choice of them as analogues to her heart insists upon the transience of fulfilling love. The need to retreat from mutability is confirmed in stanza two, in which the speaker moves away from nature and orders the erection of what can alternately be perceived as a ceremonial platform, a bed, and an ornate memorial work of art. However, the ambiguity of the initial words of command in the stanza— "Raise me"—suggest resurrection and favor the last reading. The world of art into which the rejoicing speaker withdraws in stanza two serves as a bulwark against mutability while producing a celebratory monument. The rich artistic details of the "dais" overshadow the impulse of love that generates its gothic artifice (note, for instance, the use of the archaic "vair"), and those details, in contrast with the natural images of the poem's first stanza, imply that the only true and permanent fulfillment of love is to be found in the art it gives birth to.

Love and Betrayal

Such poems as "A Bride Song" and "A Birthday" explore comparatively sanguine possibilities for attaining an ideal, wholly fulfilling love relationship in the real world. But close analysis of the poems exposes the ways in which all such possibilities ultimately prove suspect. Even so, these poems exemplify the most optimistic, albeit the smallest, group of Christina Rossetti's love poems. More dominant in her collected *Complete Poems* are ballads and lyrics that depict disillusionment and betrayal in love. I have already presented a full discussion of the various possible readings of "Maude Clare," a central poem in this context. But we can also classify as works in this category—at least in their obtrusive aspects—Rossetti's two major narrative poems, *Goblin Market* and *The Prince's Progress*, the titular showpieces of her first two volumes. Along with these can be included many minor lyrics such as "Light Love," "An Apple-Gathering," and "Grown and Flown." The women in love who appear in these poems are betrayed—at a number of levels and with varying effects—by false ideals, by false lovers, or, more simply, by what is in the background of betrayal by false ideals and false lovers: innocence, that is, innocence as a delusive obliviousness to mutability.

The effects of disappointed expectations and heightened consciousness upon Rossetti's victims of love vary a good deal. Some, like the lover in "Sister Maude," become vituperative. Some, like the bride and the would-be bride in *The Prince's Progress* and "Light Love," die or expect to die. Others are left bewildered by what amounts to the rape of their illusions, as in "An Apple-Gathering" and "Grown and Flown." Yet others, like Laura in *Goblin Market* and the speaker of "Twice," ultimately benefit from their experience and from their renunciation of illusions and earthly ideals. Much like the speaker in the *Monna Innominata*, they are led toward higher, more spiritual ideals of love (in one reading of *Goblin Market*, Lizzie is a Christ figure). By means of their suffering in love and their martyrdom to false ideals of love or pleasure, they are saved from the world.

Goblin Market and *The Prince's Progress* confront the issue of betrayed expectations in love from different perspectives. As an anonymous reviewer commented in the *Athenaeum* in 1866: "'The Prince's Progress,' like the 'Goblin Market' . . . is an allegory, and an allegory, moreover, illustrating a similar idea. In both works the argument is the power of temptation to beguile man from the worthy and earnest work of life. In 'Goblin Market' the temptations are resisted and overcome,—in 'The Prince's Progress' they triumph."[29] Moreover, in the case of *Goblin Market* the central temptations are sensory and come to be equated with sexual pleasures; in *The Prince's Progress* only one of the two central temptations that prevent the realization of an implied ideal of married bliss is sexual; the other is, ironically, a potion that promises the perpetuation of an ideal married life, an "Elixir of Life." Underlying both these poems that depict betrayal and expose illusions about love, however, is Christina Rossetti's highly aesthetic consciousness, which, like the voice in the second stanza of "A Birthday," is concerned with surmounting the inevitable betrayal of love's transient pleasures or our exalted expectations of love by memorializing such pleasures and expectations in art.

Goblin Market and *The Prince's Progress*, moreover, constitute formal and thematic assaults upon the androcentric tradition of the romantic lyric.[30] Not only do these narrative poems eschew the lyric form in which love ideals are typically presented by male speakers who aspire to fulfillment through union with their beloveds, but they also expose the corrupt (commercial and hypocritically materialist or socially prescribed) foundations upon which such false ideals are erected. Further, they palpably demonstrate the ways in which women are perceived as objects or mere ciphers by the patriarchal ideologies of romantic love that pretend to idolize women and desire union with them. These poems are, therefore, powerful social critiques of a system of romantic values that began in medieval France and had reached its institutionalized apogee in Victorian England with its apotheosis of middle-class women as Angels in the House.[31]

Presented in *Goblin Market* is an exemplary instance of betrayed expectations that the sensual delights of this world can be enjoyed with impunity. In fact, indulgence in them is shown to be dangerous and sometimes fatal. Such delights are insistently associated in the poem with love (or at least lust) by means of its much-discussed use of sexually charged metaphors and by the fatal effect of these transient pleasures on Laura and on Lizzie's friend, Jeanie, who "should have been a bride." Jeanie died from her craving for the once-sampled Goblin fruits—premature surrogates for the delights of the marriage bed.[32] "For joys brides hope to have" Jeanie "Fell sick and died / In her gay prime" (*Poems*, 1:19).[33] Following this pattern, Laura succumbs to the attractions of the Goblin fruit ("'You cannot think what figs / My teeth have met in'") and afterwards languishes "in a passionate yearning." She "gnashed her teeth for baulked desire, and wept / As if her heart would break." However, unlike Jeanie, Laura is saved by Lizzie's painful resistance to the temptations of passion symbolized by the fruit. Lizzie appears to be intuitively aware that exalted expectations of passionate pleasure are undermined by real experience, and she has renounced such pleasure. Her knowledge is reinforced by the fate of Jeanie and her sister, and she is almost martyred by her own refusal to succumb. When she seeks medicinal Goblin fruit for Laura, the Goblin men

> . . . trod and hustled her,
> Elbowed and jostled her,
> Clawed with their nails,
> Barking, mewing, hissing, mocking,
> Tore her gown and soiled her stocking,
> Twitched her hair out by the roots,
> Stamped upon her tender feet,
> Held her hands and squeezed their fruits
> Against her mouth to make her eat.
>
> (*Poems*, 1:21)

With the residue of resistance "syrup[ping] all her face," Lizzie returns to Laura as a Christ figure, symbolically introducing Laura to a new spiritual direction for her passionate impulses, one that will in all senses save her from the betrayal that inevitably follows upon false expectations of fulfillment through sensual pleasures:

> "Eat me, drink me, love me;.
> Laura, make much of me:
> For your sake I have braved the glen
> And had to do with goblin merchant men."
> *(Poems,* 1:23)

The moral tag at the end of this poem—"there is no friend like a sister"—reminds us of Coleridge's similarly understated and ironic conclusion to *The Rime of the Ancient Mariner*, a poem that parallels Rossetti's in its narrative treatment of the experience of fall and redemption, but also in its creation of a fantasy world that focuses the reader's attention more powerfully on the aesthetic and psychological experience the poem generates than on the moral precepts it is intended to convey.[34] In both poems such precepts seem, at best, anticlimactic. One anonymous reviewer, despite the moralizing conclusion, pronounced *Goblin Market* to be "purely and completely a work of art."[35] It is one whose voluptuous imagery, rather than its moral tag, remains permanently fixed in the reader's mind.

The Prince's Progress, a long narrative poem that introduces Christina Rossetti's second volume of verse, is a sequel to *Goblin Market*, and it, too, concerns false expectations of love. These expectations belong not only to the characters involved, but also, to an extent, to the reader of this quest romance whose events undercut the tradition from which it emerges. Rather than focusing, as *Goblin Market* does, on its characters' betrayed expectations of sensual delight, *The Prince's Progress* deals primarily with more philosophical issues related to betrayal in love, which here is depicted as an inevitable result of fate and human nature. On its surface this poem appears to depict a deserving Princess bride who is betrayed by an inadequately devoted lover. Yet, as in the majority of Christina Rossetti's love poems, mutability appears insistently as the culprit in the background of this narrative. It is the force that impels the characters' reactions to their circumstances and prevents fulfillment of love.

Typically in quest romances both lovers are idealized, but in Rossetti's poem only one of the central characters is admirable. The Princess dies languishing as she awaits her bridegroom's delayed arrival. As we learn in the last 60 of the poem's 540 lines, she is entirely passive, like Tennyson's

Mariana and most of the dream-poem heroines from Morris's *Defence* volume. She is beautiful, "Meet queen for any kingly king, / With gold-dust on her hair." And her temperament complements her beauty. The veiled figures who are carrying away her body when the Prince finally appears first admonish him:

> "You loitered on the road too long,
>   You trifled at the gate
> The enchanted dove upon her branch
>   Died without a mate."

(Poems, 1:108)

And then they eulogize their dead Princess:

> "We never saw her with a smile
>   Or with a frown;
> Her bed seemed never soft to her,
>   Tho' tossed of down;
> She little heeded what she wore,
>   Kirtle, or wreath, or gown;
> We think her white brows often ached
>   Beneath her crown,
> Till silvery hairs showed in her locks
>   That used to be so brown.
>
> "We never heard her speak in haste:
>   Her tones were sweet,
> And modulated just so much
>   As it was meet:
> Her heart sat silent thro' the noise
>   And concourse of the street.
> There was no hurry in her hands
>   No hurry in her feet."

(Poems, 1:109)

Significantly, these and the rest of the last 60 lines in *The Prince's Progress* were written in 1861, four years before the bulk of the narrative was composed, and clear differences in focus and technique distinguish the two parts of the poem. The lines from 1861—in a way typical of Christina Rossetti's poems of betrayed love—emphasize the character of the betrayed lover and the pathos of her fate. The 480 lines that precede the Prince's arrival carefully characterize the Prince, but they are far more philosophical in tone than the poem's final stanzas, and they make far more obtrusive use of symbolism in order to evoke a dreamlike atmosphere. The tone and atmosphere in combination produce a narrative that, in its echoes of other relevant poetic texts, once again suggests a highly self-conscious poet appropriating the work of her precursors in revisionist ways. As in the *Monna Innominata*, Rossetti manages to sustain a tension on the reader's part between sympathetic involvement with the characters and events of her poem on the one hand and intellectual detachment on the other. Such detachment is compelled by an awareness, repeatedly elicited by her text, of specific literary precedents and traditions that have helped to generate the poem.

In the course of the dilatory Prince's "progress" toward his bride, he encounters obstacles that remind us variously of man's susceptibility to sexual enchantment as it is portrayed in Keats's "La Belle Dame Sans Merci," of the futility that characterizes most of Tennyson's questers in "The Holy Grail," and of the landscape traversed by Browning's Childe Roland. Like Tennyson's Tristram, Rossetti's Prince is "Strong of limb if of purpose weak" (*Poems*, 1:96) and, also like Tristram, he is easily waylaid during the first mile of his journey by "A wave-haired milkmaid, rosy and white." After the Prince quaffs the maiden's milk, she becomes Lamia-like and Keatsian: "Was she a maid, or an evil dream?" And she compels him to remain "a day and a night fast laid / In her subtle toils." Under the "apple-tree" (which becomes an icon of fall and betrayal in Rossetti's poetry), he

> Lay and laughed and talked to the maid,
> Who twisted her hair in a cunning braid
> And writhed in shining serpent-coils
> And held him. . . .
>
> (*Poems*, 1:97)

After moving from her lair, the Prince is further delayed by a landscape as barren and hostile as that which discourages Browning's Childe Roland through most of his quest:

> . . . The grass grew rare,
> A blight lurked in the darkening air,
> The very moss grew hueless and spare,
> The last daisy stood all astunt;
> Behind his back the soil lay bare,
> But barer in front.
>
> (*Poems*, 1:98)

We are made aware of the derivative, literary quality of Rossetti's narrative not only by its conspicuous echoes of these familiar Romantic and Victorian poems, but also by its dreamlike, often nightmarish atmosphere, which recalls Tennyson's "The Lotos-Eaters" and "Mariana" as well as dream poems by Morris such as "The Blue Closet," "The Tune of the Seven Towers," "Golden Wings," and "Spell-bound." Most of these poems by Morris, like Tennyson's "Mariana" and "The Lady of Shalott," emphasize the dreamlike atmosphere surrounding a woman vainly waiting for a lover. As Margaret Lourie has quite correctly observed, reading such poems

> allows us to isolate a strain in Victorian Romanticism which perhaps began with early Tennyson poems . . . and certainly culminated . . . in the early work of . . . Yeats. It is a strain which rejects Arnold's "powerful application of ideas to life" in favor of a movement downward out of life and into primeval levels of consciousness. It is a strain which ran from Tennyson through Morris and the other Pre-Raphaelites to Walter Pater and from there, to Yeats's friends in the Rhymers' Club, whose movement out of life was all too often literal.[36]

This strain of Victorian Romanticism, specifically as it dominates Pre-Raphaelite poetry, is wholly compatible with some of Christina Rossetti's favorite religious texts. Its solipsism might be seen, in the case of Rossetti, as a literalization of the New Testament insistence (Luke 17:21) that "The kingdom of God is within you," a doctrine also taken literally and developed at length in Rossetti's much-loved *Imitatio Christi*. In that work, Thomas à Kempis admonishes: "Learn to despise outward things and to give thyself to things inward, and thou shalt perceive the kingdom of God to be come in thee. . . . All His glory and beauty is from within."[37] Clearly, in *The Prince's Progress*, in many of Christina Rossetti's other poems of vain love, and even in her children's poetry, she makes a significant, if often derivative, contribution to the genealogy of Victorian literature of "life-defying interiority," which, in its effects upon the reader, is predominantly aesthetic. Ultimately however, as Jerome McGann has suggested, such aestheticism, through its insistence upon the inadequacies and corruption of the world, serves as a social and ideological critique of Rossetti's culture (*NER*, 253–54).

Very early in *The Prince's Progress* the futility and "the doom" inevitable in love affairs on earth are emphasized by means of rich, even voluptuous imagery that we usually associate with the aesthetic temperament, from

Keats and early Tennyson to Swinburne and Pater. Before beginning his journey, the Prince requires the mysterious "voice of my doom" to tell him "Of my veiled bride in her maiden bloom." That voice describes her, significantly, as "Spell-bound," watching "in one white room," where

> "By her head lilies and rosebuds grow;
> The lilies droop, will the rosebuds blow?
> The silver slim lilies hang the head low;
>   Their stream is scanty, their sunshine rare;
> Let the sun blaze out, and let the stream flow,
>   They will blossom and wax fair.
>
> "Red and white poppies grow at her feet,
> The blood-red wait for sweet summer heat,
> Wrapped in bud-coats hairy and neat;
>   But the white buds swell, one day they will burst,
> Will open their death-cups drowsy and sweet—
>   Which will open the first?"
>
> *(Poems,* 1:96)

The voice concludes with repeated instructions to seize the day, and these are echoed by a chorus of voices, half sad and half glad:

> "Time is short, life is short," they took up the tale:
> "Life is sweet, love is sweet, use today while you may;
> Love is sweet, and tomorrow may fail;
>   Love is sweet, use today."
>
> *(Poems,* 1:96)

Two years after the publication of *The Prince's Progress*, this *carpe diem* motif found its most eloquent Victorian spokesman in Walter Pater, who, in reviewing Morris's poetry, emphasized the "awful brevity" of human experience: "A counted number of pulses only is given to us of a variegated, dramatic life. How may we see in them all that is to be seen in them by the finest senses?" (Sambrook, 115). In *The Prince's Progress* Christina Rossetti seems, in response to life's transience, almost to sanction an Epicurean quest for love, while at the same time pronouncing upon the inevitability of its failure. Almost drowned during his last adventure before arriving at the Princess's palace, the Prince desperately "clutched in one drowning hand" the phial containing the "Elixir of Life" distilled by an ancient sorcerer who had detained him. The Prince hopes, as he nears the palace, that despite his tardiness, the potion's promise of prolonged life in love "May go far to woo him a wife" (*Poems*, 1:107). Ironically, however, he is unable to outrun mutability; the Princess is dead.

> Slip past, slip fast,
> Uncounted hours from first to last,
> Many hours till the last is past,
>   Many hours dwindling to one—
> One hour whose die is cast,
>   One last hour gone.

> Come, gone—gone for ever—
> Gone as an unreturning river—
> Gone as to death the merriest liver—
>   Gone as the year at the dying fall—
> Tomorrow, today, yesterday, never—
>   Gone once for all.
>   (*Poems*, 1:105)

The final note of this poem is pathos, a sequel to the complacent happiness recorded by the sisters in *Goblin Market* who attain happiness precisely because they renounce the kind of pleasures that seduce the Prince during his journey. Though eminently desirable in *The Prince's Progress*, the beauty and joy of fulfilled love are fated to be unattainable. They constitute a temptation the pursuit of which is futile because the simple fact of mutability is insuperable. Patriarchal society's refusal to acknowledge this futility is a cruel deception that, in both poems, victimizes women. Moreover, the deception is perpetuated precisely in the fairy-tale traditions of romantic poetry that *Goblin Market* and *The Prince's Progress* parody, both formally and thematically. From these works we infer that the *carpe diem* impulse, especially in its connection with romantic ideals, must inevitably be quelled by true knowledge of *vanitas mundi*, except insofar as the impulse, its momentary fulfillment, or its disappointment can be preserved in art along with implied or explicit monitions to renounce desires for fulfillment in this world. In this way Christina Rossetti paradoxically preserves literary tradition—by appropriating and transvaluing it in parody—while she presents a critique of the ideology underlying that tradition.

ROSSETTI wrote many poems that seem designed less to warn the woman desiring to fill "love's capacity" against sensory temptation than to warn her against the false men who embody such temptation. By the last stanzas of "Maude Clare," for instance, Maude has painfully learned about the dangers of love and can readily renounce Thomas, who has betrayed her. She charges his bride, Nell, to

> "Take my share of a fickle heart,
>   Mine of a paltry love:
> Take it or leave it as you will,
>   I wash my hands thereof."
>   (*Poems*, 1:46)

The gesture of renunciation is more difficult and equivocal for the victimized heroine of "Light Love" (1856) who, during dialogue with her treacherous lover, "strained his baby in her arms, / His baby to her heart" (*Poems*, 1:137). Like Rossetti's "The Sins of the Fathers," this poignant, sentimental poem, with illicit passion and a bastard child in the foreground, is daringly un-Victorian. But the woman in "Light Love" is unlike the speaker in "The Sins of the Fathers," who renounces marriage while veiling her illegitimacy to protect her mother. The persona in "Light Love" is concerned exclusively with her own pathetic situation and is bewildered at her betrayal. She does agree, finally, to "Even let it go, the love that harms," but to her child—the issue of her "light" love who weightily perpetuates it—she entones, "We twain will never part; / Mine own, his own, how dear thou art" (*Poems*, 1:137). That child's perfidious father is about to abandon the mother for more tempting pleasures of the flesh:

> "For nigh at hand there blooms a bride,
>   My bride before the morn;
> Ripe-blooming she, as thou forlorn.
> Ripe-blooming she, my rose, my peach;
>   She woos me day and night:
> I watch her tremble in my reach;
>   She reddens, my delight;
>   She ripens, reddens in my sight."
>   (*Poems*, 1:137–38)

But the child's mother sympathetically warns this callous voluptuary against infidelity and mutability, two subjects of her own recent schooling in love:

> "Haste where the spiced garden blows:
> But in bare autumn eves
> Wilt thou have store of autumn sheaves?
> Thou leavest, love, true love behind,
> To seek a love as true;
> Go, seek in haste: but wilt thou find?"
>
> (*Poems*, 1:138)

Oblivious to her plea, her lover abandons her and she is at the end embittered: "She raised her eyes, not wet / But hard, to Heaven / And asked / 'Does God forget?'" (*Poems*, 1:138). Like Ford Madox Brown's unfinished painting, "*Take your son, Sir*" (begun in 1852), the victimized woman in this poem is in dialogue not only with her (significantly unnamed) lover, but with the entire corrupt and corrupting society he represents. Unlike the materialistic Thomas in "Maude Clare," however, this man is ironically in search of a "ripe-blooming" carnal ideal. His example exposes the hypocrisy of Victorian mythologies that portrayed women as saintly spiritual beings. These myths proliferated in conduct books of the day—most of them written by men—as well as in literature.[38]

The speaker in "An Apple-Gathering" is more perplexed than embittered by her rather abstractly represented experience of betrayal by a false lover. Here again, images of the harvest predominate, suggesting that one reaps what one sows. As the speaker views her female friends returning from the orchards with baskets full of apples, some with help from "a stronger hand," she reminisces:

> I plucked pink blossoms from mine apple tree
> And wore them all that evening in my hair:
> Then in due season when I went to see
> I found no apples there.
>
> (*Poems*, 1:43)

Like Laura in *Goblin Market*, this speaker prematurely enjoys sensual pleasures associated with love, thus betraying her own best potential, and is subsequently deserted by her lover, forfeiting the sustained fulfillment she expects. Dismayed and bewildered, she asks plaintively,

> Ah Willie, Willie, was my love less worth
> Than apples with their green leaves piled above?
> I counted rosiest apples on the earth
> Of far less worth than love.
>
> (*Poems*, 1:44)

Realizing how imprudently she has "counted," she loiters at the poem's conclusion while neighbors pass her by and while the dews, suggestive of her tears, "fell fast" as she herself had in her amorous innocence before her betrayal.

As in "An Apple-Gathering," at issue in almost all of Rossetti's poems about betrayed lovers or betrayed expectations of love is the unattainability of fulfillment. As we have seen, Rossetti often stresses ideal love's distance from reality by describing the experience of love with images of mutability. Seasonal images, images of planting and harvesting, images of ripeness and unripeness, all appear as natural analogues to naturally impelled passions, whether these are clearly erotic or more vague and ethereal. Her characters' predictable failures enduringly to fulfill passion often result in the renunciation not only of specific disappointed love relationships but also of any belief at all in attainable earthly ideals of love. We find her speakers turning away from nature and toward an internal space that can be filled with attainable spiritual ideals of love. This complete movement is the subject of her lyric, "Twice," a poem that exemplifies the transition, common to many of Rossetti's poems, from the pursuit of *eros* to its renunciation in favor of *agapē*.

"Twice" is spoken by a courageous woman who, with some reluctance, has made overtures to the man she loves. Her lover's response has shattered her faith in the value of erotic love:

> You took my heart in your hand
> With a friendly smile,
> With a critical eye you scanned,
> Then set it down,
> And said: It is still unripe,
> Better wait awhile;
> Wait while the skylarks pipe,
> Till the corn grows brown.
> (*Poems*, 1:125)

She cannot, however, wait till harvest time. Indeed, this experience has altogether destroyed her capacity to pursue earthly passion. Her lover "set [her heart] down" and "it broke." As a result,

> . . . I have not often smiled
> Since then, nor questioned since,
> Nor cared for corn-flowers wild,
> Nor sung with the singing bird.

"Twice" operates at a level of cultural criticism different from that of "Light Love" and "An Apple-Gathering." The attack implicit in its four brief stanzas is upon the powerlessness of women in a rigid patriarchal society. The man's words are spoken with absolute and final authority. But the poem subverts the premises underlying that authority by appealing to a higher one who can be imaginatively idealized as a worthy judge and lover. He can be constructed in the image of a genuinely sympathetic and receptive—that is, an ironically nonsexist—being. Along with the sanctions of love in approved social forms and contexts, the speaker here indignantly and impatiently renounces the natural world, and, now penitent for her presumptuous erotic quest, she approaches God:

> I take my heart in my hand,
>   O my God, O my God,
> My broken heart in my hand:
>   Thou hast seen, judge Thou.
> My hope was written on sand,
>   O my God, O my God;
> Now let Thy judgment stand—
>   Yea, judge me now.
>
> This contemned of a man,
>   This marred one heedless day,
> This heart take Thou to scan
>   Both within and without:
> Refine with fire its gold,
>   Purge Thou its dross away—
> Yea hold it in Thy hold,
>   Whence none can pluck it out.
>   (*Poems*, 1:125)

She thus acknowledges the uncertainty of *eros*, but also, aware that her quest for earthly love was misguided, she acknowledges her need to be chastened and "purged" in order to become worthy of God's superior love. Alienated from the arbitrary and insensitive values of her patriarchal society, the speaker in "Twice," like the persona of "A Birthday" and the lover in "Dream-Love," finds herself to be an alien in the natural world as well. Like Yeats's persona in "Sailing to Byzantium," she perceives her heart, finally, as an artifact that can be "refined" and perfected only when it is "once out of nature," projected wholly either into the world of art or the realm of the ideal. Such is the case in all of Christina Rossetti's poems whose focus is not on the possibility of fulfilling earthly love, or upon betrayal in love, but rather upon the apparently inevitable culmination of all compulsive amatory passions—renunciation.

Love and Renunciation

As is clear to any student of Christina Rossetti's poetry, *vanitas mundi* is her most frequent theme, and we have seen that this theme is as pervasive in her secular love poetry as it is in her devotional poems, where a wholesale rejection of worldly values and experiences would be expected. A philosophically crucial issue therefore—but one that is more often in the background than the foreground of the poems we have so far discussed— is the issue of choice, or (as I will term it in treating the *Monna Innominata*) directing the will. This is, of course, the central concern of Augustine's *Confessions*, and, as Charles Singleton has made clear, of Dante's cumulative works, because it is the essential issue of Christianity. In poems by Rossetti such as *Goblin Market, The Prince's Progress,* "Twice," or "An Apple-Gathering," characters appear to be doomed or saved because of amatory choices they have made, sometimes in innocence and sometimes with a degree of calculation. For the most part, however, the "salvation" Rossetti's characters achieve—through correct choice or through penitence and suffering after misguided choices—is equivocal. Or it is contingent upon the speakers' eventual death and admission to the afterlife of Love, awaiting which, they must morosely endure. It is, therefore, the voluntary renunciation of the world that her poems often scrutinize. In doing so, they display a Victorianized version of the Augustinian patterns of conversion and confession.

Examples of such poems of renunciation are "How One Chose" (1849), "From House to Home" (1858), "Memory" (part 1, 1857; part 2, 1865), "Three Nuns" (1849–50), and "The Convent Threshold" (1858). Most of these poems present choices and types of experience in life that remain for a woman who decides to renounce *eros*. In reading them we are powerfully reminded of the dominant mood in works by other Pre-Raphaelites, in which, however, renunciation is usually *not* a matter of choice. It is enforced by fate—the death of the beloved, or rejection by her, or obstacles to union with her. Moreover, in these other works the discourse of renunciation does not usually encompass a critique of the specifically patriarchal amatory values of the poets' culture, as it does, implicitly or explicitly, in most of Christina Rossetti's renunciatory love poems. The other Pre-Raphaelite poets generally accept and reinforce such patriarchal values. Their poems are avant-garde and subversive, rather, in their critique of orthodox Christian values, which neither console nor substitute for failed love. It is precisely Christian, specifically Augustinian, values, however, that Christina Rossetti's poems serve to reinforce—indeed, to recover and reinvent for her era. In their artistry and power these poems supersede the accomplishment of any other Victorian religious poetry.

Choices similar to those available to Christina Rossetti's renunciatory speakers do emerge *after* fulfillment is prevented in poems by Swinburne, Dante Rossetti, and William Morris. Their speakers must usually resign themselves to a life of stoic endurance or look forward to death as an anodyne, although they often equivocate between the two alternatives.

Such is clearly the case in Swinburne's "The Triumph of Time," whose speaker, after rejection by his beloved, first threatens suicide and then makes drowning a surrogate oedipal act of sexual consummation:

> I will go back to the great sweet mother,
>   Mother and lover of men, the sea.
> I will go down to her, I and none other,
>   Close with her, kiss her and mix her with me;
> Cling to her, strive with her, hold her fast.[39]

But soon he dejectedly resigns himself to continued existence:

> And grief shall endure not for ever, I know.
>
> .   .   .   .
>
> We shall hear, as one in a trance that hears,
>   The sound of time, the rhyme of the years;
> Wrecked hope and passionate pain will grow
>   As tender things of a spring-tide sea.
>   (Swinburne, 1:44)

The speaker here, like the female voice of the *Monna Innominata*, foresees the poignant sensations of melancholy that he must endure. Alternatively, at the end of Swinburne's *Anactoria*, the focus is not upon such "pleasures" but rather upon the achievement of death as an anodyne and release from the pains of unfulfilled passion—a goal often envisioned (as we shall see shortly) in Christina Rossetti's poems of renunciation. In *Anactoria*, Swinburne's Sappho, rejected by her would-be lover, laments,

Alas, that neither moon nor snow nor dew
Nor all cold things can purge me wholly through,
Assuage me nor alay me nor appease,
Till supreme sleep shall bring me bloodless ease;
Till time wax faint in all his periods;
Till fate undo the bondage of the gods,
And lay, to slake and satiate me all through,
Lotus and Lethe on my lips like dew,
And shed around and over and under me
Thick darkness and the insuperable sea.
(Swinburne, 1:66)

Yet, unlike any of Christina Rossetti's renunciatory speakers, Swinburne's Sappho is at last consoled by her belief that she will be immortalized through the reputation and continuing vitality of her poetry in "the world." Her poetry is invaluable precisely because it memorializes the tragic value to the human spirit of erotic passions inevitably doomed to frustration and unfulfillment. Thus, although she chooses the anodyne of death to relieve her suffering, she maintains her adherence to an ideology that places supreme value on carnal love and sees it, in fact, as a metaphor describing the interactions of all natural phenomena:

Blossom of branches, and on each high hill
Clear air and wind, and under in clamorous vales
Fierce noises of the fiery nightingales,
Buds burning in the sudden spring like fire,
The wan washed sand and the waves' vain desire,
Sails seen like blown white flowers at sea, and words
That bring tears swiftest, and long notes of birds
Violently singing till the whole world sings—
I Sappho shall be one with all these things,
With all high things for ever; and my face
Seen once, my songs once heard in a strange place,
Cleave to men's lives, and waste the days thereof
With gladness and much sadness and long love.
(Swinburne, 1:65–66)

In Dante Rossetti's poems death is not depicted, as it often is in Swinburne's, as a desirable release from the pains of disappointed love. Rather, the inevitable need to endure such pains is stressed. In Rossetti's sonnet, "Without Her" (number fifty-three from *The House of Life*), the speaker confesses his desolation at the absence of his beloved, whether through her death or her rejection of him. In the poem's sestet he asks,

> What of the heart without her? Nay, poor heart,
>   Of thee what word remains ere speech be still?
>   A wayfarer by barren ways and chill,
>   Steep ways and weary, without her thou art,
>   Where the long cloud, the long wood's counterpart,
>   Sheds doubled darkness up the labouring hill.[40]

The "labouring hill" of stoical endurance is also the immediate prospect for Rossetti's speakers in such poems as "The Woodspurge," the "Willow-wood" sonnets, "The Portrait," and even for the bereaved male lover in "The Blessed Damozel."

As in Rossetti's poems, when love fails, is renounced, or is betrayed in Morris's *Defence of Guenevere* poems, intense suffering and the need to endure it follow.[41] With Morris, however, the pain of hopeless love nearly always drives its victims to the brink of madness. In "The Haystack in the Floods," for instance, Jehane renounces her lover to save her honor. The alternative choice is to become the paramour of her lover's enemy, God-mar. Even before Godmar—avenging her refusal of him—butchers her lover before her eyes, Jehane realizes that, "I cannot choose but sin and sin / Whatever happens." At the end—aware that she must now endure "The long way back" and "The court at Paris," then "The swift Seine on some rainy day"—she

> . . . shook her head and gazed awhile
> At her cold hands with a rueful smile,
> As though this thing had made her mad.
> (Lang, 264)

Similarly, in "King Arthur's Tomb," after Guenevere finally chooses a life devoted to Christ instead of to Lancelot, Arthur's greatest knight faces the torturous and maddening prospect of a life without his beloved:

> "I stretched my hands toward her and fell down,
>   How long I lay in swoon I cannot tell:
>   My head and hands were bleeding from the stone,
>   When I rose up, also I heard a bell."
> (Lang, 181)

Like the various victims of betrayed, renounced, or ill-fated love in these poems by Swinburne, Rossetti, and Morris, Christina Rossetti's renunciatory lovers face melancholy, tormented lives. Like Swinburne's poetic characters, they frequently wish for the release of death. Some, however, have a sustaining hope unavailable to Swinburne's and Morris's failed lovers but obsessive for the bereaved lovers in such poems by Dante Rossetti as "The Blessed Damozel," "The Portrait," and "The Stream's Secret." They look forward to ideal fulfillment after death in "the flowering land of love." Such fulfillment takes two forms in Christina Rossetti's verse: it can involve ecstatic union with the beloved apart from earthly enthrallments and in the sight of God, as it is repeatedly envisioned in her brother's verse, or, more frequently, it depends solely on union with God in His transcendent Paradise of Love.

Before such fulfillment can be attained, however, the difficult choice of renunciation must be made by her women in love. "How One Chose" rehearses, in a dialogue between two lovers who are also poets and aesthetes, the idealistic and skeptical perspectives on earthly love. The voice of the former insists that the home of ideal love—"'Beyond the sea'" and "'Beyond the clouds'"—must be sought out, whatever the obstacles to its discovery. But the skeptical voice concludes the poem, renouncing the quest and the beloved:

> "Nay, seek alone: I am no mate
> For such as you, in truth;
> My heart is old before its time;
> Yours yet is in its youth:
> This home with pleasures girt about
> Seek you, for I am wearied out."
> (*Works*, 296)

In "From House to Home" (1858) the "home" is further depicted as an illusory earthly ideal, one that must be renounced in order to attain eternal fulfillment of the impulse to love. After the illusions of this life have collapsed and the consequent suffering of self-denial has been endured, the speaker envisions her reward as a Heaven of Love:

> Each face looked one way like a moon new-lit,
> Each face looked one way towards its Sun of Love;
> Drank love and bathed in love and mirrored it
> And knew no end thereof.

Glory touched glory on each blessed head,
  Hands locked dear hands never to sunder more:
These were the new-begotten from the dead
  Whom the great birthday bore.

Heart answered heart, soul answered soul at rest,
  Double against each other, filled, sufficed:
All loving, loved of all; but loving best
  And best beloved of Christ.

                                                    (*Poems*, 1:87)

This vision is the climax of Rossetti's long allegorical poem, which is, significantly, a belated but self-conscious corrective to Tennyson's "The Palace of Art."[42]

In the course of her monologue, Rossetti's speaker describes her temporary seduction by "a pleasure-place within my soul; / An earthly paradise supremely fair / That lured me from the goal" (*Poems*, 1:82). More briefly than in Tennyson's poem, this speaker describes the landscape and animal life around her "pleasure-place" of "white transparent glass" that at first appears ideal but finally is exposed as "a tissue of hugged lies" (*Poems*, 1:82). Unlike the soul in "The Palace of Art," the soul of "From House to Home" is not alone but has a lover whose beauty is a reflection of the aesthetic landscape that surrounds them:

Ofttimes one like an angel walked with me,
  With spirit-discerning eyes like flames of fire,
But deep as the unfathomed endless sea
  Fulfilling my desire:

And sometimes like a snowdrift he was fair,
  And sometimes like a sunset glorious red,
And sometimes he had wings to scale the air
  With aureole round his head.

We sang our songs together by the way,
  Calls and recalls and echoes of delight;
So communed we together all the day,
  And so in dreams by night.

                                                    (*Poems*, 1:83)

These two "singers" have clearly chosen a world of love that is insepar-able from the artistic activities it inspires.[43] But the abandonment of the speaker by her "angel," who inexplicably seeks "home," a "distant land," without her, thrusts the speaker into agonized despair: she "wailed" and "gnashed" until "my heart broke and my spirit broke" (*Poems*, 1:85). In a swoon, she dreams of a woman "incomparably pale, and almost fair, / And sad beyond expression," who symbolizes Faith and the Church, as well as her future self. This figure is remorselessly tortured but endures: "She bled and wept, yet did not shrink." Voices in the dream discuss her suffering:

> One cried: "How long? yet founded on the Rock
> She shall do battle, suffer, and attain"—
> One answered: "Faith quakes in the tempest shock:
> Strengthen her soul again."
>
> (*Poems*, 1:86)

This dream culminates with an austere description of the apocalypse— "earth and heaven were rolled up like a scroll; / . . . The day had come, that day"—and it subsides into the vision of heavenly love already quoted. By means of this allegory, then, the speaker justifies her present life of renunciation: "I would not if I might / Rebuild my house of lies" (*Poems*, 1:87). Patiently drinking of the "loathsome" cup and withstanding the "thorns" of life, without sensual pleasure and without love, and awaiting "the day when from His storehouses / God shall bring new and old," the speaker endures. But her experience, in Rossetti's imagination, is the occasion of a different kind of artistic enterprise than the hedonistic one with which the speaker begins her revelations. Rossetti's poem, as Sandra Gilbert quite rightly insists, is directed by a "moral aesthetic," but unlike the moral tag that concludes Tennyson's "Palace of Art," Rossetti's rejection of worldly pleasures is unequivocal and unambiguous.[44] The soul of the speaker in Tennyson's poem only partially renounces her pleasure palace, and even then does so specifically to enter "the world":

> "Make me a cottage in the vale," she said,
> "Where I may mourn and pray.
>
> "Yet pull not down my palace towers, that are
> So lightly, beautifully built:
> Perchance I may return with others there
> When I have purged my guilt."[45]

By contrast, Rossetti's speakers, as we have seen, generally renounce the worldly pleasures described in her poems, and the creator of those artistic edifices transposes their palpable beauties to the New Jerusalem, "the City builded without hands" (*Works*, 15).

The psychological dynamic informing "Memory" is the same as that of "From House to Home." The second part of "Memory" (*Poems*, 1:147–48), however, was not composed until 1865, when Rossetti was at the height of her artistic powers. This poem discards the elaborate dialogical and allegorical strategies of "From House to Home" and is an accomplished illustration of Rossetti's "poetics of conciseness." The first part of this terse, tensely understated poem describes the process by which the speaker—"Stripped bare of self-regard or forms or ruth"—chose to renounce her lover: "I . . . broke my heart, / Breaking mine idol." Afterwards her life nonetheless "centres" on "a blessed memory on a throne," which she secludes in a room "no one enters / Save I myself alone." Meanwhile, she endures "While winter comes and goes" and "While bloom the bloodless lily and warm rose / Of lavish summer." Sustaining a kind of sacrificial death-in-life, like the lily in its symbolic guise, she austerely bides her time on earth, as nearly all of Rossetti's renunciatory lovers do, awaiting a fulfillment inestimably superior to the transient and guilt-ridden gratifications available to lovers on earth. In autumn, "with clear eyes," she renews herself by thinking "how it will be in Paradise / When we're together." Like the speaker herself, this poem presents itself "Stripped bare of self-regard or forms." The strength of its often monosyllabic, masculine diction—the language of breaking, bracing, and choosing—not only insists upon the finality and authority of the speaker's choice to renounce earthly love. Its directness also serves to focus on the central metonymic figure in the poem, which espouses in Augustinian fashion the at once monitory and prophetic value of memory, "that human faculty whose astonishing power Augustine first really probed and praised as the preeminent path toward the experience of God."[46]

Such renunciatory conversions as those in "From House to Home" and "Memory" also form the thematic substance of "Three Nuns" and "The Convent Threshold," poems that situate the conversion experience in a traditional, institutionalized context. The ordeals of choice and the agonies of endurance that afflict the various personae of these poems force upon them a painfully heightened consciousness of the conflict and ineradicable tension between *eros* and *agapē*, between the sensual and the ascetic lives. Rossetti's speakers have chosen the latter only with great difficulty. The very titles of "Three Nuns" and "The Convent Threshold" indicate the orthodox direction of these speakers' commitment after renouncing *eros*, and their monologues suggest the extent to which the desperate characters they present need shelter, support, and continuing direction from the Church.

More important, however, these poems serve as paradigms of the specifically Augustinian pattern of renunciation and conversion common in Rossetti's poems. Understanding the operations of this pattern clarifies a number of major problems, tensions, and apparent conflicts in her poetry (and prose). As I have suggested, Augustine's *Confessions* was an important palimpsest, a textual precursor that thematically, ideologically, and even formally laid the groundwork for Rossetti's poems of renunciation.[47] Seeing the *Confessions* as palimpsest helps to explain the dialogical modes of many renunciatory poems by Rossetti, as well as the importance in them of memory, childhood innocence, lapsarian cruxes, and "severed selves."

Although "The Convent Threshold" is a more powerful and carefully crafted poem than "Three Nuns," the latter work provides a broader context for understanding the Augustinian premises, patterns of value, and behavior in Rossetti's religious poetry. Just as "A Triad" suggests the whole spectrum of impediments to the attainment by women of any ideally satisfying love relationship in the world, "Three Nuns" sets out a range of alternative motivations for an impassioned woman to choose the life of the cloister. With all three speakers here, as with the renunciatory lovers in "The Convent Threshold" and "Memory," traditional parallels between the nun's veil and that of the bride underlie decisions to reject the world. While the ascetic life serves as a self-conscious escape from the temptations of the outside world, including that posed by *eros*, it also becomes a safe, albeit painful, surrogate source of fulfillment for the same passionate impulses that make life in the world so dangerous. "Three Nuns" presents dialogically interacting soliloquies by three women who renounce the world; all three ultimately desire death either as an escape from their emotional and psychological suffering, or as a transposition to "the City builded without hands," which "Shall safely shut me in" (*Works*, 15).

The first nun seeks death primarily as escape and views life in the convent as tantamount to death:

> Shadow, shadow on the wall,
>   Spread thy shelter over me;
> Wrap me with a heavy pall,
>   With the dark that none may see.
>   (*Works*, 12–13)

Through its allusion to "Snow White," her soliloquy begins with a rejection of the mythology that culminates in fulfilled erotic love and worldly success. That mythology constitutes an invalid ideology. This nun's desperate craving for some shelter withdrawn from the world, we soon learn, results from her desire to "forget / Present sorrow and past sin." Her ambiguous "sin" clearly had to do with the speaker's vanity, which precipitated her erotic seduction. That she *had* been "full of vanity and care" when "men saw and called me fair" prompted her to renounce the world: "God was left behind, curls shorn." The last stanzas of her soliloquy expand upon this terse statement, as the speaker yearns for a return to the "dream" of childhood innocence. As a child she believed she could live

> Secret, neither found nor sought;
> Till the lilies on the stream,
> Pure as virgin purity,
> Would seem scarce too pure for me.
> (*Works*, 13)

She concludes, however, "Ah but that can never be!" This woman has succumbed to worldly temptations, but she has now moved beyond the kind of bewilderment that characterizes the speaker in "An Apple-Gathering" to a full awareness of her "sin" and the torture of her shame. To assuage it, she has sought the cloister and now seeks death, its ultimate extension: "I would be dumb."

The second soliloquy of "Three Nuns" explores the psychology of another kind of woman in love. This one, unlike the first speaker, has not "sinned" or been victim to vanity or seduction; instead, she is selflessly tenacious in seeking only the well-being of her beloved. "I prayed for him," and in the afterlife "soon with surer faith shall pray / For him" (*Works*, 14). Moreover,

> I sacrificed, he never bought;
> He nothing gave, he nothing took;
> We never bartered look for look.
> (*Works*, 14)

This nun's renunciation apparently issues from impotence and frustration in love, and her retreat to the cloister, like that of the first nun, is preliminary to a retreat to death: "Oh sweet is death that bindeth up / The broken and the bleeding heart" (*Works*, 14). Like all of Christina Rossetti's lovers who renounce *eros*, this one suffers, but unlike the first nun, who seeks death solely as an anodyne, this woman looks forward to a heavenly reward for her selflessness and her pain. Indeed, "the reward is almost won, / A crown of glory and a palm" (*Works*, 14).

The third nun presents yet another set of motives for taking the veil, unusual for Rossetti's poems in that these motives have no apparent connection with an experience of failed love. Rather, this speaker has joined the cloister from a spontaneous impulse to achieve spiritual liberation: "My heart is as a freeborn bird / Caged in my cruel breast" (*Works*, 14). This nun appears to have begun with an awareness that all things of the world are mutable and vain. She forcefully renounces the "delights and precious things" of the world, because "My heart shall beat with a new life / When thine is dead and cold." She envisions fulfillment in Paradise, where "Red roses like love visible" are "budding now for me." Her apparent complacency is redeemed, however, in the poem's last stanzas when she recalls how her renunciation of the world has been an ordeal—one that has, however, provided masochistic gratifications.

> While still the names rang in mine ears
>   Of daughter, sister, wife,
> The outside world still looked so fair
>   To my weak eyes, and rife
> With beauty, my heart almost failed;
>   Then in desperate strife
> I prayed, as one who prays for life,—
>
> Until I grew to love what once
>   Had been so burdensome.
>   (*Works*, 15–16)

Despite the fact that her heart has become "numb" in expectation of fulfillment, she is impelled to persist in her renunciation: "The Spirit and the Bride say, Come" (*Works*, 16). More interesting as a character than the first two nuns, whose retreat from life because of failure in love seems so familiar, the speaker of this last soliloquy reveals the full psychological complexity of the ways in which the language of religion—its use of bridal imagery and the idiom of love relationships—expedites the leap from *eros* to *agapē*. At the same time conversion forces upon the devotee the same pains of frustration and anticipation in pursuit of the ideal that erotic lovers inevitably endure, according to Rossetti's perceptions of romantic, especially Dantean and Petrarchan, tradition. Yet with its pains comes a hope for absolute fulfillment in the afterlife that defeats mutability and is unavailable to exclusively erotic lovers.

Each speaker in "Three Nuns" presents an autobiographical confession in the Augustinian pattern, focusing on the split between present and former selves. Memory is, therefore, the pivotal faculty in understanding the experience of conversion, on the one hand, and describing proleptically the experience of Paradise—where innocence and lost ideals are recovered—on the other. Paradise also promises unity and identity with God: "I may wake again / After His likeness." Hans Robert Jauss has demonstrated that for Augustine "the first predicate of divine identity that makes the creature conscious of its dependence on its creator is all-embracing totality. . . . [T]he child, although from the very beginning not without sin, has been created in God's image" (Jauss, 143). The first speaker in "Three Nuns" appropriately wishes that in a bird's song, "I may / Dream myself once more a child," for "while yet a child, I thought / I could live as in a dream / . . . Pure as virgin purity" (*Works*, 13). But such a dream of Wordsworthian unity of self and unity with nature is impossible to attain: "The ontological relationship between God's unity . . . and man's existence, scattered into multiplicity, becomes in Augustine's *Confessions*, the dichotomous scheme of autobiographical portrayal" that all three speakers in "Three Nuns" replicate. "Its subject is the split Christian subjectivity: an atemporal and nonlocalized writing self which . . . accusingly confronts a self lost in time. Its subject matter is very sharply divided into the state preceding and following conversion," as it is in the case of each of Rossetti's nuns (Jauss, 143). The dynamic of the unified reconstitution of self that is the aim of such self-portrayals "depends upon the capacity of . . . memory" (Jauss, 142). In "Three Nuns" Rossetti refracts the problem of bifurcated and multiple selves seeking a return to original unity, and she does so not only by depicting clear divisions between the past and present of each speaker, but also by representing three discrete versions of the "type" of the convert. Each looks back in a different way to the period before conversion—whether childhood, or the days when "men saw and called me fair," or when "still the names rang in my ears / Of daughter, sister, wife" (*Works*, 13–16). Despite conversion, however, each also remains fragmented, anticipating the attainment of self-unity, unity with renounced lovers, and unity with God in "the City builded without hands."

Significantly, Rossetti's recovery of the Augustinian pattern of conversion here and elsewhere in her poetry must be seen, according to Jauss's history of its development, as antithetical to the trend in canonical literature of the nineteenth century. For the tradition Augustine initiated, the new religious experience of an identity split into a naive self and a self that has withdrawn from the world offered the [nineteenth-century] aesthetic attitude the challenge of overcoming the heteronomy of the experience of the self and of making the "fragments of a great confession" the whole of a self-portrayal of the *individuum ineffabile*. And the history of the aesthetic experience does in fact show the process in the course of which poetry takes hold of the Augustinian scheme of the experience of self, secularizes memory as "world inner space" in love poetry, increasingly emphasizes the world-appropriating capacity of remembering aesthesis, utilizes, since Rousseau, its affective evidence to totalize the contingency of a life history and climaxes in Proust's poetics of recovered time . . . [where] in the arrogance of "saying all there is to say," he finally usurped . . . divine omniscience. (Jauss, 147)

The ideology of works by Rossetti that follow the Augustinian pattern, though ostensibly "timeless" or "medievalist," thus locates itself historically as a particular subversive (that is, conservative) reaction against the ideology of Romanticism, as that ideology presents itself in Rousseau and Proust, but also in Blake, Wordsworth, and Shelley. At the same time, by appropriating antecedent literary traditions like that of Augustine and opposing or correcting very recent ones, Rossetti reflects the paradigmatic nineteenth-century aesthetic experience. She perfects literary works that simultaneously exploit, challenge, and withdraw from the "lapsed" ideologies dominant in the literary culture of her time.

"Three Nuns" has thematic similarities to "From House to Home," but it also has significant formal and stylistic similarities. These, in fact, epitomize the dominant emotional and psychological qualities of Rossetti's renunciatory love poems. Both poems embody the tension within their speakers between aesthetic and ascetic impulses, and both also stylistically imitate that tension. With its appropriately regular iambic tetrameter and terse phrasing, "Three Nuns" reflects the predominantly ascetic directions of its speakers' lives. Yet lush aesthetic imagery and diction irrepressibly punctuate each soliloquy. For instance, the first nun wishes to "Dream myself once more a child / . . . Plucking clematis and wild / Hyacinths till pleasure grew / Tired" (*Works*, 13). The second nun, in a different Keatsian poetic mannerism, reveals that she is "half in love with easeful death": "Oh sweet is death, for I am weak / And weary, and it giveth rest" (*Works*, 14). And the third envisions heaven in voluptuous, explicitly sexual metaphors. There,

Red roses like love visible
Are blowing on their tree,
Or white like virgin purity.
(*Works*, 15)

Indeed, the "virgin purity" of all three nuns is tainted by the sensual impulses behind the aesthetic images that emerge in their speech, as well as by the sensuality of their languorous, melancholy dwelling on death. Renunciation and retreat from the world—that is, the ascetic life—allow them to savor the states of mind and emotion occasioned by erotic experience or by its transposition in the prospect of heavenly love. Such an aestheticization of experience would be disrupted, if not altogether prevented, by continued participation in the hurly-burly of life, which is not even allowed as a possibility in these solipsistic poems.

This is the case, too, in "The Convent Threshold," where an ascetic lover is shown to realize every possible advantage of renouncing *eros*. The ultimate aestheticism of her quest (and of the opportunity it provides for her creator) is exposed in the self-conscious artistry of the poem, including its form and highly polished style. "The Convent Threshold" is a dramatic monologue spoken by a woman who renounces earthly love for "the stairs that mount above, / Stair after golden skyward stair" (*Poems*, 1:61). As in "How One Chose," the lovers here are at odds. Their situation is reminiscent of the one that develops in Tennyson's *Maud*: "There's blood between us, love, my love, / There's father's blood, there's brother's blood" (*Poems*, 1:61). But here, too, Rossetti challenges the emphatically worldly ideology of Tennyson's speaker, who attempts to exorcise the guilty effects of his refusal to renounce erotic love by volunteering to fight for England in the Crimean War.[48] By contrast, Rossetti's speaker chooses the monastic life in order to purge her guilt, to wash herself clean of the "scarlet mud" that stains her "lily feet" as well as her heart. In pursuit of this goal, she associates herself, in the tradition of Thomas à Kempis, with the world's martyrs, who have become "Cherubim and Seraphim." These, "the offscouring" of the world, "bore the Cross, they drained the cup" and were "Racked, roasted, crushed, wrenched limb from limb" (*Poems*, 1:62). The speaker's final motive for renunciation and penitence, nonetheless, is to meet her lover in Heaven "as once we met / And love with old familiar love" (*Poems*, 1:65). Despite the pains she expects to endure in the ascetic life ("until my sleep begin / How long shall stretch these nights and days?"), her persistently aesthetic sensibilities are visible. In the poem's third stanza, for instance, she describes the prospect of life that appears to her unrepentent lover's eyes, and it is remarkably like the vision that confronts Arnold's Strayed Reveller as he looks down upon his companions from Circe's palace. According to the would-be nun, her lover sees

> Milk-white, wine-flushed among the vines,
> Up and down leaping, to and fro,
> Most glad, most full, made strong with wines,
> Blooming as peaches pearled with dew,
> Their golden windy hair afloat,
> Love-music warbling in their throat,
> Young men and women come and go.
>
> (*Poems*, 1:62)

The speaker's intuition of her lover's vision here is more sympathetic and nostalgic than derisive. Indeed, her agonized quest to sublimate the sensual and aesthetic inclinations this vision reflects, and to repress the erotic passion that is their corollary, is designed primarily to ensure a transposed perpetuation of both sensual and passionate experience in the afterlife. This quest is also motivated by an overpowering sense of sinfulness and, as we have come to expect in Rossetti's poetry, by a devastating sensitivity to mutability. After three tormenting dreams of her lover, she envisions herself awaking: "My face was pinched, my hair was grey" (*Poems*, 1:65). Yet she can endure mutability and the pains of her renunciation because of her knowledge that "all is small / Save love, for love is all in all" (*Poems*, 1:64) and because of her faith that this world's transient suffering and self-denial will give way finally to a paradisal eternity of "old familiar love."

UNQUESTIONABLY, Christina Rossetti had much in common with the speakers projected in her poems of renunciation, but the choices that she as an artist had to make superseded, in the complexities of their origins and operations, the choices made by the lovers she so often portrayed. Through what Jauss has termed the "aesthetic experience," Rossetti generated a set of dialogical relationships between her renunciatory poetry and "the world." Functioning at three levels, these relationships constitute one of the foremost complexities of her work. Her poems operate first, as we have seen, at the level of intercourse between each of her speakers and the world that is repudiated as unregenerate—often duplicitous, violent, and materialistic. Second, they operate at the level of interactions between the specific sociohistorical world of Victorian England (that is, the world that constitutes the audience for her poems) and the poems themselves, which enter into that world and actively abjure its dominant amatory, economic, and moral values. Finally, these poems function at the level of intertextuality, creating a dialogue between Rossetti's poems and canonized literature both past and present.

This canon's forms and ideologies can be valorized and revitalized in her own work (as with Augustine and, as we will see, with Dante) or devalued and subverted (as, most often, with Tennyson, Keats, and Wordsworth). By means of these relationships, as Jauss has suggested, the "aesthetic experience can illuminate the structure of an historical life world, its official and implied interaction patterns and legitimations, and even its latent ideology." Frequently, literature can make "palpable . . . what the historical and sociohistorical documents of the . . . life world . . . do not expressly record, or fail to mention." Aesthetic experience can therefore "form a world of its own without . . . eliding the reference back to the suspended world of everyday life or one of its provinces of meaning. Rather, the aesthetic experience can enter into a communicative relation with the everyday world or any other reality and annul the polar opposition of [art] and reality" (Jauss, 121).

Rossetti's ultimate design was not, then, merely to embody a "moral aesthetic" in verse. As the commentaries above make clear, Rossetti used her poetry largely as a medium in which to challenge what she perceived as the values of her particular historical era, as well as to discuss basic conflicts inherent in amatory and aesthetic experience. These include conflicts between desires for gratification in this life and postponement of such gratification, between the desire of pleasure and the fear of sin, between passionate impulses and a yearning for death as an end to them, between self-indulgence and self-denial, between the real and the visionary. All such painful conflicts are superseded, and in this sense reconciled, however, in the finality and the beauty of the poetic artifacts they generate.

A year before Christina Rossetti's death one of her female contemporaries wrote of the poet: "She has led a more hidden life than most nuns. . . . Her own will for seclusion and for duty has made her veil, and in some quiet Bloomsbury street or square she has pitched her cloister."[49] Rather more angrily and with less empathy, Sandra Gilbert has observed that the poet, "banqueting on bitterness, must bury herself alive in a coffin of renunciation."[50] Behind the admiration audible in the first critic's voice and the regret apparent in that of the second lies the perception that Rossetti, during her life of renunciation, wrote a large body of poetry with the dominant theme of renunciation. Yet these critics do not acknowledge two essential operations of her poetry. On the one hand, portraying speakers who adopt the pose of renunciation enabled Rossetti to dwell freely, in the discrete "subuniverse" of her poetry, on voluptuous sensations derived imaginatively from a world that had, ostensibly, been rejected. Read without awareness of its sociohistorical and intertextual commentaries, her poetry thus moves the reader, along with most of Rossetti's speakers, inward, finally, away from quotidian reality into a cloister (rather than a palace) of art. Read in its true and proper, rather than its merely self-referential, contexts, however, her poetry moves the reader to an awareness of its critical participation in social reality, as well as the reality of those literary traditions that survive to interact dialogically with social reality. For Rossetti, the single most important among such traditions was that of Dante.

CHAPTER 5.

INTERTEXTUALITY:

DANTE, PETRARCH,

AND CHRISTINA

ROSSETTI

CONTEXTUAL

I N her recent biography of Christina Rossetti, Georgina Battiscombe quite properly describes the poet as "soaked . . . in
the Dante legend."[1] More expansively, Lona Packer has explained that "as Christina grew older, she recovered from the
notion that Dante, as [her father's] special possession, was a
noxious feature of adult life. . . . Although she herself was to write several
prose studies of Dante, more important is the pervasive Dantean influence
on her poetry, an influence recognizable both in her conceptions and the
poetic techniques she used to express them. The Dantean imagery and
symbolism for the Dantean religious ideas may be found throughout her
work."[2] Rossetti herself acknowledged in 1892 that "perhaps it is enough
to be half an Italian, but certainly it is enough to be a Rossetti to render
Dante a fascinating centre of thought" (FL, 49). Almost a decade earlier,
when preparing "Dante. The Poet Illustrated out of the Poem" for *Century Magazine*, she wrote to Edmund Gosse in order to defend her use of
Cayley's translation of the *Divine Comedy* rather than Longfellow's more
popular one. In her letter of 30 January 1883, she explained that Cayley's
translation adheres "to the . . . ternary rhyme of the original poem, [and]
has gone far towards satisfying an ear rendered fastidious by Dante's own
harmony of words."[3]

Indeed, apart from the inescapable Dantean preoccupations of her entire household, we know that Rossetti began serious study of Dante in
1848 (Bell, 16); that as early as 1850 she had the opportunity to read at
least portions of Cayley's translations of the *Divine Comedy* when posting
them to William Michael (FL, 15); that she initiated (but never completed) a project to assist with the Rev. Alexander B. Grosart's edition of

Spenser's complete works by tracing allusions to Dante and Boccaccio in Spenser; and that she read Cayley's translations of Petrarch in proof during September 1878 (*FL*, 76–77).[4] Her erudition in the troubadour traditions out of which Dante's and Petrarch's works arose was indicated in small ways: for instance, in a letter to William Michael she revealed knowledge of the obscure fact that "a golden violet . . . was a provençal prize for poetry" (*FL*, 145).

The profound influence of Dante upon Christina Rossetti is, of course, neither a surprising nor a singular phenomenon. For all the Pre-Raphaelite poets, but especially for the Rossettis, Dante was a literary precursor whose importance to their art can be compared only with that of Milton to the art of the Romantics. But Dante influenced writers of all stripes during the century—sometimes enormously, as in the cases of Blake, Carlyle, and the Rossettis, and sometimes to a lesser extent, as with Keats, Tennyson, Swinburne, and Arnold. Like all writers of major influence, Dante was adapted to the particular purposes of those who alluded to him. Among Victorian writers this process of adaptation is especially clear, and differences between those aspects of Dante's poetry admired by mainstream Victorians—such as R. W. Church, Thomas Carlyle, and William Gladstone—and those emphasized by the Pre-Raphaelites, but especially by Christina Rossetti, reveal the full extent to which the Rossettis, Swinburne, and Morris can be looked upon not only as "the last Romantics," but also as harbingers of aestheticism in ways that their contemporaries were not.

Two aspects of the *Divine Comedy* especially appealed to typical Victorian readers: what they perceived as its gothic structure, and the manifest feelings of alienation shown by its author. These characteristics of the poem were admired by R. W. Church, the popular dean of St. Paul's Cathedral, who had studied under John Keble at Oxford. In an essay on Dante written in 1850 this important religious leader reveled in the gothic eclecticism of the *Divine Comedy*, exhibiting a familiar aspect of Victorian taste. He extolled Dante's masterpiece,

> so abnormal, so lawless, so reckless of all ordinary proprieties and canons of feeling, taste and composition. It is rough and abrupt; obscure in phrase and allusion, doubly obscure in purpose. It is a medley of all subjects usually kept distinct: scandal of the day and transcendental science, politics and confessions, coarse satire and angelic joy, private wrongs, with the mysteries of faith, local names and habitations of earth, with visions of hell and heaven.[5]

The immense diversity of characteristics that Church emphasized inevitably remind us not only of the expected eclecticism of the Victorian drawing room, but also of most of the basic elements of "gothic," which Ruskin later elaborated in his chapter "The Nature of Gothic" from *The Stones of Venice* (1853). Church showed sensitivity to Dante's "savageness," "changefulness," "naturalism," "grotesqueness," and "redundance." Church also found oddly attractive the extreme degree of alienation suffered by Dante, with which many Victorians could identify.[6] (It is the focal concern of Dante Rossetti's poem, "Dante at Verona.") Church described such alienation, in Dante's case, as the "price and counterpoise" of greatness. Dante was "solitary and companionless" in his "visionary world." He thought and wrote "as a friendless man—to whom all that he had held dear was either lost or embittered" (Friedrich, 339). Thomas Carlyle saw such alienation from lesser men as inevitable for the prophet-poet: "Dante burns as a pure star, fixed there in the firmament, at which the great and high of all ages kindle themselves" (Friedrich, 303).

Several crucial elements of Dante's greatest work, as extensions of the alienated great man, especially appealed to Carlyle, and these, too, reflect paramount concerns in Victorian literature and Victorian society at large. Carlyle profoundly admired the moral earnestness of the *Divine Comedy* and especially of the *Purgatorio*: "There is no book so moral as this, the very essence of Christian morality! . . . [We see in Dante] one great mind, making of himself, as it were, the spokesman of his age, and speaking with such an earnestness and depth that he has become one of the voices of mankind itself, making his voice to be heard in all ages" (Friedrich, 301). Moreover, that voice in the *Comedy* is inexorably sincere, Dante's magnum opus being "the *sincerest* of all Poems." Carlyle found sincerity to be the primary "measure of worth" in the work: "It came deep out of the author's heart of hearts; and it goes deep, and through long generations into ours" (Friedrich, 302). For Carlyle, a characteristic of Dante's work even more poignant than his earnest morality and sincerity, however, is the elegiac tone of his poem. Beneath the surface of Carlyle's commentary is the dolorous yearning for lost ideals, the remorse for failed potential that literary Victorians inherited from the Romantic poets and that pervaded the literature of Victoria's reign, existing in tension with its utilitarian faith in progress. Carlyle pronounced Dante "great above all in his sorrow!" (Friedrich, 301).

Other aspects of Dantean thought were attractive to William Gladstone, who felt a kinship with Dante in political principles, but he valued Dante's religious precepts still more highly. In a letter written near the end of his life, Gladstone expressed the enormous debt he felt to Dante's work as a kind of *magister vitae*. He described the "supreme poet" as "a 'solemn master' for me" and explained that "the reading of Dante is not merely a pleasure, a *tour de force*, or a lesson; it is a vigorous discipline of the heart, the intellect, the whole man. In the school of Dante I have learnt a great part of that mental provision . . . which has served me to make the journey of life up to the term of nearly seventy-three years" (Friedrich, 322). Gladstone actually translated touchstone passages from the *Divine Comedy*, and one of his favorites—presumably a source of moral as well as ontological instruction—was the speech of Picarda, daughter of Simone Donati, in *Paradisio* 3. Speaking to Dante, she explains how in heaven,

> Within the will Divine to set our own
> Is of the essence of this Being blest,
> For that our wills to one with his be grown.
> So, as we stand throughout the realms of rest,
> From stage to stage, our pleasure is the King's
> Whose will our will informs, by him imprest.
> In His Will is our peace. To this all things
> By Him created, or by nature made,
> As to a central Sea, self-motion brings.
> (Friedrich, 321)

Dante's paradisal ideal of loving union between man's will and God's provided a goal to be pursued by Gladstone, one that probably often reinforced the prime minister's faith in the moral rectitude of his political actions as well as his social endeavors.

From Church, Carlyle, and Gladstone—a fairly representative sampling of influential Victorian readers of Dante—we can generalize about the uses to which the less avant-garde contemporaries of the Pre-Raphaelites put Dante. The crucial values they perceived in or projected upon the *Divine Comedy* derive from the poem's eclectically varied form and content, a feature reminiscent of gothic architecture. But those values also clearly hinged upon their sensitivity to the profound and inescapable feelings of alienation incurred by men who attempt great work in the world. Dante's typical Victorian readers admired his intense sincerity of tone (for them a facet of all profoundly earnest moral endeavors), his great poem's undercurrent of sorrow that laments and foreshadows fallen experience, and his serious celebration of the providential ways in which God designed the world and operates within it to align man's will with His own.

The emphases we find in Church, Carlyle, and Gladstone upon these elements of Dante's vision of the world differ substantially from the values extrapolated by the Pre-Raphaelites from Dante. One such value was Dante's self-conscious concern with literary traditions and genealogies, and their importance to him in pursuing and perfecting his art. As a corollary to this, and equally important, was the Pre-Raphaelites' obsessive concern with the great Italian poet's transposition of erotic passion to a spiritual object and condition. Christina Rossetti describes the central movement in Dante's work as one in which "the lost love of earth is found again as one higher, lovelier and better loved in paradise."[7] This movement begins for Dante in the *Vita Nuova* and culminates in the *Paradisio*. It is therefore appropriate that Dante Rossetti's first extensive published work included a meticulous translation of Dante's first major literary enterprise.

In his preface to the first edition of *The Early Italian Poets* (1861) Dante Rossetti broaches (but does not subsequently pursue) a discussion of those areas of his life in which literary culture subsumes biography. He begins the penultimate paragraph of his preface with the statement that "In relinquishing this work, . . . I feel, as it were, divided from my youth." He explains: "The first associations I have are connected with my father's devoted studies [of Dante], which, from his own point of view, have done so much towards the general investigation of Dante's writings. Thus, in those early days, all around me partook of the influence of the great Florentine; till, from viewing it as a natural element, I also, growing older, was drawn within the circle."[8] Significantly, when this "only contribution" of Rossetti's "to our English knowledge of old Italy" was revised and reissued in 1874, it was also retitled as *Dante and His Circle*, suggesting that Rossetti had by then achieved a more powerful awareness of his position within the historically expanded circumference of Dante's circle of influence. After having published his own first volume of poems in 1870, Rossetti could implicitly acknowledge that throughout much of his creative life he saw himself and his own work as an extension of a literary tradition that his namesake had redefined and perpetuated.

Similarly Christina Rossetti, near the end of her life, wrote to her brother William of "all too late . . . being sucked into the Dantean vortex" (*FL*, 188). This remark appears at the conclusion of some brief statements about Canon Moore's volume, *Dante and His Early Biographers*, and is perplexing because Christina Rossetti had throughout her life been surrounded and influenced by Dante scholars. The comment nonetheless reflects her sense of inadequacy as a commentator on the great poet whose life and works had absorbed such an enormous amount of her family's intellectual energy. Up to 1892 her attention to Dante had been primarily imaginative rather than scholarly, and her anxieties on that score are enunciated very early in her second major essay on Dante (1884). She explains that,

> If formidable for others, it is not least formidable for one of my name, for *me*, to enter the Dantesque field and say my little say on the Man and on the Poem; for others of my name have been before me in the same field and have wrought permanent and worthy work in attestation of their diligence. My father, Gabriele Rossetti, in his "Comento Analitico sul' Inferno di Dante" ("Analytical Commentary upon Dante's Hell"), has left to tyros a clew [*sic*] and to fellow-experts a theory. My sister, Maria Francesca Rossetti, has in her "Shadow of Dante" eloquently expounded the Divina Commedia as a discourse of most elevated faith and morals. My brother Dante has translated with a rare felicity the "Vita Nuova" . . . and other minor (political) works of his great namesake. My brother William has, with a strenuous endeavor to achieve close verbal accuracy, rendered the Inferno into English blank verse. I, who cannot lay claim to their learning, must approach my subject under cover of "*Mi valga . . . il grande amore*" ("May my great love avail me"), leaving to them the more confident plea, "*Mi valga il lungo studio*" ("May my long study avail me").[9]

This passage elucidates Christina Rossetti's perspective on that engrossing tradition of love poetry that began with the troubadours and culminated in the works of Dante and Petrarch. It was a tradition that deeply influenced Dante and Christina Rossetti, and with which all of the Rossetti children felt compelled to deal in their literary efforts, each of them reading and assimilating Dante as both a literary father—that is, an authenticating authority—and as a liberator of the imagination. As the two preceding quotations make clear, for all four Rossettis the culture of Dante was inescapable. It affected their values, their patterns of thought, their emotions, and their spiritual lives. The ambiguous title of Maria Rossetti's *A Shadow of Dante* appropriately reveals the range of influence Dantean literature had, especially on Dante and Christina Rossetti; as a great poet, but also as a representative of a tradition, he provided the enabling conditions for their art.[10] As early as 1867, she wrote in her first essay on Dante: "Viewing the matter of nationality exclusively as one of literary interest, now in this nineteenth century when it is impossible to be born an ancient Greek, a wise man might choose not unwisely to be born an

Italian, thus securing Dante as his elder brother, and the 'Divina Comme-dia' as his birthright."[11] It is hardly surprising, therefore, that Rossetti introduces what may be her most fascinating love poem, the *Monna Inno-minata*, with a preface that identifies a point of origin and the literary backgrounds for the *Monna Innominata* sonnets, but that also does a good deal more. (See Appendix for the complete text of the preface and poem sequence.) It raises a whole constellation of questions concerning matters of literary historicity, as well as the intertextual qualities, and therefore the full range of meanings, displayed by Christina Rossetti's love poetry. As we know, she began to write poetry dealing with the problems of attaining fulfillment in love at an age far too young for it to have originated from her own emotional experience with a man; rather it must have come from the "Poet mind," that is, from aesthetic and emotional responses to fundamentally literary experience.[12] Rossetti's apparent fa-miliarity with the troubadours—"a school of less conspicuous poets"—once again belies assumptions that she was virtually ignorant of most nonreligious literature produced before the nineteenth century. We might well infer some familiarity on her part with medieval romances and lyrics, which were probably of interest to her close friend, Charles Cayley (the translator of Dante), and which were being fervently researched at the British Museum during the various periods of Christina's own work there in the 1870s and 1880s. Moreover, the last paragraph of her preface reconfirms her faith in "the Poet mind," the ability of the creative imagi-nation to appropriate all materials—especially, in this case, literary my-thologies—in order to generate works of art that extend and develop those mythologies.

INTERTEXTUAL

Thomas Sebeok has recently described the concept of intertextuality as "Janus-faced," working "as much prospectively as . . . in retrograde scape." Extending Bakhtin's "hardly precise formulation of heteroglossia, dialo-gism, and polyphony," Sebeok emphasizes the ways in which "works of art—especially literature—are produced in response not to social reality but to previous works of art and the codes and conventions governing them." For him the concept of intertextuality helps us to understand all that is most *ahistorical* about a work of art: to the degree that it is in-tertextual, a novel, poem, or film "becomes distorted, opaque even, a darkly specular reflection of actuality—as, for instance, a myth. It becomes a lattice of signposts, regressing into, effectively, infinity, and thus capable of sustaining many alternative interpretations."[13]

In opposition to Sebeok, Claus Uhlig perceives the intertextual dimensions of a literary work as a precise barometer of the text's self-conscious historicity:

> It is exactly in the intertext [as palimpsest] . . . that historically conditioned tensions come to the fore: tensions not only between calendar time and intraliterary time but also between the author's intention and the relative autonomy of a text, or between the old and the new in general. What in this way contradicts the obsolete aesthetic ideal of an organically structured work of art appears from the literary historian's point of view as a necessary consequence of that history within the text the palimpsest preserves. . . . Any text will the more inevitably take on the characteristics of a palimpsest the more openly it allows the voices of the dead to speak, thus . . . bringing about a consciousness of the presentness of the past.[14]

Such speculation brings Uhlig to the startling and problematic conclusion that many literary works, because of their deliberate intertextuality, concern themselves preeminently with their own histories or genealogies. "It is doubtlessly true, and all the more so since the Romantic era," he insists, "that the aging of poetic forms and genres constantly increases their self-consciousness as knowledge of their own historicity. Through this progressive self-reflection, whose sphere is intertextuality, literature is in the end transformed into metaliterature, mere references to its own history."[15] The intriguing difference between the positions of Sebeok and Uhlig—for those who study the evolution of literary forms in their relations with cultural value systems, that is, with ideology—is that Sebeok assumes an absolutist view of history and Uhlig sustains a relational concept of history. Whereas Sebeok is what Hayden White would describe as an "historicist," Uhlig is a "radical relativist."[16] Both critics agree, however, that self-consciously intertextual literary works usually have little concern with "social reality." As is evident in her intertextual uses of Dante, Christina Rossetti proves an exception to this rule and employs parodic reworkings of literary palimpsests, their forms and themes, precisely in order to present a critique of particular deficiencies and false values basic to the social reality of Victorian England.

Sebeok and Uhlig also agree that views of history and of the self in relation to history—especially our creations or works in relation to past works—are deeply ideological.[17] Yet the preoccupation with such relations might be said to have begun only in the nineteenth century. It was during the nineteenth century that "the modern discipline of history first came fully into its own as a truly rigorous inquiry into the past."[18] Ultimately, however, because of "the very success of scientific history at reconstituting the past," the powerful awareness of the past itself became "burdensome and intimidating, . . . revealing—in Tennyson's metaphor—all the models that could not be remodeled." In fact, the apocalyptic aims of the Romantic poets early in the century reflected "the idea that history, simply by existing, exhausts possibilities, leaving its readers with a despairing sense of their own belatedness and impotence. And this despair in turn leads to anxious quests for novelty, to a hectic avant-gardism, and in the end to an inescapable fin de siècle ennui."[19]

As self-appointed heirs of the Romantics, the Pre-Raphaelite poets, including Christina Rossetti, display in their works an extraordinary degree of historical self-consciousness. As we have seen, with Rossetti such historical self-awareness can be either elided or explicit, as is the case in the *Monna Innominata* sonnets. When Rossetti's work operates openly and directly in the sphere of literary historical relations—that is, of intertextuality—it becomes deliberately parodic in the full and true sense of the term. Moreover, when her poetry functions parodically it can simultaneously accomplish solipsistic, aestheticist effects on the one hand, and the aims of a cultural critique on the other.

Some especially useful theoretical discussion of parody has appeared in recent years in the writing of Roland Barthes, Gerard Genette, Michael Riffaterre, and Mikhail Bakhtin. But these theorists have done work that serves, finally, to marginalize, bracket, or in other ways delimit and deflate parody both as a literary genre (or subgenre) and as a medium for self-conscious ideological discourse. Linda Hutcheon's recent book, *A Theory of Parody*, however, largely succeeds in rehabilitating parody by cogently redefining it as a specific mode of discourse and by enlarging our notions of what constitutes parody and what literary parody can accomplish.[20] In doing so, she forcefully demonstrates the interrelations between parody and some central issues that emerge in recent semiotic, formalist, and new historical approaches to literature and literary theory.

According to Hutcheon, "a parodic text [is] defined as a formal synthesis, an incorporation of a backgrounded text into itself. But the textual doubling of parody (unlike pastiche, allusion, quotation, and so on) functions to mark difference. . . . [O]n a pragmatic level parody is not limited to producing a ridiculous effect (*para* as 'counter' or 'against'), but . . . the equally strong suggestion of complicity and accord (*para* as 'beside') allow[s] for an opening up of the range of parody" (Hutcheon, 54). Thus there exist "both comic and serious types of parody." Indeed, as Hutcheon points out, "even in the nineteenth century, when the ridiculing definition of parody was most current . . . reverence was often perceived as underlying the intention of parody" (Hutcheon, 57). Further, parody "is never a mode of parasitic symbiosis. On the formal level, it is always a paradoxical structure of contrasting synthesis, a kind of differential dependence of one text upon another." Parody, moreover, can involve a whole ethos or set of conventions rather than a single text; parodoxically, "parody's transgressions [or transvaluations of a text or a set of conventions] ultimately [are] authorized by the very norm it seeks to subvert. . . . In formal terms, it inscribes the mocked conventions onto itself thereby guaranteeing their continued existence." But of course, "this paradox of legalized though unofficial subversion . . . posits, as a prerequisite to its very existence, a certain aesthetic institutionalization which entails the acknowledgement of recognizable, stable forms and conventions" (Hutcheon, 75).

But the texts, conventions, traditions, or institutions encoded by an author in his or her parodic text often require a sophisticated reader to recognize them and to decode the text, that is, to perceive the work at hand as parodic and dialogic, as transcontextual and transvaluative. Most works thus understood are also perceived finally as avant-garde. They engage in a form of what Barthes termed "double-directed" discourse, often "rework[ing] those discourses whose weight has become tyrannical." For Christina Rossetti, as well as her brother Dante Gabriel and A. C. Swinburne, one of the most important among such "discourses" is found in the tradition of Dante.

Swinburne, who greatly admired the *Monna Innominata*, had since 1866 sent Christina Rossetti copies of nearly all his volumes of poetry.[21] In his poems and prose he had written copiously on the subject of literary inheritance and its influence on the poetic imagination. Many of his poems are richly and complexly intertextual and parodic (in Hutcheon's sense of the term). Such is the case with "Ave Atque Vale," his Dantean elegy on the death of Charles Baudelaire (himself greatly influenced by Dante), and with his "Prelude" to *Tristram of Lyonesse* (a volume Christina Rossetti described as "a valued gift").[22] In the "Prelude" he specifically alludes to Dante and Dante's career as emblematic of the poetic vocation and activity. As he is about to launch into his epic poem on the well-worn subject of the love between Tristram and Iseult, Swinburne, like Rossetti at the beginning of her *Monna Innominata*, is careful to place his imaginative enterprise in its full and proper historical context. In doing so he identifies himself with all great lover-poets, and specifically with Dante. Re-envisioning Dante's image of Tristram and Iseult that appears in the *Inferno*, Swinburne asserts that "these my lovers," at the moment of their encounter with the poet,

> Saw Dante, saw God visible by pain,
> With lips that thundered and with feet that trod
> Before men's eyes incognisable God;
> Saw love and wrath and light and night and fire
> Live with one life and at one mouth respire.[23]

Commenting on this passage, Jerome McGann has elucidated Swinburne's point that, like every great poet, "Dante created the world anew. . . . Therefore, Swinburne has been called to explain a fuller significance for Dante's own creation, just as Blake knew himself called to explain the 'true' meaning of the Bible and Milton."[24] At the end of his "Prelude" Swinburne explains his own vocation, identifiable metaphorically as an intense and essential impulse, or "heart." He questions his motives for (and implicitly the value of) writing yet another grand love poem based upon the myth of Tristram and Iseult:

> So many and many of old have given my twain
> Love and live song and honey-hearted pain,
> Whose root is sweetness and whose fruit is sweet,
> So many and with such joy have tracked their feet,
> What should I do to follow? yet I too,
> I have the heart to follow, many or few
> Be the feet gone before me.[25]

Christina Rossetti invokes precisely this pattern of self-justification in her writing of the *Monna Innominata* sonnets, as her preface and epigraphs make clear. At work in her awareness of literary precedents (and in Swinburne's) is a phenomenon more complex than mere "anxiety of influence" or the inescapable activity of interpretation (though both of those are involved in Rossetti's endeavors).

In her preface to the *Monna Innominata* Rossetti lays claim to an already intertextual tradition that her sonnets appropriate, extend, and transvalue for her own particular historical moment. Discussing the nineteenth-century love lyric as the "successor to the Petrarchan love lyric," Margaret Homans has acknowledged that "women writers did not often choose to write romantic lyrics, for to do so was either to repeat the traditional quest plot, in linguistic drag, or to take up the position of the silent object [of desire] and attempt to speak from there."[26] Rossetti, she insists, in the *Monna Innominata* "provides an example of the challenges and pitfalls of the second of these strategies. In her self-consciously anti-Petrarchan sonnet sequence . . . she writes love lyrics from the position of the silent object in the complete awareness that she is attempting to reverse centuries of tradition when she does so, but in the end tradition writes her perhaps as much as she rewrites tradition" (Homans, 574). A brief overview of the structure and the "plot of desire" in Rossetti's sonnet sequence will help demonstrate some important oversights in Homan's critique, however, and will help elucidate the work's true historical relations and value.

The thematic structure of the *Monna Innominata* is at first difficult to discern, and once perceived, it includes a good deal of repetition and variation. However, like her brother's *House of Life*, the structure of this sequence echoes that of the Petrarchan sonnet itself.[27] Four discrete thematic units appear within this "sonnet of sonnets," or macrosonnet.[28] These roughly correspond to the first and second quatrains of the octave within a Petrarchan sonnet and the two triplets of the sestet. The first sonnet of the series establishes the aesthetic context (sustained through all fourteen sonnets) identifying "song" with "love"; it also strikes the dominant thematic note for the first four sonnets—the desire for fulfillment of erotic passion. The first sonnet states the need for the beloved's physical presence. The second expresses a poignant wish to generate memories of the lovers' first meeting. The third acknowledges that, at present, perfect union between the lovers occurs only in the speaker's dreams. And in sonnet 4 the desires expressed in sonnets 1 and 2 and the fantasies of sonnet 3 are abruptly realized. The lovers are apparently together, their respective feelings of love for each other at first in open competition but finally yielding unity between them. Such union has been achieved, as far as the reader can tell, exclusively through the exercise of the poetic imagination, in an operation reminiscent of Keats's comparison of that faculty's workings to Adam's dream: "He awoke and found it truth."

The focus in the second quatrain of sonnets (5 through 8) is the role of God in the speaker's secular love relationship. In sonnet 5 (analogous to the first line of the macrosonnet's second quatrain) the speaker renounces the service proffered by her lover in favor of his granting it to God. This psychological turn occurs as abruptly as the realization of unity between the lovers in sonnet 4. Sonnet 6, however, tempers the renunciation that precedes it and reasserts the indissoluble unity of the lovers. It also asserts an absolute dependency of the speaker's love for her innominate earthly lover upon her love of God. The tension between earthly and religious devotions culminates in sonnet 7 with a vision of relief from this tension and a perfect union between the lovers "as happy equals" in the afterlife. Sonnet 8 perplexingly reinforces the speaker's hope for such a union by prefacing a prayer for God's sanction of her earthly love with an elaborately sensualized rendition of the book of Esther.

In the first triplet of the macrosonnet's sestet (sonnets 9 through 11), the speaker now fully resigns herself to renouncing any earthly fulfillment of her love. Yet she retains hope for a preferable fulfillment in the afterlife. Sonnets 12 and 13 reassert the speaker's inexorable belief in her feelings of union with the beloved whether she renounces him in this world in favor of another woman (12) or God (13). Sonnet 14 reinforces the themes of renunciation and resignation but introduces a new emphasis on the speaker's melancholy awareness of mutability. Despite the dolorous tone of this sonnet, its extended implications for the macrosonnet's themes are salubrious, for without mutability, the wished-for heavenly reunion of the lovers could not take place. The sequence concludes with a description of the same "longing . . . heart pent up forlorn" that began the sequence but which now, having explored possible routes for the release and fulfillment of its longing, adopts the silent pose of "love that cannot sing again."

With this overview of the *Monna Innominata*'s structure in mind, we can observe that the sequence self-consciously uses for experimental purposes the guise of an unrequited poet-lover and the tradition of song as a medium of release for such a figure. The sequence is an experiment in aesthetic and psychological exploration that also tests the boundaries of literary and religious traditions, especially as these appear to conflict and to intersect with each other. Optimistic about the power of song and imagination early in the sonnets, the speaker is apparently pessimistic by the end. Neither one alone nor both in combination have sufficed to relieve the speaker's pent-up longing heart or satisfy her passion, whether intended by the author to appear real, fictionalized, or a psychologically realized fiction. The reader can envision, through the aesthetic enterprise of the sequence, an author steeped in Dantean and Petrarchan tradition, the poetry of Keats and biblical texts, and the literature of confession and renunciation trying in verse to work out the problem of love. The origins of the author's Romantic endeavor and of the speaker's romantic expectations appear to include both literature and social reality because of the extent to which actual Victorian patterns of behavior in love (especially among the Pre-Raphaelites) were conditioned more radically than our own by literary paradigms. We are reminded of this fact by the focus in the symmetrical framing sonnets on "song," on the value (or lack of it) of the poetic mode as a medium for filling "love's capacity."

For the Victorian "poetess" who speaks in the sequence, however, the Petrarchan paradigm fails to yield satisfaction, exposing the social, moral, and spiritual inadequacies of the tradition itself and of her own historical moment. The sonnets conclude with her resignation to unfulfillment, with

> The longing of a heart pent up forlorn,
>   A silent heart whose silence loves and longs;
>   The silence of a heart which sang its songs
> While youth and beauty made a summer morn,
> Silence of love that cannot sing again.
>
> (Poems, 2:93)

Yet this voice has, of course, already sung, and done so eloquently, in a radical, avant-garde fashion. This conclusion to the *Monna Innominata* follows thirteen sonnets that powerfully and with unconventional assertiveness articulate a female poet-lover's committment to her passion and her struggle to overcome all temptation to mere earthly fulfillments of love. The posture of silence she assumes at the end is, therefore, not one whereby the speaker simply relapses into the role of the silent object of desire, but one in which she deliberately defies that role as traditionally conceived, having not only renounced the typical patterns and expectations of experience found in ritual Petrarchan love lyrics, but having also instructed her traditionalist lover to yield to such conventions if he must: in sonnet 12 she unjealously "commends" him to any woman with "nobler grace, / And readier wit than mine." In sonnet 4 she has asserted their equality: "With separate 'I' and 'thou' free love has done, / For one is both and both are one in love"; and in sonnet 7 she envisions transcendent fulfillment of passion, when the two shall "stand / As happy equals in the flowering land / Of love." Rossetti thus subverts the post-Dantean values and expectations of her genre while defiantly resisting the conventional role of silent object and overturning the gender relations usually accepted in Petrarchan sonnet sequences.

Margaret Homans thus ignores at least two important implications of

Rossetti's preface to the *Monna Innominata* that become increasingly significant as we read through this sequence of sonnets, which moves from desire to transient union with the beloved to the female speaker's renunciation of him in this world. The first implication is that, for Rossetti, Laura and Beatrice are "resplendent with charms but . . . scant of attractiveness" precisely *because* they are silent objects of desire, powerless to respond to their lovers. When Rossetti gives the *donna innominata* a voice, she also gives her a *character* rather than the merely idealized "charms" traditionally projected upon such female objects of desire. Rossetti's speaker subverts Petrarchan tradition, however, not only by becoming a personality and abjuring all expected courtly compliments from her beloved, but also by assuming the role of an equal (rather than a subordinate and powerless idol) in the relationship. Yet she goes further than this, taking full control of the relationship after sonnet 9; in order to preserve the integrity of her love, she repudiates all possibility of the sort of earthly fulfillment often desperately sought by male love poets after Petrarch. As a final gesture, she abjures even the literary form in which such fulfillment has been traditionally sought. Her sequence thus serves to expose the corrupt and fraudulent ideology the form itself has come to represent.

Such a strategy is made clearer still by the immediate historical context Rossetti invokes in her preface. She refers explicitly to the "Great Poetess of our own day and nation" as a prospective writer of these sonnets had she "only been unhappy instead of happy" in love. With this curious invocation Rossetti announces further parodic dimensions of her work, inviting the reader to compare and contrast her sonnets of renounced love with Elizabeth Barrett Browning's *Sonnets from the Portuguese*, which speak of fulfilled love and do so with inferior craft in more than thrice the number of poems.[29] Unlike Rossetti's sequence, Browning's surrenders entirely to tradition. As all readers of her sonnets are aware, Browning's speaker repeatedly embraces her subordinate role in the relationship with her beloved.

Accepting the traditional "charms" and courtly compliments projected upon *donne innominate* (as well as ritual conventions such as the exchange of locks of hair in such relationships), Browning's speaker fully identifies with the tradition she employs. She thus lacks genuine character as an individual. Whereas Rossetti's speaker insists upon equality and refuses to be objectified as a "charming" idol, Browning's implicitly adopts this conventional role by reciprocating the discourse of courtly compliment and embracing its economy of artifices, one that claims to worship women while disempowering them in praxis:

I should not love withal, unless that thou
Hadst set me an example, shown me how,
When first thine earnest eyes with mine were crossed.[30]

Browning's emphasis upon her speaker's subordinate and protected position runs as a dominant motif throughout her sequence: "Thou art more noble and like a king, / Thou canst prevail against my fears and fling / Thy purple round me" (Browning, 217). By further contrast with Rossetti's heroine, who loves "God the most"—her love being such that "I cannot love you if I love not Him" (*Poems*, 2:89)—Browning's speaker, "who looked for only God" but "found *thee*," is content with her earthly lover and the baggage of conventional Petrarchan desires, expectations, and fulfillment that accompany him: "I find thee; I am safe, and strong, and glad" (Browning, 220). Unlike Browning's poet-lover in another way, Rossetti's speaks characteristically in imperatives, ultimately renouncing all the modes of fulfillment and happiness to which traditional Petrarchan sonneteers aspire.

In this sense, once again, the intertextual qualities of Rossetti's poem function as a corrective to the lapsed Dantean tradition that she recovers by a process Jerome Bump has termed metalepsis; it is "the attempt to establish priority over the precursor by being more true to the precursor's own sources of inspiration."[31] Reconstituting and purifying the love lyric tradition, whose most eminent practitioner, for Rossetti, was Dante, her speaker becomes, unlike Browning's complacent poetess, a genuine type of Beatrice leading her beloved to salvation and their relationship ultimately to a transcendent, rather than an earthly, level of fulfillment. At the same time, Rossetti—the poet behind the fictitious "poetess" of the sonnet sequence—represents herself obliquely as a cultural critic whose special concern is with the presently corrupt relations, not only between men and women, but also between love and religion, especially as those relations are expressed in a particular artistic tradition.

Within the projected action of the sonnets themselves, however, any direct cultural criticism is elided. In repudiating the values of love as they are typically enacted in "the world," the speaker attains an aestheticist and solipsistic distance from the amatory issues the sequence raises. The poems she generates succeed in the forceful expression of a yearning—indeed, a passion—for death, peace, and an amorphous but ideally fulfilling afterlife in "the flowering land" where "all is love." At the same time, however, art itself (as the process of creation) demonstrably provides a psychological and imaginative space in which a kind of fulfillment—as redemption from intense, unsatisfied longings—takes place, even while it expresses and reinforces the desire for fulfillment. Describing a frustrated passion for the ideal in a sense achieves that ideal, for it is exclusively in the tension between longing and a vision of fulfillment that the ideal exists. And art gives that tension palpable form.

For Rossetti's speaker, as for Dante in Rossetti's own reading of him (and in that of other, more modern critics of Dante), art thus attains a unique primacy and autonomy. It becomes a mode of redemption, a simultaneously aesthetic, spiritual, and emotional pursuit. As Franco Ferrucci explains, "Dante's genius lies in his deep-rooted conviction that heaven is attainable through a poetic masterpiece, and his profound faith rests upon the vast expressive possibilities that the Christian hereafter offers to his imagination. Spiritual evolution can never be separated from its representation. *To believe is to represent*, and vice versa; consequently, spiritual flowering cannot be separated from creative rebirth."[32] In this sense, then, "heaven" becomes the embodiment of an imaginative ideal in the real world and can be attained only in art.

IN its complex relations with the text of the *Monna Innominata*, the literary genealogy that prefaces the poem illuminates the values, patterns of meaning, and origins of many poems by Christina Rossetti. The preceding analysis of the preface—as it bears upon the generalized action, the themes, and literary form of the poem—helps us also more fully to understand how Rossetti's poetry operates within its special Pre-Raphaelite contexts, as well as the larger contexts of formal and thematic developments in canonical Victorian poetry.

Because Christina Rossetti appears in her poetry to be an "orthodox" devotee of both amatory and religious literary traditions that dominate the Victorian scene, her works are more fascinating than those of her brother or Swinburne or Morris, all of whose poems are often overtly subversive of accepted ideologies. Christina Rossetti's poems reflect an historically more complex set of cultural tensions than do the works of the other Pre-Raphaelites. Her works, in fact, simultaneously illustrate two of the three dominant post-Romantic directions in nineteenth-century literature for social, cultural, and (ultimately) spiritual amelioration. The central direction, which Rossetti generally eschews in her poetry, is found in the realistic and topical, often openly didactic, literature of the Victorians, which can be seen as a reaction against the potential solipsism of the Romantics. Another direction is visible in the early literature of aestheticism, which (as it is fully realized in Pater and the decadents) accepts—

indeed revels in—the solipsism so feared by the Romantic poets themselves. The final direction appears in the ascetic withdrawal advocated by participants in the Oxford Movement. While the aesthetes focus their attention on secular passions or empirical beauties and the religious writers focus on love of God, both groups ultimately move toward withdrawal and transcendence of the phenomenal world. In that sense the art of both is generally self-reflexive and self-sustaining, rather than mimetic or topical.

Christina Rossetti's poetry, as we have seen, combines characteristics visible in aesthetic as well as Tractarian poetry. It is in every sense idealistic, has largely literary origins, and forcefully delineates the struggle between the ascetic and aesthetic alternatives while at the same time synthesizing them. Yet the effect of such a synthesis in Rossetti's work is, finally, to distance her poetry from its immediate historical contexts and by doing so—paradoxically, it would seem—to present a forceful ideological critique of those contexts. Her work's focus on broad cultural issues and traditions—religious, amatory, philosophical—draws attention to the inadequacies, hypocrisies, and false values of her society as well as the literary work that has preceded her and that proceeds around her.

In accomplishing this goal she finds her purest precursor in Dante. Looking at Christina Rossetti's love poems, many of which either explicitly or implicitly extend Dantean tradition, one might say about the exemplary value of these traditions for Rossetti what she said about the symbolic value of Beatrice for Dante: "either [they] literally, or else that occult something which [the poetry they produced] was employed at once to express and to veil, must apparently have gone far to mold [her] . . . ; to make [her] what [she] was, to withold [her] from becoming such as [she] became not."[33] Ultimately, it is the Dantean contexts for Rossetti's poetry that allow us to arrive at some holistic view of her work, which seems, at the superficial level, to be divided into secular and religious categories. Those contexts enable us, as well, to understand the full and complex relations between Rossetti's project as a writer and the work of the other Pre-Raphaelites on the one hand; and, on the other, between her project and the directions and ideologies of other major Victorian poets.

In the *Monna Innominata* Rossetti operates at a self-consciously intertextual level, as we have seen. She succeeds in integrating not only Dantean, but also troubadour, Petrarchan, and biblical tradition in a fashion similar to that which Claude Lévi-Strauss originally defined as *bricolage*. This method is common also in her brother's work (and that of his subsequent imitators). Ron Bannerjee has described the results of *bricolage*, for instance, in discussing T. S. Eliot's allusions in "La Figlia che Piange" (1917) to D. G. Rossetti's "The Blessed Damozel." In Eliot's poem "a new system of myths not only reorganizes the fragments of the preceding system, but . . . the 'ends' of that system become its 'means.' . . . What looks like reorganization is also a process of transvaluation." Rossetti generated a purely aesthetic mythology that Eliot wished to supersede with his own. But clearly such an effect is also accomplished in Christina Rossetti's own uses of Dante. Although the effect of *bricolage* in the *Monna Innominata* sonnets is different from that achieved by Eliot and by Dante Rossetti, the method itself is certainly at work in Christina Rossetti's poem. It involves "the ambivalence, indirection, synthesis of heterogeneous elements, the quality of myth embodying repetition. Multiple analogues are functional in the same way as exemplary universality of myth is. . . . Allusions serve as myths, not to control the poem, but to define its boundaries of suggestion."[34]

Thus, assembled in the *Monna Innominata*—along with direct allusions to Dante, to troubadour tradition, and to Petrarch—are biblical echoes, evocations of Shelleyan Platonism and of some eighteenth-century treatments of love (we are reminded powerfully here of Pope's Eloisa), and an atmosphere and language familiar from gothic and sentimental nineteenth-century fiction. Although the poem's most wrenching emotional effects may come simply from the speaker's personality and her final tone of loss and discouragement, the poem's total effect upon the reader results in large part from its yoking together of only partially compatible traditions, which it attempts simultaneously to revive, sustain, and critique. Ultimately, the framework of literary allusions that surrounds the speaker reinforces her eclectic Victorian voice.

That voice seems intensely Victorian, in part because of the standard of taste implied by its ornamental but weighty literary *bricolage*, but also because of its sentimentality that depends upon the use of commonplace —especially religious—allusions, language, and images. Such a procedure, though fairly rare in Rossetti's secular poetry, is typical in her devotional verse with its many subjectively employed biblical allusions, and it reflects a pervasive tendency in much Victorian art to use such images and diction as code words. This procedure dominates Rossetti's prose works, especially *Seek and Find* and *The Face of the Deep*, but it also characterizes the *Monna Innominata* sequence. In sonnet 6, for instance, the speaker describes herself as "the sorriest sheep Christ shepherds with His crook." Earlier, in sonnet 5, the speaker with a loose biblical allusion compares her love, which will extend from this life into the next, to "the Jordan at his flood," which "sweeps either shore." And in sonnet 9, she alludes to the story of Jacob wrestling with God's angel (Gen. 3:2). Transvaluing for spiritual purposes images that are at once economic and sexual, the speaker compares Jacob's struggle to the conflict within her between love of God and the passion she feels for her earthly beloved:

> . . . love may toil all night,
> But take at morning, wrestle till the break
>   Of day, but then wield power with God and man:—
>   So take I heart of grace as best I can
> Ready to spend and be spent for your sake.
>
> (Poems, 2:91)

Sonnet 11 provides us with an example of yet another peculiarly Victorian element of the *Monna Innominata* sequence: its free, almost reckless adaptation of the medieval traditions of poetry concerning obstacled love. Rossetti's female troubadour focuses upon her "love and parting in exceeding pain / Of parting hopeless here to meet again, / Hopeless on earth, and heaven is out of view." Yet her love "foregoes you but to claim anew / Beyond this passage of the gate of death, / . . . at the judgment" (*Poems*, 2:91–92). Rossetti's procedure here reflects a characteristic more specific to the Pre-Raphaelites than the general tendency among Victorian writers to take liberties with medieval values and tradition.[35] Dante Rossetti, Morris, and Swinburne in their poems repeatedly project upon this tradition their own compulsions to sublimate sexual energies and redirect them as aesthetic or spiritual (often mystical) aspirations.[36] Just as Morris appropriates Malory and Froissart in his *Defence of Guenevere* volume, as Dante Rossetti exploits Dante for aesthetic effects and psychological backgrounds in much of his verse, and as Swinburne uses for his own purposes Romantic and various medieval literary sources and precedents, so in the *Monna Innominata* Christina Rossetti projects an imagined psychological resonance with troubadour and Dantean tradition. She is manifestly enamored of this special literary tradition, and the poet-speaker she depicts as born of it craves union with a fantasy lover. Yet the speaker finally feels compelled to sublimate the psychological reality of her love to religious aspirations that conflict with it; and she does so in a manner represented as true to the originary Dantean tradition, which is at once amatory, literary, and religious.

Dante and his early successors were able, in their art, to build upon and enhance erotic impulses so as to translate them finally into all-pervading and all-encompassing spiritual passions. While Rossetti attempts to parody and thus recover the fundamental ideological values of that art, her brother, Morris, and Swinburne generally allude to medieval tradition in order to flaunt or sublimate erotic impulses. In the latter case, the result can be either an unsatisfactory conflation of erotic and spiritual yearnings, or an ultimately unsuccessful attempt to redirect erotic passions in vaguely spiritual directions, or (more rarely) an ineffective and seemingly affected attempt to disguise *eros* as *agapē*. Because troubadour and Dantean cultural values are psychologically irrecoverable in Christina Rossetti's positivist and post-Romantic era, however, her own Victorian poet-lover's attempted reconstitution of Dantean tradition in the *Monna Innominata* is doomed to fail. She, too, appears merely to conflate the erotic and the spiritual, or to sublimate passion, or to place supreme value on an art that is generated by the insatiable "craving heart." But *her* failure constitutes *Rossetti's* avant-garde exposé of a spiritually bankrupt culture. Thus Rossetti's Dantean works, like her other amatory poems, function as a cultural critique, simultaneously idealizing and lamenting a lost age of spiritual opportunity and unified, rather than fragmented, sensibilities. These works, like love poems by the other Pre-Raphaelites, most often culminate in pathos and aestheticism, but for different reasons. Moreover, although the radical appropriation of literary tradition upon which Rossetti's poems depend for such effects is—like that strategy in the work of the other Pre-Raphaelites—virtually unique in her era, the resulting *mood* of her amatory poetry (and theirs) is in many respects typically Victorian.

The speaker's voice in the *Monna Innominata* sonnets would therefore have seemed comfortably familiar to Christina Rossetti's contemporary readers. In its spirit of melancholy resignation, it resembles the voices we find in Meredith's *Modern Love*, Dante Rossetti's *The House of Life*, and even Arnold's "Marguerite" poems. The *Monna Innominata*, like these love poems, seems characteristically Victorian in its false starts, its equivocations, and its dominant tone of frustration. Ultimately Rossetti's sonnet sequence exposes its speaker's immobility in the quest for fulfillment and transcendence. Wandering between two worlds, she pursues an archaic, no longer functional set of ideals, to which she is, nonetheless, wholly committed. Thus, rather than shoring up the fragments of tradition against her ruin, the speaker's adherence to traditional ideologies and the poetic forms used to express them ensures her psychological ruin and finally her spiritual malaise. As a result, the poem reflects at a highly generalized level the Victorian poet's typical condition: torn between past ideals, primal (that is, universal) emotional, spiritual, and intellectual needs, and modern scientific and social realities that subvert those ideals and threaten the satisfaction of those needs.

At this level the *Monna Innominata* may appear to be an historically inevitable poem. Yet Christina Rossetti differs significantly from most other important Victorian poets in the value system that underlies her work and belies the apparent similarities between her poetry and theirs. The others are perpetually questing for alternative ideals to those discovered in the traditional literature they most admired. The alternatives they generate, however, yield only partial fulfillment or the promise of it. For Arnold, religion and the literary culture associated with it in providing a sustaining system of beliefs and ideals must be replaced with a more monolithic "culture," whose heart is poetry. For Tennyson—in a more limited, personal way—fame, the laureateship, and the Victorian prophet's podium appear to have allowed some compensation for lost ideals. For Morris (and Ruskin), art and its power for social amelioration promised hope. And—more radically but in the same direction—for Dante Rossetti and for Swinburne, art and devotion to beauty itself became an ultimately melancholy substitute for the less limited (and limiting) spiritual and emotional values of the writers they viewed as their own precursors. More conservative, finally, than any of these writers, Christina Rossetti returned with fierce determination to the no longer functional religious and amatory ideals of her literary fathers, especially those of Dante.

HISTORICAL AND INTERTEXTUAL

As we have seen, Christina Rossetti's preface to the *Monna Innominata* sonnets discusses the specifically literary culture from which the sonnets emerge. In doing so, it accomplishes a number of complex effects. At one level it insists upon a very precise place in literary history for the work that follows it. The preface invokes an historically distant tradition, thus evoking for the reader a powerful sense of estrangement from some of the conventions and emotional components of that tradition. Yet the sense of estrangement generated by the preface also causes us to suspend whatever proclivities we might feel to disbelieve and to criticize; the preface in this way encourages feelings of sympathy and even imaginative identity with the speaker. Paradoxically, therefore, through the very self-conscious artificiality of the work in which she figures, the speaker's tone of sincerity is reinforced. The preface in these ways thrusts upon the reader an awareness (of which we are reminded by the Dantean and Petrarchan epigraphs to each sonnet in the sequence) that the author is writing in a parodic literary mode. Because of the interaction within the sequence between originality and imitation (or appropriation), the reader is constantly moving between complex levels of response, including an emotional level elicited by the "sincere" voice of the melancholy or hopeful or ascetically resigned speaker, and a more detached but still emotionally fraught literary-historical level evoked by the poem's preface, with its biblical, Dantean, and Petrarchan allusions. These allusions reinforce our feelings of estrangement, our suspension of disbelief, and hence our emotional responses at the first level. But at the same time the preface and the allusions remind us that we are engaged with a work of art in which a fictionalized speaker (as in Dante and Petrarch) creates a visionary reality (largely distant from any true events) in order to generate specific kinds of emotional and spiritual responses that satisfy specific, even primal, needs. In short, the work's effectiveness is enhanced by its self-conscious historicity and the awareness it evokes of its own artifices.[37] Its power is also reinforced and extended (as usually is the case in such allusive poems) by the emotional and spiritual weight brought to it by the literary works it invokes as contexts. These authenticate the *Monna Innominata*, bringing to bear upon the reader's responses his or her memories of a previous set of related literary experiences.

The cultural and specifically literary traditions upon which Rossetti's art depend are enormously complex. The history of European literature is often the history of attempts to reconcile *eros* and *agapē*. For Dante and Petrarch, clearly, both kinds of love are compatible and interdependent. Both, too, are internal, matters for the imagination. The inherent dangers of their attempted reconciliation, however, are ones that Christina Rossetti does not easily escape. As Jean Hagstrum has observed in this regard, "One of the mischiefs of love is that, while turning us to another person, it can also turn the gaze inward and lead to dangerous self-preoccupation. Freud saw that such preoccupation could produce what he called 'the narcissistic overestimation of subjective mental processes' [in 'The Uncanny,' 1919]. . . . Apparently a nexus exists between love in any form and imagination, whose tendency is to lead away from life."[38] Moreover, the dangers of erotic solipsism are magnified by the "ambiguity of the entire Judeo-Christian heritage" in its attitudes toward love:

On the side of positive encouragement, the great tradition made marriage a sacrament, proclaimed that God was love, required in its two greatest commandments (on which hang all the law and the prophets) both love of God and love of man, made love between man and woman the most important type for the relations of God and Israel, Christ and the Church, made marriage the metaphor for the consummation of all things, and sought to make the blessed and chosen community a fraternity of love and service. . . . The whole matter of how deeply religion affected social behavior and indeed the mind of the artist at the moment of creation is a vexed one.[39]

The vexations for the student of European love poetry culminate with the tradition initiated by the troubadours, Dante, and Petrarch, within which Christina Rossetti locates the *Monna Innominata*.

Rossetti's impulse to reconcile *eros* and *agapē* has its roots in southern European literature of the thirteenth and fourteenth centuries, in the Augustinian Platonism that preceded it, and in the many varieties of Neoplatonism that followed it. Murray Krieger quite rightly acknowledges that "the Petrarchan mode itself, with its sources in Courtly Love, serves to institutionalize a symbolic [literary] form consecrated to the transformation of earthly love to spiritual." In the mythology which that form propagates, "the [beloved], both agent and object of transformation, becomes ritualized beyond [his or her] historical reality. As Idolatry merges with typology, the metaphorical play on the divine-human paradox of Christianity fuses the [beloved] into an eschatological figure."[40] Such is exactly the process attempted in the visionary métier of the *Monna Innominata* sequence. Yet it first appeared among the late troubadours to whom Christina Rossetti alludes in her preface to the *Monna Innominata*, crystallizing most clearly, perhaps, in the works of Arnaut Daniel. As Dante himself acknowledges in canto twenty-six of the *Purgatorio*, Arnaut was the most important precursor of the system of attitudes toward love that Dante reshaped (and that the Rossettis perpetuated in their work). Dante praises Arnaut as the greatest among previous vernacular poets. Moreover, as L. T. Topsfield—the most helpful among the many recent commentators on troubadour tradition—observes, "the . . . rules which apply to Dante's *Divine Comedy* can also be used for some poems by Arnaut Daniel in which we can see a literal sense, and a moral and Christian sense."[41]

Indeed, because there are specific correspondences between Arnaut's poetry and basic elements of the *Monna Innominata*, one is led to specu-

late that Christina Rossetti's introduction to the troubadour poet through
Dante had led her to read him. For within the larger tradition that attempts to reconcile *eros* and *agapē*, we find in Arnaut's lyrics the same
psychopathology of erotic solipsism, the same expected longing for the
physical closeness of the beloved (*MI* 2), the same faith in the Paradisal
reunion of lovers (*MI* 7 and 10), and even the same concern with slander-
ers (*MI* 11) (Topsfield, 216). Like Christina Rossetti's "poetess," and like
Dante and Petrarch before her, Arnaut the poet practices "in his attempt
at conscious self-absorption in the courtly ethic . . . a form of self-forget-
fulness, the *s'oblidar* of earlier troubadours. He turns his love inward upon
itself and shrinks from the outward sensual expression of love" (Topsfield,
204). Yet like the speaker in the first two *Monna Innominata* sonnets, he
"longs for the closeness of his beloved's physical reality" (Topsfield, 216).
He feels caught between the spirit and the flesh, and in attempting to
reconcile *eros* and *agapē*, "refers explicitly to . . . the New and Old Testa-
ments." He believes his soul will "have double joy in Paradise, if one can
enter there through loving well." Moreover, his adherence to *Fin 'Amors*
involves the renunciation of earthly fulfillment and "raises him to the
moment of ultimate happiness, the *summum bonum* or *mielhs* of the early
troubadours, in which moral, spiritual and Christian doubts are resolved,
and the lover can hope for happiness in Paradise" (Topsfield, 217). Indeed, "behind his poetry there is . . . the basic Augustinian debate of the
struggle between carnal desire of the body and the soul's desire for God.
[Ultimately] Arnaut affirms the excellence of *Fin 'Amors* by equating it
with love of God" (Topsfield, 216).

Most of these elements are expanded upon, indeed mythologized, by
Dante and, to a lesser extent, by Petrarch. But with Arnaut, at least from
Dante's view, they crystallized in their purest form, and it is inevitable
that the allusion to Arnaut appears in the *Purgatorio*, for purgatory is in
Dante's cosmology the special habitation of Provençal poet-lovers and the
dolce still nuovo poets.[42] Not surprisingly, nine of the fourteen Dantean
epigraphs to the *Monna Innominata* sonnets are taken from the *Purgatorio*. These draw attention not only to the purgatorial psychic effects of
love upon the speaker in the poem, but also to the self-conscious concern
in both Rossetti and Dante with the role of "song" in transforming *eros*
into *agapē* and thus in achieving salvation (*MI* 1, 4, 14). Significantly, the
Purgatorio begins, "I will sing of that second realm where the human spirit
is purged, and becomes fit to ascend to heaven."[43] For Rossetti's speaker,
as for Dante, the very experience of singing, of generating in poetry a
vision of love's development, becomes a melancholy mode of purification,

enforcing upon her the suffering that accompanies unfulfilled earthly passion, renunciation, and an awareness of mutability. In short, the female troubadour Christina Rossetti envisions in her preface—an imaginative counterpart of Arnaut Daniel—purges her passion and purifies her soul through her poetry, just as Rossetti perceived Dante to have done.

The general movement of the sonnet sequence is clear. On its most basic level it begins with an exclusive focus on *eros* and the desire for physical union with the beloved. But the speaker's desire for earthly love gives way to spiritual aspirations that subsume *eros*, but which her beloved apparently does not share. Thus, while contemplating the prospect of love's apotheosis through death and transcendence, and while suppressing her yearning for a full sensory apprehension and exploration of passion, the speaker exposes her fears of betrayal and of mutability. These fears culminate in a complete this-worldly renunciation of her beloved. Repressive and self-chastening impulses come to dominate her. Like Arnaut, she weeps and sings as she goes, enduring the fire that purifies (*Purgatorio* 26). Shortly, the speaker succumbs to a desire for death that sustains her because it promises an end to the emotional turmoil she suffers as well as a translation to "the happy land" where "all is love" and where passion is disencumbered of its painful earthly complications and disappointments. In the speaker's vision of heaven, *eros* is transmuted into *agapē*.

As I suggest above, this movement attempts to imitate what Rossetti perceived as the Dantean pattern of spiritual development through love. Thus, for her the work simultaneously fulfills sincere and parodic impulses, just as Dante's poetry does. Charles Singleton has observed that Dante repeatedly "concern[s] himself with the *literary* tradition of courtly love." Significantly, Christina Rossetti accepts and imitates Dantean tradition rather than attempting to supersede or transform it as her brother does, and as Dante transformed the tradition he absorbed. (Such radical conservatism, however, can be seen as equally avant-garde in the contexts of Victorian topical literature, sentimental poetry, or even Spasmodicism.) Singleton explains that although Dante "awarded the crown of excellence" to Arnaut Daniel in dealing with *venus*, or the spark of earthly passion, he acknowledged that he himself was supreme in compositions that must be classified "beyond (and above) the poetry of courtly love." Ultimately, in the *Divine Comedy*, "Dante is a poet of *rectitudo*, his concern is with *directio voluntatis*," that is, directing the will toward transcendence, the transformation of *eros* into *agapē*. Indeed, this concern developed into his "program . . . his working principle," and it unifies the movement of his major works, Singleton persuasively claims, from the *Vita Nuova* through the *Divine Comedy*.[44] Singleton expands upon his thesis in a way that is relevant to any serious discussion of the *Monna Innominata*:

> With the *Vita Nuova* (which makes its beginning with the courtly tradition, so that it can clearly and explicitly register the manner and degree in which it *leaves* that tradition behind), Beatrice becomes the vehicle, the God-given means, by which the will of the poet is directed to God. And with the *Vita Nuova*, in this sense, Dante becomes the poet of *directio voluntatis* and remains such a poet through the fragmentary *Convivio*, and then, triumphantly and completely, in the *Commedia*. And all the while . . . Dante can play, sometimes, at courtly love. . . . Dante . . . it was who showed us, excelling as he did in the mode of *directio voluntatis* . . . that courtly love can be perfected beyond itself—without being abolished.[45]

In the *Monna Innominata* we discover in highly compressed form the speaker's derivative program involving not only the transvaluation of passion through song, but also the suppression of its erotic elements. But that program for the speaker eventually founders and is overwhelmed by fears of failure and mutability.

Still, the experience of imaginatively embedding such a speaker in such a literary tradition proves salutary for the poet behind the speaker, as it did for Dante. Throughout the *Divine Comedy* Dante represents himself as the supreme visionary actively learning in the course of his poetic production. Christina Rossetti appears in such a role only in her preface to the *Monna Innominata*, having learned from the precursors she cites. But in both cases the authors' personae—Dante's self-depiction and Rossetti's speaker—are to an extent perfected. Through the painful ordeals they experience, their authors (and audiences, presumably) gain spiritual direction and an awareness of artistic excellence, learning from the ideals they poetically describe as well as from the failures of such ideals. On Dante's epic scale in the *Divine Comedy*, of course, both the poet and the reader gain spiritual direction from many speakers. Especially in the *Purgatorio*, on which Christina Rossetti focuses in her epigraphs, the examples of misguided lovers, and specifically lover-poets, perfect Dante's understanding of love as the guiding force and principle of the universe. A passage from *Purgatorio* 17 is crucial in understanding how the poet's depiction of "failed" poet-lovers not only extends tradition but serves to purge the poet (through his sympathies for those he treats) and to educate him. In this passage Virgil instructs Dante, just as, by extension, Dante has instructed Christina Rossetti, and as her work will guide future poets writing of love:

"Neither Creator nor a creature ever,
  Son," he began, "was destitute of love
  Natural or spiritual; and thou knowest it.
The natural was ever without error;
  But err the other may by evil object,
  Or by too much, or by too little vigour.
While in the first it well directed is,
  And in the second moderates itself,
  It cannot be the cause of sinful pleasure;
But when to ill it turns, and, with more care
  Or lesser than it ought, runs after God,
  'Gainst the Creator works His own creation.
Hence thou mayst comprehend that love must be
  The seed within yourselves of every virtue
  And every act that merits punishment."[46]

Thus, in Dante and in Rossetti the central concern is *directio voluntatis*, and their works constitute an exercise in learning to redirect the passions by means of imaginatively viewing the successes and failures of lovers, poets, and poet-lovers. In this way, the aestheticization of passion becomes the most accessible pathway to salvation, one which, Rossetti believes, must be reopened for her culture by work "directed to that which is true and right," like her own.

Although Christina Rossetti's most important use of Dante, then, appears in her speaker's failed reenactment in the *Monna Innominata* of his program for simultaneous aesthetic and spiritual purification, other significant thematic echoes proliferate. I have already mentioned the sanction for renouncing the beloved, which appears in *Purgatorio* 15 and which shapes Rossetti's seventh sonnet. But also in the *Divine Comedy* we find the pervasive atmosphere of solipsism that distinguishes Arnaut's poetry as well as Dante's. Christina Rossetti chooses from *Purgatorio* 2 an epigraph for sonnet 12 that suggests the visionary quality of the described experience throughout her sequence: "Love, that discourses in my mind." Further, Rossetti's twelfth and thirteenth sonnets irresistibly suggest the *vanitas mundi* theme that often dominates her other works and that punctuates the *Purgatorio* (see especially *Purgatorio* 11 and 12).

More specifically, in *Purgatorio* 17 Dante alludes to the book of Esther in a visionary context whose power may well have inspired Rossetti's eighth sonnet. Although it reinforces the *Monna Innominata*'s motif of self-sacrifice for the good of the beloved, this sonnet's appearance in the sequence is rather puzzling because it constitutes a lengthy digressive allusion involving a biblical theme that at first appears to be relevant only on the most general level to the experience of the speaker in the sonnets.

This difficulty can, however, be explained by the crucial visionary images that open *Purgatorio* 17 and by the brief but very important theory of imagination expressed in the canto's first thirty-three lines. In these lines Dante directly addresses the faculty within his mind that generates images without external stimulation.[47]

> O imagination, that do sometimes so snatch us from outward things that we give no heed, though a thousand trumpets sound around us, who moves you if the sense affords you naught? A light moves you which takes form in heaven, of itself, or by a will that downward guides it.
>
> Of her impious deed who changed her form into the bird that most delights to sing, the impress appeared in my imagination, and at this my mind was so restrained within itself, that from outside came naught that was then received by it. Then rained down within the high fantasy one crucified, scornful and fierce in his mien, and so was he dying. Round about him were the great Ahasuerus, Esther his wife, and the just Mordecai who was in speech and deed so blameless. And . . . this imagination burst of itself, like a bubble.[48]

This passage would have attracted Rossetti's attention because of her interests not only in Dante but also in the Bible, Keats, and the operations of the poetic imagination. These converge here in suggestive ways. The first literary allusion in this passage is to the myth of Philomel, who in Ovid's *Metamorphoses* is transformed into a nightingale. In Keats's famous ode "the bird that most delights to sing" becomes a symbol of the poetic imagination. The second allusion is to Esther. And immediately following the quoted text is a reference to the *Aeneid*. The allusive technique in the passage may well have seemed to Rossetti an exemplary instance of her own methodology in the *Monna Innominata*, which I have described as *bricolage*. More significantly, the brief theory of imagination Dante states here would have appealed to Rossetti as a simple way of solving the central problem of Keats's poetry, which finds one of its clearest expressions in his "Ode to a Nightingale"—the apparent impossibility of reconciling the escapist tendencies of the imagination with its utilitarian potential, indeed, with the potential of the poet to become a "physician to all men" rather than a mere visionary or "dreamer." This solution would have been unavailable to Keats as a non-Christian, but it was inescapable for

Rossetti as a Christian Platonist in the tradition of Dante. According to Dante, in this passage from *Purgatorio* 17, poetic images "descend into the mind directly from God, whose will directs them downward."[49] The extended implications of this notion for Rossetti's solipsist "poetess" and devout lover in the *Monna Innominata* are crucial: passionate impulses and the visionary experience of love are not only sanctioned by God, but also "willed" by him in order ultimately to direct the lover to pursue an ideal of Love, *agapē*, that transcends *eros*. The poet-lover eventually thus gains Love by desiring and then renouncing love. But to do so, the poet-lover, like Dante, must first traverse purgatory. He or she must imaginatively suffer and poetically express the pangs of unfulfilled love. Moreover, the poet behind this persona becomes a poet-prophet, generating an art that may, like Dante's, lead its audience toward salvation. Thus, for Christina Rossetti the story of Esther, the savior of her people, becomes, through its context and uses in Dante, a crucial touchstone for Rossetti's entire poetic enterprise.

In addition to the many Dantean resonances in the *Monna Innominata*, we find pervasive echoes of numerous images and motifs from Petrarch's *Canzone*, from which Christina Rossetti takes her second set of epigraphs.[50] The speaker in the *Monna Innominata* is, like Petrarch's persona, a poet extremely self-conscious about the relations between love, song, the beloved's approval of her verses, and the promise of salvation through love and heavenly reunion with the beloved. The depiction of song (in Petrarch's thirty-seventh poem, for example) mediating between two lovers reminds us of the central concern in the two sonnets that frame the *Monna Innominata* sequence. Petrarch concludes his long poem with an address to personified "Song":

> Song, if in that sweet place
> Our lady you will see,
> You think perhaps like me
> That she will offer you her lovely hand
> From which so far I stand.
> Do not go near; kneeling respectfully,
> Tell her:—I come as soon as can be done,
> Either bare soul or man of flesh and bone.[51]

But the compulsion to generate song, to poeticize love, to strive even for the "laurel" crown that is punningly identified with the beloved Laura, is ubiquitous in the *Canzone*. (See, for instance, poems 6, 23, 37, 60, 61, 70, 72, 73.) This is so despite the speaker's occasional lamentations over his inability to versify (see poem 20). But even this lament, of course, reminds us of Christina Rossetti's sonnet 14.

Visible also in Petrarch's thirty-seventh poem are two motifs that Rossetti adapts and that appear repeatedly in the *Canzone*: the desire to touch the beloved's hand and the motif of the lovers' reunion in Paradise. These are seen also, for instance, in poems 58, 270, 275, and 278. Indeed, any full discussion of Petrarchan antecedents for elements in the *Monna Innominata* would be very long. More briefly, we must at least note Petrarch's repeated attempts to portray his first meeting with Laura (*Can.* 13, 20, 61; *MI* 2); his concern with attaining God's sanction for his love and salvation through it (*Can.* 4, 13, 15, 29, 59, 72, 277; *MI* 5, 6, 8, 9, 13); the self-conscious renunciation of love's earthly pleasures (especially *Can.* 1, 13, 56; *MI* 5, 11); his desire for death as a comfort and release from the torments of unfulfilled passion in this world (*Can.* 8, 14, 18, 30, 36; *MI* 10, 11); the speaker's sense of profound inadequacy (*Can.* 20; *MI* 9, 12–14); his concern with the reputation that his behavior in love will yield (*Can.* 72; *MI* 11); the intense consciousness of mutability (*Can.* 12, 30, 32, 272; *MI* 10, 14); and finally, the profound melancholy elicited by a love that remains unfulfilled in this life (*Can.* 9, 10, 21; *MI* 14).

Such echoes of Petrarch, Dante's great emulator, interact with Christina Rossetti's biblical allusions, as well as with her uses of Dante and of troubadour motifs, to generate the complexly sincere and parodic quality of her poem. The *Monna Innominata* must therefore be seen finally as a highly intertextual work. The detached author displays herself on one level as a student of those tormenting but essential human yearnings for completion and fulfillment that are visible in the traditional quest to transform erotic into spiritual passion and thereby to transcend mortality. On another level she is a student of literary traditions that glorify, diffuse, and assuage those yearnings by making art of them.

Such traditions (especially that of the sonnet sequence)—having been virtually dormant in England since the early seventeenth century—were fervently revived not only by the Pre-Raphaelites, who used them uniquely, but also by many mainstream Victorian writers as well, for perhaps obvious reasons. On the one hand, of course, the renewal of interest in things medieval burgeoned during the nineteenth century in England, and the Victorian fascination with medieval romance, troubadour poetry, and Dantean tradition can be seen simply as one aspect of this phenomenon. On the other hand, the interest in medieval traditions of love literature clearly resulted from a peculiarly Victorian perception—one seen by Rossetti as misguided and hypocritical—that the high Middle Ages was an era parallel to their own in its manner of reconciling the demands of the flesh with the aspirations of the spirit. For most canonical Victorian poets who dealt with the subject of love (except Swinburne), erotic passion had to be, in one way or another, made "respectable." The quest for purity and sanctity was, at least in art and social intercourse, an inescapable product of socialization, and it resulted in the compulsive evasion, suppression, or transposition of erotic desire into acceptable forms. Thus, for Victorian love poets the traditions of great medieval love poetry served an exemplary function, not just as fine art, but also as models of the necessary psychological process of suppression and rechannelling.

In this largely superficial way, then, Christina Rossetti's love poems resemble those of Arnold, Browning, Elizabeth Barrett Browning, and even Dante Rossetti, as well as the major relevant poems of Tennyson, including the *Idylls of the King* and *In Memoriam*. *In Memoriam* is an especially useful poem in comparing Christina Rossetti's uses of Dantean tradition to those of other mainstream Victorian poets. As early as 1909, T. H. Warren made clear the extent of Dantean influences on Tennyson.[52] The pervasiveness of Dantean tradition among Victorian intellectuals, poets, and religious thinkers in the nineteenth century is strikingly previewed in the undergraduate writings of Arthur Hallam, the most dazzling of the Cambridge Apostles in the 1830s and, of course, the single most important influence on Tennyson's poetry. Hallam's own attitudes toward the issue of love and literary treatments of it had an immeasurable impact upon young Tennyson, and those attitudes were derived in large part from his studies of medieval Italian literature: "His enthusiasm for Dante and to a lesser extent Petrarch he was able to communicate to Tennyson. For what there is in Tennyson's conception of love that is consciously Neoplatonic he absorbed in large measure from Hallam's energetic espousal of . . . Italian Platonism."[53] In addition to writing his Dantean poem, "A Farewell to the South" (1828), Hallam also delivered a prizewinning declamation, "The Influence of Italian upon English Literature," in 1831. More significantly in the context of the present discussion, Hallam wrote "Remarks on Professor Rossetti's 'Disquisizioni Sullo Spirito Antipapale' " in response to Gabriele Rossetti's *Analytic Commentary* on the *Divine Comedy*, a volume that we might well expect Christina Rossetti to have read at some point.

Gerhard Joseph quite rightly suggests the influence of Hallam upon Tennyson's Christian idealism, and considering Gabriele Rossetti's influence upon Hallam, it is not surprising that we find in the latter's writings and in Tennyson's poetry an essentially Dantean interaction between *eros* and *agapē* similar to that which we discover throughout Christina Rossetti's love poems and paradigmatically in the *Monna Innominata*. Summarizing Hallam's conclusions to his remarks on Rossetti's "Disquisizioni," Joseph explains, "Hallam equates the emotion that Christian man lavishes upon God and upon His clearest surrogate on earth, woman. . . . It is on the base of such a perception of woman analogous to God that western man has erected a religion whose essence is an erotic relation to God." Thus, "Hallam insisted on the inseparability of true spiritual emotion and the language of eroticism in western civilization. He furthermore argued that as a result the ascent toward God would be facilitated by the presence of female influence or by the male's attribution of a polar femininity to the object of his apotheosis. *In Memoriam* describes the transformation of Hallam into an analogue of Christ; to render this Hallam-Christ accessible, Tennyson eroticizes him, giving him female attributes."[54] This development in *In Memoriam* can, of course, be seen as analogous to Dante's treatment of Beatrice and Petrarch's of Laura, which Christina Rossetti invokes in her preface to the *Monna Innominata*.

In her particular and highly self-conscious uses of this tradition that demands an apotheosis of the beloved, however, Christina Rossetti's procedure and achievement is in certain ways more complex than that which Hallam perceives in Dante or that Tennyson undertakes in *In Memoriam*. For, while retaining all of the effects accomplished by the presentation of a sincere speaker struggling between *eros* and *agapē*, Rossetti objectifies that speaker's experience and elaborately locates it in a special literary tradition, making of it an aesthetic object and ultimately creating a poem whose emotional power is superseded by its power as a stimulus for detached contemplation of both amatory and literary-historical issues.

EXEGETICAL

The central critical issue of the *Monna Innominata*, and of almost all Christina Rossetti's poetry, is, finally, how the deliberately failed (or postponed) quest of her poetic personae for the ideal operates within her art. Although most of Rossetti's admiring critics have insisted that various poetic virtues are visible in the *Monna Innominata*, a number have made the usual mistake of reading the sonnets biographically, that is, as a commentary on Rossetti's own alleged love relationships that were never fulfilled.[55] Yet none has presented a full exegesis of the sequence or an extensive discussion of the poem's manipulation of its literary-historical contexts.[56] Because these contexts largely determine the "meaning" and help us understand the extended effects of the sonnet sequence, such an exegesis allows us to locate the poem's ideological, formal, thematic, and stylistic centrality to Rossetti's corpus. More important, a full discussion reveals the poem's true value as a cultural document, one that illuminates the place of uniquely Pre-Raphaelite sensibilities and literary procedures within the larger context of Victorian taste and representative Victorian poetic practices.

The first sonnet of the *Monna Innominata* laments the absence of the speaker's beloved with a traditional Petrarchan figure: "My world is you." This sonnet focuses upon the psychology of "longing" in its relations with love and "song." Significantly, the sonnet's otherwise perplexing last two lines make clear that the crucial issue (both what comes forth and the crux) of this love is "song": "Ah me, but where are now the songs I sang / When life was sweet because you called them sweet?" At one level of intertextuality, this sonnet enters complexly into dialogue with sonnet 7 of Browning's *Sonnets from the Portuguese*. At the end of that poem, Browning's poet-lover—sententiously, artlessly, and simplistically, by comparison with Rossetti's speaker—acknowledges that ". . . this lute and song . . . loved yesterday, / (The singing angels know) are only dear / Because thy name moves right in what they say" (Browning, 216). By contrast, Rossetti's sonnet ends with a syntactically and intellectually complex question that seems, on deliberation, to require an answer. Not only does the question imply some skepticism about the sincerity of the beloved's compliment, but the lines further imply the primacy not of "you" but of "songs." We can't be sure whether happiness is achieved primarily through reciprocated love or through the creative process that results in poetry. Sonnet 1 thus prepares for the increasingly significant concern, as the sequence proceeds, with literary matters, with the quality and value of "song" as well as the prototypes, sources, and touchstones for this speaker's largely derivative, perhaps wholly imaginary emotional and psychological experiences. Significantly, throughout these sonnets, "song" or poetry reflects and at times seems even to generate the poetic vision of transcendent love. Only in song can that vision be realized.

Taking its associative cue from sonnet 1, sonnet 2 reveals its speaker's unsuccessful attempt to recall the time she first met her beloved.

> I wish I could remember that first day,
> First hour, first moment of your meeting me,
> . . . .
> So unrecorded did it slip away.
> . . . .
> A day of days! I let it come and go
> As trackless as a thaw of bygone snow.
> *(Poems*, 2:87)

The poem thus dwells on the speaker's awareness that experience is frustratingly ephemeral. Her psychological condition is especially noteworthy because her situation is so uncommon—romantic lovers traditionally remember in vivid detail their first meetings with the beloved. This sonnet seems to make a deliberate attempt to overturn tradition. It is anti-Romantic (specifically, un-Wordsworthian) in that its central problem does not hinge on a recollection that overshadows present thought and intensifies present joy, but rather on the absence of any emotionally sustaining memory at all. Here Rossetti depicts the opposite of a Wordsworthian "spot of time." All the subjunctives in the poem, as well as the concerns they express, lead us to wonder even whether the first meeting that the speaker seeks to recall ever occurred. Perhaps she desires not really to remember it, but rather to imagine it adequately so as to sustain or justify a set of exalted emotions, which she feels and finds irresistible, but which attach only to a constellation of traditional, literarily derived ideals and expectations comprehended by the term "love." All this occurs to the informed reader, especially because Dante and Petrarch spend many words idealizing the precisely remembered first moments of meetings with Beatrice and Laura. The sonnet's epigraph from Petrarch deliberately draws our attention to this fact: "I recur to the time when I first saw thee" (*Works*, 462). In this way Rossetti suggests the possible fictionality of her speaker's love. The experience may be a projection of idealities, of emotions, even of intellectual strivings for fulfillment and completion.

With references to "empty shades" (from Dante) and to "an imaginary guide" (from Petrarch), the epigraphs of sonnet 3 reinforce suspicions aroused by sonnets 1 and 2 that the experience of love depicted here may be largely imaginary. So far, we have been informed only of a lover's absence, not his presence. He is an ideal: "only in a dream we are at one." The speaker desires "that I might / Dream of you and not wake but slumber on" (*Poems*, 2:87). The movement inward (as with Keats's Madeline), the solipsistic impulse, is so powerful here that it finally yields a desire for death as providing the only possible, permanent achievement of the ideal:

> If thus to sleep [and dream] is sweeter than to wake,
>   To die were surely sweeter than to live,
> Though there be nothing new beneath the sun.
>
> (Poems, 2:88)

The allusion to Eccles. 1:9 in the last line here reinforces perceptions of the ideality of the speaker's experience; dreams can yield novel and desired experiences unavailable "under the sun" of the phenomenal world. But also by the simple act of alluding to the Bible, as well as by the contents of the passage alluded to, this last line reminds us of the ideality of the whole endeavor the author and we readers are engaged in. It reminds us that this poem is an imaginative recreation of the contents of an imaginatively generated (Dantean and Petrarchan) mythos, extending a long tradition of such love poetry. (Eccles. 1:9 reads in full: "The thing that hath been, it is that which shall be; and that which is done is that which shall be done: and there is no new thing under the sun.")

By sonnet 4 the "problems" treated in the first three sonnets have been solved, apparently by virtue of the imagination's ascendancy within the speaker. Song or poetry seems to have made love real according to the traditional pattern of desires projected in the first three sonnets. Suddenly the beloved is present (the speaker addresses him), and the early period of their love is remembered (that is, created):

> I loved you first: but afterwards your love
>   Outsoaring mine, sang such a loftier song
> As drowned the cooings of my dove.
>   Which owes the other most? my love was long,
>   And yours one moment seemed to wax more strong.
>
> (Poems, 2:88)

Here Rossetti reinvents the Petrarchan tradition by innovatively reconstituting the love relationship in the expressly competitive convention of the pastoral singing contest. The speaker's antitraditional emphasis is not only on the equality of the lovers, but also, as a result of that equality, on their harmonious unity demonstrated in an exchange and interplay of songs. Neither partner is silent. Their love can be perfected and fulfilled only through their art. Indeed, given the orientation of the preceding sonnets, it appears that dream and desire have been realized wholly in song. Art can from this point perpetuate the fictive love relationship by dwelling upon its nature, alluding to its shaping literary heritage, and by raising new obstacles to its adequate fulfillment. In this sonnet we are reminded that love, like the power of expressive song, is ultimately impalpable. It exists in an ideal realm—not subject to "weights and measures"—and requires interpretation: "I loved and guessed at you, you construed me / And loved me for what might or might not be."

In sonnet 5 the "love which makes us one" becomes for the first time transcendentally transvalued, directed to God for sanction, completion, and perfection. In the form of a benediction, the octave reinforces the extreme identification between the lovers asserted in sonnet 4, but through the use of chiasmus and paradoxical juxtaposition it also directs us forcefully to the transcendent world within the speaker: "Oh my heart's heart, and you who are to me / More than myself myself, God be with you." The grammatical ordering within these lines tends to conflate self, beloved, and God. In the course of the octave, the speaker prescribes for her lover devotion to God "whose noble service setteth free." In that ambiguously liberating service, she will assist by means of her literally undying love— "Today, tomorrow, world without an end." This allusion to Gal. 5:1 suggests that the speaker wishes to be to her lover as Paul was to the Galatians, liberating them from the tyranny of Jewish law, and as Christ is to man, liberating him from earthly (that is, erotic and material) enthrallments.

Here we begin to see the relationship between human and divine love that is developed through the rest of the sonnet sequence. As with Dante and his predecessors, the opposition between love and Love (*eros* and *agapē*) is portrayed ultimately as a false dichotomy, but here the attempt to reconcile the two is strained. The central impulse in both varieties of love, according to Rossetti's speaker, is pursuit of the ideal, the transcendent, and the mystical. Ultimately, love of man is to Love of God as emotion is to spirit. The love relation with God supersedes but should also encompass love of man. The allusions to Matthew and to Hebrews, here elucidating the speaker's desire that God "perfect" her beloved, indicate that she perceives herself as a Beatrice figure, a guide to her lover's salvation. Here, too, the speaker replicates the theme of her identity with her lover. Matt. 5:48 exhorts, "Be ye therefore perfect, even as your Father which is in heaven is perfect." But as the concluding echo of Genesis ("Since woman is the helpmeet made for man") insists, the beloved will not be alone in his perfection and identity with God.

By this point in the sequence the speaker has progressed from the wish for a physical meeting with her beloved, to a powerful desire for memories of their "First touch of hand in hand," to transfiguring dreams of a union that transcends any relationship accessible in life, to a sudden realization of those dreams in a complete spiritual union with the beloved ("love makes us one"), and finally to a desire for perfection of the beloved, which would yield a transcendent union of the lovers with God. We have moved inward and upward well beyond phenomenal reality at this point. In a Dantean pattern, throughout these sonnets "song" or poetry has not merely reflected but seemed even to generate the poetic vision of transcendent love, while enabling that vision to be realized.

However, in sonnets 5 through 8 obstacles arise that halt any continuation of the speaker's projected perfectible love relationship. Sonnets 5 and 6 introduce a concern with God as (paradoxically) both a barrier to the lovers' absolute union and a mediator in accomplishing it. Commending her lover to God's service leaves the speaker unacceptably isolated and subordinate: "So much for you; but what for me, dear friend?" In sonnet 6, a dispute arises between the lovers' respective commitments to *eros* and *agapē*. The beloved, in lapsed Dantean and Petrarchan fashion, apparently remains committed to *eros* and "the world." Unlike the speaker, the earthbound beloved rebukes her. By implication like Lot's wife, he is "Unready to forgo what [she willingly] forsook." While the speaker insists that she loves "God the most," she is nonetheless torn between love of God in purist Dantean tradition, on the one hand; and *eros* and corrupt Petrarchism on the other: "I cannot love you if I love not Him, / I cannot love Him if I love not you" (*Poems*, 2:89). In sonnet 7 the love that began as an apparently secular passion with an apparently specific object, and that has by sonnet 6 taken on metaphysical dimensions, becomes even further etherealized and idealized. Its culmination and fulfillment are envisioned in the posthumous future, "the flowering land / Of love, that knows not a dividing sea." This land is clearly a realm that combines images from Dante's *Paradisio* and the heaven depicted in Dante Rossetti's "The Blessed Damozel." In it "love is strong as death." Yet this vision severely tests the speaker's willingness to sacrifice and sublimate erotic desires: "My heart's a coward though my words are brave." And in sonnet 8 the speaker takes unprecedented liberties with the biblical story of Esther. She attempts to reconcile her passion and her spiritual ideals by envisioning herself as an Esther-Beatrice-Damozel figure, who will risk her salvation to cull God's ("Love's") sanction for her "prayer"—apparently that perfect union with the beloved *will* be achieved despite his recalcitrance. But this impulse is transient and is implicitly renounced.

Sonnets 5 through 8 are pivotal in the sequence. After the seventh sonnet the speaker's previously articulated quest for the physical presence of the beloved, for sensations of union with him, and for the beloved's perfection through service to God give way to increasingly frequent thoughts of death and decay, as well as to convictions of inadequacy. The ideal has failed in a culture projected (through the depiction of the beloved) as one dominated by a corrupted (that is, insistently patriarchal, erotic, and materialist) ideology of romance. Still, the speaker's frustration ultimately serves to perpetuate, complicate, and enrich the projected love relationship. Her own mutability now becomes her dominant preoccupation, and, as a result, she repeatedly offers (and resigns herself to her beloved's acceptance of) surrogate lovers. The denouement of the sequence begins with the ninth sonnet's nostalgia for the ideal of "all that might have been and now can never be." Sonnets 5 through 8 are also much more densely allusive than the first four poems of the sequence, which contain only one major biblical reference (as compared to fourteen in the second quatrain of sonnets). These allusions reflect the central tension in this section of the *Monna Innominata* between secular love and love of God. The speaker now uses the language of the Bible far more frequently than she does the conventional language of love poetry.

Sonnet 8 is perhaps the most perplexing and certainly the most "Pre-Raphaelite" of the *Monna Innominata* sequence. From the perspective of the concluding sonnets, it serves to critique the purely sensory and erotic values of other Pre-Raphaelite love poetry. This sonnet flaunts sensually evocative details and is extremely self-conscious in its artificiality. It also displays the most radical transformation and redirection of sources that Christina Rossetti employs in the *Monna Innominata*, or indeed anywhere in her poetry. In the sonnet's first line Rossetti makes clear its source in the Old Testament book of Esther: "'I, if I perish, perish,' Esther spake." However, Rossetti's version of Esther is Keatsian in its sensuality, whereas the biblical text is unembellished. Rossetti's seductive Esther—with the "lustre of her perfumed hair," her "smiles that kindle longing but to slake," her "beauty for a snare, / Harmless as doves and subtle as a snake"—is a morally equivocal figure, rather than a prototype of Christ who risks martyrdom to save the Jewish people (mankind) in mediating on their behalf with King Ahasuerus (God). Making Esther into a Lamia figure and thus altering and imaginatively enhancing her source, Rossetti calls attention, as she does throughout the sequence, to the issue of intertextuality in these sonnets, but also to the parodic power of her imagination to assimilate and transvalue a text in order to generate a poem that carries the critical weight of myth. This appropriation of Esther, then, like so many of the sonnets' other allusions (including those in the epigraphs from Dante and Petrarch) reminds us that this poetry is simultaneously "literary" (that is, parodic), self-reflexive, and self-fulfilling, and at the same time critical of an entire cultural ideology of romance that victimizes women who are subject to it and objectified by it. Rossetti's speaker not only fails to "trap" and "vanquish" her beloved but quickly realizes that such an objective is wholly misguided and based upon false values.

The speaker thus reacts, in sonnet 9, with dejection but also with courage to the fact that her fantasy of success "can never be" realized. The Dantean epigraph to this sonnet insists on the speaker's retention of a "dignified and pure conscience" (*Works*, 462). With an allusion to Corinthians, she ironically announces herself "unworthy of the happier call." As if contaminated by the romantic desires she has earlier indulged while employing the traditionary values and expectations of Petrarchism, she now renounces any love union in this world and determines to "abide even as" Christ. But she does not surrender her more important and pervasive vision of transcendent union in the "flowering land of love" after death. That ideal returns here and in sonnet 10 as the new focus of her attention. She is "yet not hopeless quite nor faithless quite, / Because not loveless."

In sonnet 11 the speaker worries about accusations of caprice in love that she imagines will now be lodged against her (because of her renunciation) by "idle women" who know nothing of "Love and parting in exceeding pain"; that is, by those who know nothing of the tradition of renunciation established by the troubadours, embellished by Dante and Petrarch, but afterward trivialized and corrupted in western literary culture. Her parodic counter to such charges is a literalized convention of the tradition: she calls upon her beloved to "make it plain" at "the judgment" that "My love of you was life and not a breath." And once again before this triplet of the macrosonnet concludes, we are reminded of the extent to which the misguided "love" initially aspired to here has been nurtured by, if it is not entirely the product of, an imaginative and originally religious literary tradition that has become secularized. But this fact is also a source of the speaker's hope for eventual salvation and fulfillment. It is a tradition that has *created* cultural reality. Solipsistic and self-reflexive, its prelapsarian (that is, Dantean and Petrarchan) originals may be rehabilitated by the individual lover who renounces the amatory (and therefore social and moral) deficiencies of her culture. Even though "Hopeless on earth, and heaven is out of view," she vows to reconstitute her "love that you can make not void nor vain" in the afterlife ("Beyond this passage of the gate of death"). That is, she vows spiritually and literarily to treat the figure of her beloved just as Dante and Petrarch had employed Beatrice and Laura. Her fallen beloved's commitment to the pleasures and false values of this world becomes tantamount, in her Victorianized Dantean mythology, to the death of the beloved in its original.

Indeed, so self-sufficient and self-sustaining is the speaker's passion that she invents a challenge to it even more daunting than the one broached in sonnet 5: she invites her beloved to marry any woman who "can take my place" by virtue of a "nobler grace," "readier wit," and "sweeter face." Because of the imaginatively projected and ineradicable spiritual identity between her and the now-idealized beloved, the speaker claims that she would only gain by his taking a bride other than she:

> . . . since the heart is yours that was mine own,
> Your pleasure is my pleasure, right my right,
> Your honourable freedom makes me free,
> And you companioned I am not alone.
>
> (*Poems*, 2:92)

This rhetoric of renunciation functions simultaneously on two imaginative levels. For the speaker, whose psychic raison d'être is unfulfilled passion that yields a motive for self-purification and a creative impetus (and thus these sonnets recording the psychopathology of love), such renunciation creates a challenge to her passion that can only serve to sustain it. At a complementary level, the speaker's act of renunciation benefits from its expression in an allusion to Dante's *Purgatorio* 15.[57] This allusion reminds us once again that we are engaged with a deeply intertextual poem whose parody of a pervasive western literary tradition constitutes a metalepsis whose design is to recover the ideology and the poetic stature of its earliest eminent palimpsest.

Appropriately, an alternate gesture of renunciation dominates sonnet 13. This gesture implicitly reinforces the speaker's sense of inadequacy and "impotence" both in "the world" and for the afterlife once she has succumbed, even transiently, to its corrupting values. Rather than another woman, she now recommends God as a surrogate:

If I could trust mine own self with your fate,
  Shall I not rather trust it in God's hands?
Without Whose Will one lily doth not stand,
Nor sparrow fall at his appointed date;
  Who numbereth the innumerable sand,
Who weighs the wind and water with a weight,
To Whom the world is neither small nor great,
  Whose knowledge foreknew every plan we planned.
Searching my heart for all that touches you,
  I find there only love and love's goodwill
Helpless to help and impotent to do,
Of understanding dull, of sight most dim;
  And therefore I commend you back to Him
  Whose love your love's capacity can fill.
                           (*Poems*, 2:92–93)

Four biblical allusions reinforce the speaker's assertions of God's omniscience, omnipotence, and omnipresence, which contrast with her own deficiencies.[58] Moreover, both epigraphs to this poem emphasize the speaker's self-chastening adherence to a belief in her spiritual inadequacies. But also, in Dantean manner, they insist upon the inextricable dependency of earthly love upon divine love for fulfillment. "And we will direct our eyes to the Primal Love" is William Michael Rossetti's translation of the epigraph from Dante; and its rationale from Petrarch is, "I find a burden to which my arms suffice not" (*Works*, 463).

The paradox of Rossetti's play with both originary and corrupted Petrarchan romantic traditions is that her speaker is represented as a "fallen" Beatrice-figure with her own poetic voice, whose diminished efficacy has been inevitably determined by a recalcitrant culture. Through Rossetti's own metalepsis of literary tradition, nonetheless, she can present in exemplary fashion a mode of redemption, a poetic pattern of return to grace. To accomplish this goal, Rossetti's speaker must renounce love and therefore abjure any hope of her own redemption through the power of *eros* to lead to *agapē*. She becomes a martyr to the redemption she desires for her culture, and her silence in the end does not indicate a relapse into the role of "silent object," as in Petrarchan tradition, but rather the completion of her self-sacrifice in opposition to that culture's ideological lapses from the Dantean model. In this way, then, poetry becomes the unique vehicle for Rossetti's prophecy and depends for its moral as well as aesthetic accomplishment on parody—the appropriation, critique, and transvaluation of literary prototypes. The composite procedure serves as a revelation of one (literary) mode through which "Primal Love" operates in the world.

The fourteenth sonnet's symmetry with the first therefore reinforces our awareness that the experience portrayed in these sonnets is literary and derivative, ideal and artificial, self-generating and self-sustaining. Sonnet 14 deliberately employs the standard Petrarchan theme of beauty's transience: "Youth gone, and beauty gone . . . / What remains of bliss?" It also rehearses expected flower images to support this theme, albeit in renunciatory directions:

> I will not bind fresh roses in my hair,
> To shame a cheek at best but little fair,—
>   Leave youth his roses, who can bear a thorn,—
> I will not seek for blossoms anywhere,
>   Except such common flowers as blow with corn.
>   (*Poems*, 2:93)

And the sonnet concludes on the conventional note of "a heart which sang . . . songs." But—acting against most authors of love sonnets since Petrarch, including Sidney, Spenser, and Shakespeare—this heart now condemns itself to silence because it had initially followed the misguided pattern of worldly, post-Dantean love songs. These have created a fallen and patriarchal culture of *eros* dominated by false expectations and desires, a culture that has become blind to the only genuine possibility of fulfilling "the craving heart" and "love's capacity": in "the flowering land" of spiritual love. The sequence comes full circle when we are left, at the end, with precisely that which we encountered at the beginning of the sonnets:

> The longing of a heart pent up forlorn,
>   A silent heart whose silence loves and longs;
>   The silence of a heart which sang its songs
> While youth and beauty made a summer morn,
> Silence of love that cannot sing again.
>   (*Poems*, 2:93)

The movement from desire to renunciation, the realization that the romantic and literary tradition that has taught her to feel, to write, and to idealize is duplicitous—these have been wrenching for the speaker.

The psychological effects of her experiences appear in the elegiac tone of this concluding sonnet of the sequence. Implicit in the speaker's final renunciation, the renunciation of "song," is Rossetti's awareness that the speaker's achievement in merely sublimating earthly to spiritual passions is antithetical to the earliest and best models from the literary tradition out of which the impulse to portray such a speaker emerges. Whereas Dante and Petrarch ascended by means of *eros* to *agapē* and celebrated their ascent in poetry, this speaker must altogether reject her erotic desires, the poetry they might generate, and the salvation both might lead to. In this deeply intertextual and self-consciously historical work, Rossetti's creation, her female counterpart of a troubadour poet or her regendered Dante, has failed because her love, her beloved, and her poetic project are circumscribed by Victorian cultural values and informed by Victorian rather than medieval sensibilities. Rossetti's "fancy" of a "'donna innominata' drawn . . . from feeling" by "the great Poetess of our own day"—Elizabeth Browning, had she been "unhappy instead of happy" in love—has exposed an extremely significant incompatibility between Dante's system of values and poetic practice on the one hand, and, on the other, the corrupt amatory, spiritual, and even aesthetic values of Rossetti's own era. But, as I have suggested, in at least two other important respects her speaker's failure to reconcile erotic and spiritual passions is the grounds of Rossetti's artistic success.

First, in the *Monna Innominata* sequence Rossetti depicts a pattern for sublimating and redirecting erotic impulses, for chastening and "perfecting" the will of the tempted earthly lover. That pattern, and even its sadly sentimental outcome, would have appealed to the psychological and emotional as well as the social needs of her Victorian audience. Second, in the distance between the literary potential of love in medieval times and in the Victorian period, Christina Rossetti can discover a limited but congenial field for the operations of her imagination, a mental space in which to exist, as in an aesthetic cloister. In it she finds freedom for her art, just as her brother, Swinburne, and Morris did. But such freedom requires that she renounce all commitments to her own historical era. By promising herself to archaic literary ideals and practice (as in the case of the *Monna Innominata*), or to God (as in the exclusively religious poetry), or to a life of pure fantasy (as in *Goblin Market* and *Sing-song*), she can wander between two worlds, cloaked attractively and protectively in aesthetic garments. In the *Monna Innominata*, perhaps more than in any of her other works, Christina Rossetti fully exposes the psychological, emotional, and spiritual tensions that inform her poetry, and at the same time she attempts to recover and espouse the Dantean ideology that originally transformed such tensions into great religious art.

BIOGRAPHICAL
EPILOGUE

DISCUSSING the influence of John Henry Newman's style during the last quarter of the nineteenth century, David DeLaura has explained that "the cult of Newman the supreme artist in prose . . . establishes [a] . . . crucial line of that still rather puzzling continuity descending from Newman and the Oxford Movement to aestheticism."[1] Christina Rossetti, a great admirer of the central figures of that movement, can be seen as a major Pre-Raphaelite poet who establishes yet another crucial line of this continuity, one that exposes the connection between *ascesis* and aestheticism, and that perhaps in part explains how the earnest repressiveness of the Victorians could ultimately explode into the sensual extravagance of the decadents.

In his essay, "Style," Walter Pater suggests—albeit in a limited context—the complex relations between *ascesis* and aestheticism as those relations are directly applicable to Christina Rossetti's poetics of "conciseness":

> Self-restraint, a skillful economy of means, *ascesis*, that too has a beauty of its own; and for the reader supposed there will be an aesthetic satisfaction in that frugal closeness of style which makes the most of a word, in the exaction from every sentence of a precise relief, in the just spacing out of word to thought, in the logically filled space connected always with the delightful sense of difficulty overcome.
>
> Different classes of persons, at different times, make, of course, very various demands upon literature. Still, scholars, I suppose, and not only scholars, but all disinterested lovers of books, will always look to it, as to all other fine art, for a refuge, a sort of cloistral refuge, from a certain vulgarity in the actual world. A perfect poem . . . has for them something of the uses of a religious "retreat."[2]

Extrapolating from Pater's observations, we can see how, in the case of Christina Rossetti's poetry, *ascesis* becomes significantly more than a matter of style, although it is certainly that, too. The concept, when applied to her life as well as her work, comprehends a pervasive system of values and renunciatory psychological and emotional compulsions. These mold her poetic vision. The chastening impulse of abnegation allowed Rossetti to create repeatedly in her poetry—as Dante did in his—a program for redirecting sensual desires and erotic passions to spiritual ends. In the process she wrote poems in which the striving for artistic perfection, the self-conscious and sometimes experimental craftsmanship, corresponds to the pursuit of spiritual perfection that the speakers in her poems often enact. Thus, ascetic impulses generate aestheticist effects. The renunciation of sensuality and passion, as well as the sensory beauties of nature that most often image these, becomes matter out of which another order of passion and beauty emerges. Rossetti's renunciatory art, however, often paradoxically enters the world of particular historical contexts that partly inspire it; it operates as a powerful cultural critique, as we have seen. It can serve to expose dangerously misguided social, moral, and spiritual value systems as well as the literary traditions in which they are grounded and replicated.

Ultimately for Rossetti, art *was* a kind of cloistral refuge from the demands and constraints that threatened to impinge upon her because of her special position as a devoutly religious female poet living in Victorian England. It was also her response to a world that appeared to her "fallen," corrupt in many important respects. Her writing allowed her to mediate between conflicting aspirations: to success as a poet; to success as a "prophet" (albeit in a minor key); to success in her often difficult roles as daughter, sister, and aunt; and to success in renouncing the vanities of this world in favor of the "hope deferred" for absolute fulfillment in the next. Her poetry enabled her simultaneously to live in the world, to comment on its lapsed values and behavior, to use it as a source of self-chastisement and thus of poetic inspiration, but also temporarily to transcend the world through the projected idealities of religious belief and through the ideals of beauty concretely realized in her art. As she suggested in her early letter to William Edmonston Aytoun, her vocation as a poet provided her with an unassailable position from which to pursue what all respectable Victorians would have perceived as "aims" that were "pure and directed to that which is true and right." And her art enabled her to do so in all aspects of her life. Largely through her writing, Rossetti attained a certain level of earthly fulfillment. Yet, toward the end she clearly found the rewards of her work inadequate.

In unpublished correspondence with her close friend, Caroline Gemmer, during her last decades, Rossetti discloses the pattern of expectation and disappointment that she retrospectively imposed upon her life.[3] She insists that a position *in* the world, no matter how marginal, has been more suited to her needs and desires than any complete cloistral refuge. "So you think I once trembled on 'The Convent Threshold,'" she responds, apparently to Gemmer's inquiry. "Not seriously ever, tho' I went thro' a sort of romantic impression on the subject like many young people. No, I feel no drawing in that direction: really, of the two, I might perhaps have less unadaptedness in some ways to the hermit life. But I suppose the niche really suited to me is the humble family nook I occupy; nor am I hankering after a loftier." Rossetti's complacency was, however, temporary and limited entirely to the domestic sphere. Elsewhere, speaking in broader terms, she more fully reveals her equivocation between the worldly and the otherworldly:

> "Surviving" is the lot of old age. . . . No, I don't exactly take the *tantalization* and *delusion* view of past years. They all have led me up to what now I am, and the whole series is leading me to my final self. I trust all I have vainly wished for here will be more than made up to me hereafter if—an all-momentous if!—I endure to the end. After all, life is short, and I should not immerse myself too deeply in its interests. Please note that I say, "I should not"—I dare not pretend "I do not."[4]

From her earliest sallies into the competitive literary marketplace, it is clear that Rossetti wanted professional success but wished also to retain complete artistic and ideological integrity. Doing so required much in the way of renunciation and self-sacrifice. Hence her highly self-conscious efforts at self-effacement in her poetry, prose works, letters, and social relations. Like the other Pre-Raphaelite poets, she was acutely sensitive to life's inevitable disappointments and losses, as well as to her own unfulfillment. These subjects often generated the elegiac subtexts of her poetry. In 1882, the year of Dante Gabriel's death, she wrote to Gemmer of the "struggle life is to many of us, and not least to many a 'love lorn' woman." And ten years later, more conclusively, she confessed: "do you wonder that I feel life a saddened period? Surely not. Look without or look within, *feel* without or feel within, and it is full of trial." At that time, despite her "literary success" with which she claimed to be "fully satisfied," she felt the hollowness of her accomplishment in light of all she had lost and, by implication, all she had deliberately renounced. Approaching her last decade, she acknowledged that "literary success cannot be Mother, Sister, dear friend to me." Sadly, the prospect of a heaven other than her "heaven of art" also dimmed in her final years. In what appears to be her last extant letter, she wrote to Frederick Shields (5 September 1894) to say "good-bye for this life." She was dying of cancer and wished to thank Shields for his "precious" friendship. She also begged him for "your prayers for the poor sinful woman who has dared to speak to others and is herself what God knows her to be."[5]

APPENDIX

MONNA INNOMINATA[1]
A Sonnet of Sonnets

Beatrice, immortalized by "altissimo poeta . . . cotanto amante"; Laura, celebrated by a great tho' an inferior bard,—have alike paid the exceptional penalty of exceptional honour, and have come down to us resplendent with charms, but (at least, to my apprehension) scant of attractiveness.

These heroines of world-wide fame were preceded by a bevy of unnamed ladies "donne innominate" sung by a school of less conspicuous poets; and in that land and that period which gave simultaneous birth to Catholics, to Albigenses, and to Troubadours, one can imagine many a lady as sharing her lover's poetic aptitude, while the barrier between them might be one held sacred by both, yet not such as to render mutual love incompatible with mutual honour.

Had such a lady spoken for herself, the portrait left us might have appeared more tender, if less dignified, than any drawn even by a devoted friend. Or had the Great Poetess of our own day and nation only been unhappy instead of happy, her circumstances would have invited her to bequeath to us, in lieu of the "Portuguese Sonnets," an inimitable "donna innominata" drawn not from fancy but from feeling, and worthy to occupy a niche beside Beatrice and Laura.

1.

"Lo dì che han detto a' dolci amici addio."—DANTE
"Amor, con quanto sforzo oggi mi vinci!"—PETRARCA

Come back to me, who wait and watch for you:—
   Or come not yet, for it is over then,
   And long it is before you come again,
So far between my pleasures are and few.
While, when you come not, what I do I do
   Thinking "Now when he comes," my sweetest "when:"
   For one man is my world of all the men
This wide world holds; O love, my world is you.
Howbeit, to meet you grows almost a pang
   Because the pang of parting comes so soon;
   My hope hangs waning, waxing, like a moon
      Between the heavenly days on which we meet:
Ah me, but where are now the songs I sang
      When life was sweet because you called them sweet?

2.

"Era già l'ora che volge il desio."—DANTE
"Ricorro al tempo ch'io vi vidi prima."—PETRARCA

I wish I could remember that first day,
   First hour, first moment of your meeting me,
   If bright or dim the season, it might be
Summer or Winter for aught I can say;
So unrecorded did it slip away,
   So blind was I to see and to foresee,
   So dull to mark the budding of my tree
That would not blossom yet for many a May.
If only I could recollect it, such
   A day of days! I let it come and go
   As traceless as a thaw of bygone snow;
It seemed to mean so little, meant so much;
If only now I could recall that touch,
   First touch of hand in hand—Did one but know!

3.

"O ombre vane, fuor che ne l'aspetto!"—DANTE
"Immaginata guida la conduce."—PETRARCA

I dream of you to wake: would that I might
  Dream of you and not wake but slumber on;
  Nor find with dreams the dear companion gone,
As Summer ended Summer birds take flight.
In happy dreams I hold you full in sight,
  I blush again who waking look so wan;
  Brighter than sunniest day that ever shone,
In happy dreams your smile makes day of night.
Thus only in a dream we are at one,
  Thus only in a dream we give and take
    The faith that maketh rich who take or give;
  If thus to sleep is sweeter than to wake,
    To die were surely sweeter than to live,
Tho' there be nothing new beneath the sun.

4.

"Poca favilla gran fiamma seconda."—DANTE
"Ogni altra cosa, ogni pensier va fore,
E sol ivi con voi rimansi amore."—PETRARCA

I loved you first: but afterwards your love
  Outsoaring mine, sang such a loftier song
As drowned the friendly cooings of my dove.
  Which owes the other most? my love was long,
  And yours one moment seemed to wax more strong;
I loved and guessed at you, you construed me
And loved me for what might or might not be—
  Nay, weights and measures do us both a wrong.
For verily love knows not "mine" or "thine;"
  With separate "I" and "thou" free love has done,
    For one is both and both are one in love:
Rich love knows nought of "thine that is not mine;"
    Both have the strength and both the length thereof,
    Both of us, of the love which makes us one.

5.

"Amor che a nulla amato amar perdona."—DANTE
"Amor m'addusse in sì gioiosa spene."—PETRARCA

O My heart's heart, and you who are to me
  More than myself myself, God be with you,
  Keep you in strong obedience leal and true
To Him whose noble service setteth free,
Give you all good we see or can foresee,
  Make your joys many and your sorrows few,
  Bless you in what you bear and what you do,
Yea, perfect you as He would have you be.
So much for you; but what for me, dear friend?
  To love you without stint and all I can
Today, tomorrow, world without an end;
    To love you much and yet to love you more,
  As Jordan at his flood sweeps either shore;
Since woman is the helpmeet made for man.

6.

      "Or puoi la quantitate
Comprender de l'amor che a te mi scalda."—DANTE
"Non vo'che da tal nodo amor mi scioglia."—PETRARCA

Trust me, I have not earned your dear rebuke,
  I love, as you would have me, God the most;
  Would lose not Him, but you, must one be lost,
Nor with Lot's wife cast back a faithless look
Unready to forego what I forsook;
  This say I, having counted up the cost,
  This, tho' I be the feeblest of God's host,
The sorriest sheep Christ shepherds with His crook.
Yet while I love my God the most, I deem
  That I can never love you overmuch;
    I love Him more, so let me love you too;
  Yea, as I apprehend it, love is such
I cannot love you if I love not Him.
    I cannot love Him if I love not you.

7.

"Qui primavera sempre ed ogni frutto."—DANTE
"Ragionando con meco ed io con lui."—PETRARCA

"Love me, for I love you"—and answer me,
   "Love me, for I love you"—so shall we stand
   As happy equals in the flowering land
Of love, that knows not a dividing sea.
Love builds the house on rock and not on sand,
   Love laughs what while the winds rave desperately;
And who hath found love's citadel unmanned?
   And who hath held in bonds love's liberty?
My heart's a coward tho' my words are brave—
   We meet so seldom, yet we surely part
   So often; there's a problem for your art!
      Still I find comfort in his Book, who saith,
Tho' jealousy be cruel as the grave,
   And death be strong, yet love is strong as death.

8.

"Come dicesse a Dio: D'altro non calme."—DANTE
"Spero trovar pietà non che perdono."—PETRARCA

"I, if I perish, perish"—Esther spake:
   And bride of life or death she made her fair
   In all the lustre of her perfumed hair
And smiles that kindle longing but to slake.
She put on pomp of loveliness, to take
   Her husband thro' his eyes at unaware;
   She spread abroad her beauty for a snare,
Harmless as doves and subtle as a snake.
She trapped him with one mesh of silken hair,
   She vanquished him by wisdom of her wit,
      And built her people's house that it should stand:—
      If I might take my life so in my hand,
And for my love to Love put up my prayer,
   And for love's sake by Love be granted it!

9.

"O dignitosa coscienza e netta!"—DANTE
"Spirito più acceso di virtuti ardenti."—PETRARCA

Thinking of you, and all that was, and all
    That might have been and now can never be,
    I feel your honoured excellence, and see
Myself unworthy of the happier call:
For woe is me who walk so apt to fall,
    So apt to shrink afraid, so apt to flee,
    Apt to lie down and die (ah, woe is me!)
Faithless and hopeless turning to the wall.
And yet not hopeless quite nor faithless quite,
Because not loveless; love may toil all night,
    But take at morning; wrestle till the break
        Of day, but then wield power with God and man:—
        So take I heart of grace as best I can,
    Ready to spend and be spent for your sake.

10.

"Con miglior corso e con migliore stella."—DANTE
"La vita fugge e non s'arresta un' ora."—PETRARCA

Time flies, hope flags, life plies a wearied wing;
    Death following hard on life gains ground apace;
    Faith runs with each and rears an eager face,
Outruns the rest, makes light of everything,
Spurns earth, and still finds breath to pray and sing;
    While love ahead of all uplifts his praise,
    Still asks for grace and still gives thanks for grace,
Content with all day brings and night will bring.
Life wanes; and when love folds his wings above
    Tired hope, and less we feel his conscious pulse,
        Let us go fall asleep, dear friend, in peace:
        A little while, and age and sorrow cease;
    A little while, and life reborn annuls
Loss and decay and death, and all is love.

11.

"Vien dietro a me e lascia dir le genti."—DANTE
"Contando i casi della vita nostra."—PETRARCA

Many in aftertimes will say of you
   "He loved her"—while of me what will they say?
   Not that I loved you more than just in play,
For fashion's sake as idle women do.
Even let them prate; who know not what we knew
   Of love and parting in exceeding pain,
   Of parting hopeless here to meet again,
Hopeless on earth, and heaven is out of view.
But by my heart of love laid bare to you,
   My love that you can make not void nor vain,
Love that foregoes you but to claim anew
     Beyond this passage of the gate of death,
   I charge you at the Judgment make it plain
     My love of you was life and not a breath.

12.

"Amor, che ne la mente mi ragiona."—DANTE
"Amor vien nel bel viso di costei."—PETRARCA

If there be any one can take my place
   And make you happy whom I grieve to grieve,
   Think not that I can grudge it, but believe
I do commend you to that nobler grace,
That readier wit than mine, that sweeter face;
   Yea, since your riches make me rich, conceive
   I too am crowned, while bridal crowns I weave,
And thread the bridal dance with jocund pace.
For if I did not love you, it might be
   That I should grudge you some one dear delight;
     But since the heart is yours that was mine own,
   Your pleasure is my pleasure, right my right,
Your honourable freedom makes me free,
     And you companioned I am not alone.

13.

"E drizzeremo glí occhi al Primo Amore."—DANTE
"Ma trovo peso non da le mie braccia."—PETRARCA

If I could trust mine own self with your fate,
   Shall I not rather trust it in God's hand?
   Without Whose Will one lily doth not stand,
Nor sparrow fall at his appointed date;
   Who numbereth the innumerable sand,
Who weighs the wind and water with a weight,
To Whom the world is neither small nor great,
   Whose knowledge foreknew every plan we planned.
Searching my heart for all that touches you,
   I find there only love and love's goodwill
Helpless to help and impotent to do,
     Of understanding dull, of sight most dim;
     And therefore I commend you back to Him
Whose love your love's capacity can fill.

14.

"E la Sua Volontade è nostra pace."—DANTE
"Sol con questi pensier, con altre chiome."—PETRARCA

Youth gone, and beauty gone if ever there
   Dwelt beauty in so poor a face as this;
   Youth gone and beauty, what remains of bliss?
I will not bind fresh roses in my hair,
To shame a cheek at best but little fair,—
   Leave youth his roses, who can bear a thorn,—
I will not seek for blossoms anywhere,
   Except such common flowers as blow with corn.
Youth gone and beauty gone, what doth remain?
   The longing of a heart pent up forlorn,
     A silent heart whose silence loves and longs;
     The silence of a heart which sang its songs
   While youth and beauty made a summer morn,
Silence of love that cannot sing again.

The following are William Michael Rossetti's translations of the epi-graphs to each sonnet of the *Monna Innominata* (*Works*, 462–63).

1. The day that they have said adieu to their sweet friends.
   Love, with how great a stress dost thou vanquish me today!

2. It was already the hour which turns back the desire.
   I recur to the time when I first saw thee.

3. Oh shades, empty save in semblance!
   An imaginary guide conducts her.

4. A small spark fosters a great flame.
   Every other thing, every thought, goes off, and love alone remains there with you.

5. Love, who exempts no loved one from loving.
   Love led me into such joyous hope.

6. Now canst thou comprehend the quantity of the love which glows in me towards thee.
   I do not choose that Love should release me from such a tie.

7. Here always Spring and every fruit.
   Conversing with me, and I with him.

8. As if he were to say to God, "I care for nought else."
   I hope to find pity, and not only pardon.

9. O dignified and pure conscience!
   Spirit more lit with burning virtues.

10. With better course and with better star.
    Life flees, and stays not an hour.

11. Come after me, and leave folk to talk.
    Relating the casualties of our life.

12. Love, who speaks within my mind.
    Love comes in the beautiful face of this lady.

13. And we will direct our eyes to the Primal Love.
    But I find a burden to which my arms suffice not.

14. And His will is our peace.
    Only with these thoughts, with different locks.

NOTES

PREFACE

1. McGann, *Beauty of Inflections*, 344. See also Butler, "Against Tradition"; Weimann, *Structure and Society*; and Lindenberger, "New History." Harrison, "Reception Theory," presents a generalized theoretical exploration of what is required in a full-scale project in reception history (as a major component of the comprehensive project of a new historicist criticism).

CHAPTER I

1. Quoted by Sandars, *Christina Rossetti*, 85. The original of this letter is in the Yale University Library Special Collections.

2. As Jerome J. McGann has observed, Crump's new edition will have a "salutary, restorative effect" on Rossetti criticism (*NER*, 208).

3. McGann quite correctly describes this as the "most treacherous of all 'schools' of Rossetti criticism" and cites Lona Mosk Packer's "speculative psychobiography," *Christina Rossetti*, as a work that "carries this kind of criticism to its self-destructive limits" (*NER*, 238). However, this "tradition" is pervasive and difficult to escape in Rossetti criticism. As William Fredeman observes, "biographical has long outstripped critical interest in Christina Rossetti" ("The Pre-Raphaelites," 291). The most influential precursors of Packer include William Michael Rossetti (see his "Memoir" in *Works*); Rossetti's official biographer, Mackenzie Bell (*Christina Rossetti*); and Maurice Bowra (*Romantic Imagination*, 245–70). Even two of Rossetti's most recent critics use her poetry to interpret her life (see Owen, "Christina Rossetti," and Fass, "Christina Rossetti and St. Agnes' Eve"). In a recent major anthology of Victorian poetry, Donald Gray, an otherwise impeccable editor, begins his discussion of Rossetti's poetry by insisting that her works "are often personal in the sense that they express her feelings about herself and her connections with others, with the possibilities of life outside her narrow bound, and with God" (*Victorian Literature: Poetry*, 543).

4. For the most important recent discussions of this issue, see Ball, "Sincerity"; Davie, "On Sincerity from Wordsworth to Ginsberg"; Trilling, *Sincerity and Authenticity*; and Mellor, *Romantic Irony*.

5. Apart from McGann, a number of important recent critics do not succumb to the powerful temptation to read Christina Rossetti's poetry exclusively as autobiography. Among the most recent is Joan Rees (*Poetry of Dante Gabriel Rossetti*, 152–60, 167–75). Rees usefully but sketchily introduces an approach to Christina Rossetti's poetry in terms of the Dantean and the sonnet traditions. Gisela Hönnighausen studies religious traditions of flower imagery behind Rossetti's verse ("Emblematic Tendencies"), and Winston Weathers eschews the psychobiographical approach, insisting that Christina Rossetti was able to transcend the "simply

autobiographical and environmental" elements in her work ("Christina Rossetti"). See also Blake, *Love and the Woman Question*; Wenger, "Influence of the Bible"; Gilbert and Gubar, *Madwoman in the Attic*; Kent, "Sequence and Meaning" and "'By thought word and deed'"; D'Amico, "Christina Rossetti" and "Reading and Rereading"; Shaw, "Projection and Empathy"; Connor, "Speaking Likenesses"; Homans, "'Syllables of Velvet'"; and Mermin, "Heroic Sisterhood."

6. We need a full-scale, dependable biography, an edition of her complete letters, an annotated bibliography of her reading, and clear-minded critical treatments of her previously unstudied poems (that is, the bulk of them).

7. Like "Maude Clare," a number of Rossetti's published poems consist of stanzas selected from works much longer in manuscript form. See especially "Thy Friend and thy Father's Friend forget not," "Easter Monday," and "There Remaineth Therefore a Rest to the People of God." Although Rossetti herself did not publish the deleted stanzas under their original manuscript titles during her own lifetime, William Michael Rossetti often did so in his edition of her works. See, for instance, *Poems*, 2:426, 433, 435, 437, 438, 442, 445, 448, 453, 456, 462, 465, 469, 472, 475.

8. "Forty-three stanzas or thereabouts" according to William Michael Rossetti (*Works*, 481), but, as Crump explains, in the only extant manuscript in the British Library "the last page of the MS is missing from the notebook, and the last two stanzas of the published version are not in the MS as it now stands" (*Poems*, 1:244). In my comments below I do not assume that the last two stanzas of the published version originally appeared on the last MS page.

9. In Crump's first volume see, for instance, the following heavily revised poems: "Song," "Echo," "Shut Out," "Bitter for Sweet," "The Poor Ghost," "Songs in a Cornfield," "The Bourne," "Summer," "A Royal Princess," "Bird or Beast," "After This the Judgment," "By the Sea," "The Lowest Room," and "Who Shall Deliver Me?"

10. For a fuller commentary on Rossetti's acceptance and employment of the doctrine of "Soul Sleep," see *RP*. A central biblical text from which the doctrine of soul-sleep or psychopannychism originates (but which McGann does not cite) is 1 Thess. 4:13–17.

11. This letter is in the Troxell Collection of the Princeton University Library.

12. See William Fredeman's remarks on the biographical approach to Rossetti criticism ("'From Insult to Protect'" and "Impediments and Motives").

13. The critical and editing activities of William Michael Rossetti are well known, but his translation of Dante is not. And Victorianists at large are even less familiar with Maria Rossetti's *A Shadow of Dante*, which Christina admired enormously (and which was widely used as a classroom text in the nineteenth century). See *FL*, 75, 171.

14. Rossetti reveals her extensive interest in the troubadour roots of Petrarchan and Dantean tradition in the preface to her sonnet sequence, *Monna Innominata*, which was composed over perhaps as long as a fifteen-year period (see Rees, *Dante Gabriel Rossetti*, 152–53).

15. These must, of course, be distinguished from the poem's central *moral* values of humility, fidelity, and courage.

16. See Symons, "Christina Rossetti," in *Two Literatures*, 48; Woolf, *Second Common Reader*, 264; and DeWilde, *Christina Rossetti*.

17. Quoted in Sandars, *Christina Rossetti*, 86.

18. Christina Rossetti to William Michael Rossetti, 31 Jan. 1850, Troxell Collection, Princeton University Library.

19. Christina Rossetti to William Michael Rossetti, 13 Aug. 1853, ibid.

20. 4 Feb. 1874, in Packer, *Rossetti-Macmillan Letters*, 99.

21. Troxell, *Three Rossettis*, 143.

22. Bloom, *Walter Pater*, 6.

23. Pater, *Plato and Platonism*, 139–40.

CHAPTER 2

1. Sharp, "The Rossettis," 427.

2. Bowker, "Literary Centre," 827.

3. Sharp, "The Rossettis," 429.

4. See Hamilton, *Aesthetic Movement in England*, and more recently, Hunt, *Pre-Raphaelite Imagination*. Both of these now-standard works convincingly argue that the aesthetic movement was generated largely by Pre-Raphaelitism and that its participants self-consciously looked to Pre-Raphaelite aesthetic values as the source of their own.

5. [Dennet], "Miss Rossetti's Poems," 47.

6. "Christina Georgina Rossetti," *Dial*, 38.

7. "The Rambler," 21.

8. Gosse, "Christina Rossetti," 214.

9. Hunt, *Pre-Raphaelite Imagination*, xi–xii.

10. Ibid., xii.

11. Hunt does, however, devote several pages to the similarities between aspects of Christina Rossetti's *Commonplace* stories and the elements of aestheticism.

12. Lang, *Pre-Raphaelites and Their Circle*, xxvi–xxvii.

13. Ibid. Lang does, of course, retain a sampling of Christina Rossetti's verse in his historically founded anthology of Pre-Raphaelite poetry.

14. La Gallienne, review of *Poems*, 131.

15. [Dennet], "Miss Rossetti's Poems," 47.

16. Review of *The Prince's Progress*, 824.

17. Ibid., 825.

18. Law, "Poetry of Christina Rossetti," 452.

19. Ibid., 447.

20. George Landow properly reminds us that the Pre-Raphaelites "read not only the first volume of *Modern Painters*, which emphasized truth to nature, but the second volume, which contained Ruskin's theories of beauty and imagination" (*Victorian Types*, 4).

21. Dante and Christina Rossetti are, of course, the crucial figures in maintaining this continuity.

204 Notes to Pages 29–37

22. For the clearest presentation of this view of Pre-Raphaelite poetry, see Edward Engelberg's anthology, *The Symbolist Poem*.

23. Of course, these same precepts also lead, ironically, to the Paterian and Wildean aestheticist impulses that dominated the 1890s and enabled the modernist poetry of Yeats, Eliot, and Pound to emerge. See Bloom, *Walter Pater*, 1–21.

24. There were two poems in the January issue; three in the February issue; and two in the March number, retitled *Art and Poetry, Being Thoughts Toward Nature, Conducted Principally by Artists*.

25. The most illuminating commentary on Dante Gabriel Rossetti's adaptation of Christian symbolism is McGann's "Rossetti's Significant Details," reprinted in Sambrook, 230–42. On the Ruskinian influence on Pre-Raphaelitism, see Sussman, "The Brotherhood Aesthetic" (*Fact*, 33–46).

26. A late letter makes this clear. Even in 1883, despite Ruskin's "annoying" criticism of her late brother's painting, she confided to her sister-in-law, Lucy, "I cannot help admiring much of [Ruskin's] work" (*FL*, 137–38).

27. Landow, *John Ruskin*, 110.

28. Ibid.

29. See, for instance, my discussion of "An Old World Thicket" later in this chapter.

30. See Landow, *John Ruskin*, 372–91.

31. Ibid., 391.

32. For his critical response, see William Michael Rossetti, *Ruskin*, 258–59. Christina Rossetti's interest in Ruskin extended at least from the mid-1850s when Dante Gabriel was seeing a good deal of his patron and her sister Maria apparently became attracted to him (see Battiscombe, *Christina Rossetti*, 87). In all likelihood, however, she was reading the early volumes of *Modern Painters* along with her brothers somewhat earlier than this. Her concern with the power and value of Ruskin's work continued well into her later years. On 16 May 1885 she wrote to her close friend, Caroline Gemmer, "Yes, indeed, I do warm towards Mr. Ruskin. . . . I was talking to another Oxford anti-V[ivisectionist] yesterday 'Lewis Carroll' and he shares my respect for the 'ex' Slade Professor" (unpublished letter, Koch Collection, Pierpont Morgan Library).

33. Landow, *John Ruskin*, 373.

34. Ibid.

35. Ibid., 115.

36. Ibid., 148–49, 151.

37. See, for instance, "In an Artist's Studio," "Wife to Husband," "Listening," "The Convent Threshold," "Cousin Kate," "L.E.L.," "Three Nuns," and "Is and Was."

38. Rossetti, *Time Flies*, 62, 122.

39. Jerome Bump acknowledges this important fact in "Hopkins' Imagery," 115–16, n. 31.

40. Courthope, "Latest Development in Literary Poetry," 63.

41. See, for instance, the persuasive case McGann makes for such a view (*NER*, 241–47).

42. In addition to Hunt, see especially Lang (preface to *The Pre-Raphaelites*); Fredeman (introduction to *Pre-Raphaelitism* and "The Pre-Raphaelites"); Buckley

(introduction to *The Pre-Raphaelites*); and Rees (introduction to *Dante Gabriel Rossetti*, 1–16).

43. Like Walter Hamilton and John Dixon Hunt, Renato Pogglioli acknowledges without complication the evolution of Pre-Raphaelitism (as an avant-garde movement) into aestheticism, noting simply "the message handed down by the Pre-Raphaelite Brotherhood to the aesthetic movement at the fin de siècle" (*Theory of the Avant-Garde*, 226–27).

44. Sussman, "Pre-Raphaelite Brotherhood," 7.

45. As Sussman explains, "the Brotherhood self-consciously engaged in the familiar avant-garde strategy of defamiliarization through radical stylistic innovation" in order to "restore intensity to the perception of familiar subject matter" (ibid., 8).

46. The other paradox crucial to the movement, as I have indicated, is its use of the sensuous to figure the noumenal.

47. Sussman notes the stylistic innovativeness of Swinburne and Morris but not their revival of old forms ("Pre-Raphaelite Brotherhood," 8–9).

48. On this subject, see Bump, "Hopkins, Christina Rossetti, and Pre-Raphaelitism," 5–6.

49. In Pater, *The Renaissance*, 106.

50. Gosse, "Christina Rossetti," 211–12.

51. Ford, *Critical Attitude*, 179.

52. Rossetti, *Ruskin*, 258–59.

53. As Janet Camp Troxell has observed, the only previous explanation for Ruskin's remarks "is that Ruskin felt it was damaging to Gabriel to have another Rossetti in the market" (*Three Rossettis*, 30–31).

54. Curran, "Lyric Voice of Christina Rossetti," 289, 293.

55. See especially Blake, *Love and the Woman Question*, 3–25; and Connor, "Language and Repetition."

56. W. M. Rossetti, *Rossetti Papers*, 77.

57. Ibid., 88. For Christina's brief remarks on her revisions of the poem, see also p. 94.

58. See chapter five for a full discussion of the intertextual qualities of Rossetti's poetry.

59. [Dennett], "Miss Rossetti's Poems," 47.

60. Law, "Poetry of Christina Rossetti," 450.

61. "Christina Georgina Rossetti," *The Critic*, 21.

62. Gosse, "Christina Rossetti," 214.

63. As William Michael Rossetti notes in his brief biographical memoir to his sister's *Works*, Saint Augustine and Thomas à Kempis were two of her favorite authors (p. lxix), and one is often surprised, in her prose works, to come upon detailed knowledge of such medieval matters as those concerning the life of Gregory the Great which she reveals in *Time Flies*, 50–52.

64. Bump, "Hopkins' Imagery," 100.

65. Hough, *The Last Romantics*, 24.

66. Christina Rossetti, *Called to Be Saints*, xiii.

67. Hunt, *Pre-Raphaelite Imagination*, 103.

68. Stubbs, "Pre-Raphaelitism and the Aesthetic Withdrawal," originally pub-

lished in *The Darkling Plain*, 147–78. Reprinted in Sambrook, 166–85. This comment appears on page 167 of Sambrook.
69. Law, "Poetry of Christina Rossetti," 444–45.
70. Hunt, *Pre-Raphaelite Imagination*, 223–25.
71. Ibid., 77.
72. Symons, *Studies in Two Literatures*, 142, 143.
73. Gosse, "Christina Rossetti," 215.
74. La Gallienne, review of *Poems*, 132.

CHAPTER 3

1. For Bump's position, see "Hopkins, Christina Rossetti, and Pre-Raphaelitism," 1–6.
2. Courthope, "Latest Development in Literary Poetry," 63.
3. Riede, "Erasing the Art-Catholic," 50.
4. Courthope, "Latest Development in Literary Poetry," 63. Also see J. C. Shairp's even more vitriolic attack, on similar grounds, in "Aesthetic Poetry."
5. The letter is dated 13 May 1851 (*WJR*, 12:319–23).
6. Fredeman, *P.R.B. Journal*, 9, 13. See Sussman, *Fact*, chapter 4, for a full discussion of scripture as history among the Pre-Raphaelites.
7. Chapman, *Faith and Revolt*, 175–96, passim.
8. See the sale catalog, *Books from the Libraries of Christina, Dante Gabriel, and William Michael Rossetti*, 27. Rossetti's possession of Keble's *Christian Year* is noted by Battiscombe (*Christina Rossetti*, 180) and Packer (*Christina Rossetti*, 7); the book is now in the possession of Helen Angeli Rossetti.
9. See Kent, "Sequence and Meaning."
10. The medieval revival was, of course, a phenomenon that affected many areas of Victorian life, literature, art, and architecture. A number of major studies of Victorian medievalism have appeared since Kenneth Clark's pioneering work on the gothic revival in architecture. These include: Chandler, *Dream of Order*; *Browning Institute Studies* 8 (1980); Girouard, *Return to Camelot*; and Harrison, *Swinburne's Medievalism*.
11. For a concise, helpful commentary on Rossetti's medievalism, see Stein, *Ritual of Interpretation*, 121–30.
12. On the Tractarian concept of Analogy, see especially *VDP*, 52–56, 93–96, 146–51. On Reserve, see 41–47.
13. *Tracts for the Times*, 6:143.
14. Newman, *Apologia*, 29.
15. See, for instance, McGann, "Rossetti's Significant Details," in Sambrook, 230–42.
16. Morris, *Earthly Paradise*, 2:199.
17. Swinburne, *Complete Works*, 1:13.
18. Christ, *Finer Optic*, 60–61.
19. Keble, *Lectures on Poetry*, 1:143.
20. See, for instance, "To What Purpose Is This Waste" (*Works*, 305).
21. Warren, *English Poetic Theory*, 10.

22. These are by no means always dream visions, as McGann insists, however.

23. For the best available discussion of Keats's influence on Rossetti, see Fass, "Christina Rossetti and St. Agnes' Eve."

24. See, for instance, Keble's "Fourth Sunday in Advent."

25. Among Rossetti's relevant poems, see "The Portrait," "He and I," "Lost Days," "The Soul's Sphere," "Without Her," and "Severed Selves."

26. For a full and useful elucidation of those values, see Gorham, *Victorian Girl*, and Poovey, *Proper Lady and the Woman Writer*.

27. Christina Rossetti to Caroline Gemmer, 3 Jan. 1888, Frederick Koch Collection, Pierpont Morgan Library.

28. Among such works I would include the great bulk of paintings by Rossetti, Burne-Jones, and Waterhouse, as well as poems like "The Blessed Damozel," "The Portrait," and the "Willowwood" sonnets already cited. Also see Morris's *Earthly Paradise* and Swinburne's "Rococo," "Before a Mirror," "Hermaphroditus," "A Nympholept," "The Lake of Gaube," and "The Queen's Pleasance" from *Tristram of Lyonesse*.

29. Keble, *Occasional Papers*, 16.

30. For a summary of this view of Pre-Raphaelitism, see Lourie, "Embodiment of Dreams."

31. Ibid., 194.

32. Other Pre-Raphaelite works that embody the same self-sustaining and self-reflexive qualities as Dante Rossetti's poems include Morris's "Concerning Geffray Teste Noir," "The Day Is Coming," and the introductory lyric in *The Earthly Paradise*; and Swinburne's "Thalassius," "Hermaphroditus," *Anactoria*, and, among his essays, "Charles Baudelaire" and *William Blake*.

33. Newman, *Works*, 1:23.

34. See especially D'Amico, "Reading and Rereading"; and Kent, "'By thought word and deed.'"

35. See, for instance, Swinburne's "The Triumph of Time," "The Garden of Proserpine," and "Hertha."

CHAPTER 4

1. "The thematic unity of the work [of literature] is not the combination of its words and individual sentences. . . . Theme always transcends language. . . . The theme of a work is the theme of the whole utterance as a definite socio-historical act. Consequently it is inseparable from the total situation of the utterance to the same extent that it is inseparable from linguistic elements. . . . Further, it becomes clear that the forms of the whole, i.e., the genre forms, essentially determine theme." Thus, "the thematic unity of the work is inseparable from its primary orientation in its environment, inseparable, that is to say, from the circumstances of place and time" (Bakhtin, *Formal Method in Literary Scholarship*, 132).

2. See, for instance, "We 'Other Victorians,'" in Foucault, *History of Sexuality*.

3. See Adorno, "Lyric Poetry and Society."

4. Important in this context is Rossetti's letter to Augusta Webster explaining her refusal to support women's suffrage. She refuses on the grounds of the patriar-

chal doctrines, values, and hierarchy of Christian orthodoxy, but with a very significant caveat: "On the other hand if female rights are sure to be overborne for lack of female voting influence, then I confess I feel disposed to shoot ahead of my instructresses, and to assert that female *M.P.'s* are only right and reasonable. Also I take exceptions at the exclusion of married women from the suffrage,—for who so apt as Mothers—all previous arguments allowed for the moment—to protect the interests of themselves and of their offspring? I do think if anything ever does sweep away the barrier of sex, and make the female not a giantess or a heroine but at once and full grown a hero and giant, it is that mighty maternal love which makes little birds and little beasts as well as little women matches for very big adversaries" (Bell, *Christina Rossetti,* 112).

5. Heath-Stubbs, "Pre-Raphaelitism and the Aesthetic Withdrawal." On Dante Rossetti, see William Fredeman's now-classic study, "Rossetti's 'In Memoriam.'" Cecil Lang correctly insists that the *Defence* volume is not only "the first, as well as the most, Pre-Raphaelite volume of poems," but also Morris's last Pre-Raphaelite volume (*Pre-Raphaelites,* 19).

6. The most extensive discussion of Keats's influence on the Pre-Raphaelites appears in Ford, *Keats and the Victorians.* But see also Fass, "Christina Rossetti and St. Agnes' Eve."

7. Both Dante Rossetti and Swinburne did, of course, write a good deal of poetry with explicit moral and political themes. Rossetti's "The Burden of Nineveh" and "Jenny" are such poems, and political verse dominates Swinburne's two volumes of the early 1870s, *Songs Before Sunrise* and *Songs of Two Nations.* On Rossetti's political poetry, see Bentley, "Political Themes in the Work of Dante Gabriel Rossetti." However, even such works by Swinburne and Rossetti generally "aestheticize" their moral and political themes by presenting them statically, as matter for abstract contemplation rather than action.

8. See Keats to Benjamin Bailey, 22 November 1817, in Rollins, *Letters of John Keats,* 1:185.

9. The final effect of Tennyson's *Maud* (1855) is, after all, precisely to renounce the solipsism, the perversely aesthetic mentality, and the fully melancholic malaise of its central character.

10. The seminal treatment of the subject is Hamilton, *Aesthetic Movement in England.*

11. Symons, *Studies in Two Literatures,* 138.

12. Keats to Bailey, in Rollins, *Letters of John Keats,* 1:185.

13. The indisputable influence of Plato and Augustine upon Rossetti is made clear by Bellas (*Christina Rossetti,* 17–19), Packer (*Christina Rossetti,* 94, 142–43, 195, 231, 259, 316); and W. M. Rossetti ("Memoir," in *Works,* lxix–lxx).

14. W. D. Shaw approaches, but does not quite endorse, this conclusion about Christina Rossetti's aesthetics ("Projection and Empathy in Victorian Poetry," 324–29).

15. Packer, *Christina Rossetti,* 195. Hereafter cited in the text as "Packer." Packer also traces the image of the revered but dreaded lover in "My Dream" (1859) to Plato's *Phaedrus* as well as to Shelley (p. 94). Later, in commenting on "Mirrors of Life and Death," she quite correctly remarks that for Christina Rossetti, "The external world of nature symbolizes the inner world of the spirit. Christina visual-

izes 'the two worlds, visible and invisible' as 'doubling' against each other,' 'Wind, water, fire, the sun, a star, a vine, a door, a lamb . . . will shadow forth mysteries.' This Platonic conception of nature providing an endless series of 'terrene mirrors' as images of a nonsensuous reality is [her] theme" in this poem (p. 316).

16. The article was republished in 1895 in *Plato and Platonism*.

17. Pater, *Plato and Platonism*, 134–36.

18. The full comments by William Michael Rossetti and Ralph Bellas concerning Augustine's influence are helpful at this point. Rossetti explains that, "theology [Christina] studied, I think, very little indeed: there was the Bible, of which her knowledge was truly minute and ready, supplemented by the *Confessions* of Augustine and *The Imitation of Christ.* . . . I question whether, apart from this one book of Augustine, she ever read any 'Father,' Latin or Greek, or desired to read him" (*Works*, lxix). Extending Rossetti's remarks, Ralph Bellas observes that, "next in importance [to the Bible] were *The Confessions* of St. Augustine and the *Imitation of Christ* by Thomas à Kempis. Christina's religious sensibility resembled Augustine's and Thomas's in her acute awareness of worldly temptations, of man's sinfulness, and of his unworthiness in God's eyes. Augustine's . . . Christian Platonism especially appealed to her" (*Christina Rossetti*, 18).

19. See *FL*, 65, 87, 92, 164.

20. Colish, *Mirror of Language*, 35.

21. This influence is perceived, it seems, even by students of Augustine. In his classic commentary, *Amor Dei: A Study of the Religion of St. Augustine*, John Burnaby appropriately places Christina Rossetti's poem "Passing Away" as an epigraph to his chapter, "The Platonist's Christianity."

22. That mentality surfaces repeatedly in her family letters. For instance, to William Michael in Italy she wrote (5 February 1887): "It sounds earthly-paradise-like, your sketch of San Remo: but even there it would behove me to feel, Arise ye and depart, for this is not your rest" (*FL*, 159). Just over a year later (10 December 1888) she wrote to her brother, "Beautiful, delightful, noble, memorable, as is the world you and yours frequent,—I yet am well content in my shady crevice: which crevice enjoys the unique advantage of being to my certain knowledge the place assigned me" (*FL*, 168). We must, of course, balance our sense of Rossetti's apparently profound selflessness with the knowledge that she *did* expect heavenly rewards for her self-denial on earth. In this context, Janet Camp Troxell cites a passage from Rossetti's *Letter and Spirit* in which "we get an idea of the compensation she expected to receive for [her various] renunciations: 'For the books we now forbear to read, we shall one day be endued of wisdom and knowledge; for the music we will not listen to, we shall join in the song of the redeemed. For the pictures from which we turn, we shall gaze unabashed on the Beatific Vision. For the companionship we shun, we shall be welcomed into angelic society, and the communion of triumphant saints. For the amusements we avoid, we shall keep the Supreme jubilee. For the pleasures we miss, we shall abide, and forever abide, in the rapture of heaven'" (*Three Rossettis*, 148).

23. Colish, *Mirror of Language*, 29.

24. See Augustine *Confessions* 7, 8; and Colish, *Mirror of Language*, 42–45.

25. Colish, *Mirror of Language*, 68.

26. Gosse, "Christina Rossetti," 216.

27. Quoted in Packer, *Christina Rossetti*, 106.

28. Indeed, Jerome McGann praises the poem as an exposé of the sexual and social constraints on Victorian women, which undermined their integrity and prevented true fulfillment in love relationships (*NER*, 245).

29. Review of *The Prince's Progress*, 824.

30. Margaret Homans has convincingly demonstrated this point for *Goblin Market* (see "'Syllables of Velvet'").

31. For backgrounds to the evolution of this ideology, see Rougement, *L'Amour et L'occident*, and Rabine, *Reading the Romantic Heroine*.

32. Two radically different perspectives on the poem are articulated by Jerome McGann and Sandra Gilbert. McGann reads the poem as a "prophetic" critique of Victorian marriage markets. For him, the poem is designed to convey "the need for an alternative social order" (*NER*, 254). For Gilbert, the goblin men's fruits represent the "fruit of art" whose serious pursuit was forbidden to Victorian women (*Madwoman in the Attic*, 569–71). The most forceful feminist reading of *Goblin Market* appears in Homans's essay. She argues that *Goblin Market* "is about poetic language as well as about female sexuality" and that Rossetti subverts patriarchal and androcentric traditions of romantic lyric in her poem by showing Lizzie "turning [the goblin men's] assault against their intentions, reappropriating their objectification of her body and transforming that objectification into her own positive strategy. Having been reduced to mere body within a metaphoric [androcentric] economy by the goblins' assault, Lizzie, by understanding herself as inhabiting instead a metonymic economy . . . experiences that body as a source of power." According to Homans's reading, *Goblin Market* demonstrates that "the cure of female sexuality subjected to romantic desire is the cure of metaphor into metonymy" ("'Syllables of Velvet,'" 589).

33. "Gay" was a familiar Victorian term applied to prostitutes.

34. Such resemblances between *Goblin Market* and Coleridge's *Rime* were observed by early readers. For instance, Mrs. Charles Eliot Norton, in her review of Rossetti's first volume of poems, asserts that *Goblin Market* may "vie with Coleridge's 'Ancient Mariner' . . . for the vivid and wonderful power by which things unreal and mystic are made to blend and link themselves with the everyday images and events of common life" ("'The Goblin Market,'" 404).

35. Review of *Goblin Market*, 230.

36. Lourie, "Embodiment of Dreams," 202–3.

37. Thomas à Kempis, *Imitation of Christ* 2.1.

38. For a full discussion of this literature, see Gorham, *Victorian Girl*.

39. Swinburne, *Poems*, 1:24. Hereafter cited in the text as Swinburne.

40. Dante Rossetti, *Works of Dante Gabriel Rossetti*, 92. Hereafter cited in the text as Rossetti.

41. All citations to poems from Morris's *Defence of Guenevere and Other Poems* are from Cecil Lang's edition in *The Pre-Raphaelites and Their Circle*. Hereafter cited in the text as Lang.

42. In line 13, for instance, the speaker describes her house as a "castle," but, significantly, this term substitutes for her original word "palace" (*Poems*, 1:263).

43. Sandra Gilbert explains that the "pleasure-place" is "quite clearly a paradise

of self-gratifying art" inhabited by a "female poet-speaker" (Gilbert and Gubar, *Madwoman in the Attic*, 571).
44. Ibid.
45. Tennyson, *Poems*, 418.
46. Jauss, *Aesthetic Experience*, 146. Hereafter cited in the text as Jauss.
47. For a full theoretical discussion of intertextuality in these terms, see Uhlig, "Literature as Textual Palingenesis."
48. The conclusion to Tennyson's poem continues to perplex critics. For one explanation of its operations, see Harrison, "Irony in Tennyson's 'Little *Hamlet.*'"
49. Hinkson, "Poetry of Christina Rossetti," 78.
50. Gilbert and Gubar, *Madwoman in the Attic*, 575.

CHAPTER 5

1. Battiscombe, *Christina Rossetti*, 129.
2. Packer, *Christina Rossetti*, 14.
3. Christina Rossetti to Edmund Gosse, 30 Jan. 1883, Ashley Manuscripts, The British Library. Quoted by Packer, *Christina Rossetti*, 360.
4. Bell suggests that Rossetti began her work assisting Grosart in 1855, but the effort probably came later. Grosart's ten-volume Spenser did not appear until 1882–84 (*Christina Rossetti*, 36).
5. Quoted in Friedrich, *Dante's Fame Abroad*, 339. To simplify references to Victorian commentators on Dante, all future citations for such commentary will be cited in the text as Friedrich.
6. For two standard discussions of the sense of alienation that pervades Victorian literature and culture, see Houghton, *Victorian Frame of Mind*, esp. 77–89; and Johnson, *Alien Vision of Victorian Poetry*.
7. Christina Rossetti, "Dante, an English Classic," 201.
8. Dante Rossetti, *Early Italian Poets*, 3.
9. Christina Rossetti, "Dante. The Poet Illustrated out of the Poem," 566–67. Mackenzie Bell observes that Christina Rossetti "was herself a student of Dante, though not in so profound a sense as her father, her sister, or William. As to this aspect of her character Mr. [William Sharp] reports a very interesting utterance: 'I wish [she said] I too could have done something for Dante in England! Maria wrote her fine and helpful book, William's translation of the "Divina Commedia" is the best we have, and Gabriel's "Dante and His Circle" is a monument of loving labor that will outlast either. But I, alas, have neither the requisite knowledge nor the ability'" (*Christina Rossetti*, 63–64). Bell also cites Christina Rossetti's letter of 28 March 1892 to Patchett Martin, editor of *Literary Opinion*, in which she volunteers to review for him any new book on Dante: "Perhaps enthusiasm for my subject might make up for scant learning," she proffers modestly. However, as Bell observes, "She did not [in the end] write on Dante for *Literary Opinion*" (p. 131). For brief, general remarks about the Dantean influence on Christina Rossetti, see also Bell, *Christina Rossetti*, 355; and Bellas, *Christina Rossetti*, 18–19.
10. Bell observes Christina Rossetti's extreme admiration for her sister's *A*

Shadow of Dante, and he cites Christina's frequent references to it in her *The Face of the Deep* (*Christina Rossetti*, 64–67). Lona Packer has located two copies of *A Shadow of Dante* that fully reveal Christina's interest in the work. One, which is in the collection of Harold Rossetti, she describes as containing "copious marginal notes and illustrations in pencil by Christina Rossetti." The other, in Oliver Rossetti's private collection, also has "marginal notes by Christina Rossetti commenting on the text" (*Christina Rossetti*, 438).

11. Christina Rossetti, "Dante, an English Classic," 200.

12. Battiscombe reinforces the point: "In Sept. 1847 she wrote two poems, *Heart's Chill Between* and *Death's Chill Between* . . . in which she deals with a tragedy of thwarted love. If ever poems read like a cry from the heart these are they; yet it is all but certain that the sixteen-year-old Christina had never been in love. . . . These two linked poems should be sufficient warning of the danger of reading an autobiographical meaning into Christina's early poetry" (*Christina Rossetti*, 42). Also see Bell who makes the same point about "Love Attacked" and "Love Defended" (*Christina Rossetti*, 219).

13. Sebeok, "Enter Textuality," 657–58.

14. Uhlig, "Literature as Textual Palingenesis," 502.

15. Ibid., 503.

16. White, "Historical Pluralism," 482–86.

17. On this topic in connection with nineteenth-century literary studies, see the recent work of Jerome J. McGann and Hayden White, as well as that of Marilyn Butler, Terry Eagleton, Fredric Jameson, and Jane Tompkins.

18. Gilbert, "Female King," 866. Also see Culler, *Victorian Mirror of History*, and Dale, *Victorian Critic and the Idea of History*.

19. Gilbert, "Female King," 866.

20. Hutcheon, *Theory of Parody*. Hereafter cited in the text as Hutcheon.

21. In a letter to his sister dated 7 September 1881, Dante Rossetti describes Swinburne's reaction to *A Pageant and Other Poems*, in which *Monna Innominata* first appeared: "Swinburne's delight with the [volume] amounted to a dancing and screaming ecstacy" (Doughty and Wall, *Letters of D. G. Rossetti*, 4:1920). It is clear that Christina read Swinburne's poetry with some care. See *FL*, 120, and Packer, *Christina Rossetti*, 353.

22. Packer, *Christina Rossetti*, 353.

23. Swinburne, *Poems*, 4:11.

24. McGann, *Swinburne*, 140.

25. Swinburne, *Poems*, 4:12.

26. Homans, "'Syllables of Velvet,'" 574. Hereafter cited in the text as Homans.

27. For a similar argument regarding Dante Rossetti's sonnet sequence, *The House of Life*, see William Fredeman's now-classic discussion, "Rossetti's 'In Memoriam.'"

28. Hereafter I have adopted the "macro" designation when discussing the structure of the sequence, as opposed to its thematic and psychological movements.

29. Joan Rees has convincingly demonstrated the superiority of Rossetti's craft in the *Monna Innominata*. Rees insists that Rossetti exercises "the utmost econo-

my and simplicity of statement" in the sequence, while exhibiting "taughtness" and "firm intellectual control" (*Poetry of Dante Gabriel Rossetti*, 146–60).

30. Browning, *Poetical Works*, 217. Hereafter cited in the text as Browning.

31. See Bump, "Hopkins, Metalepsis, and the Metaphysicals."

32. Ferrucci, *Poetics of Disguise*, 121.

33. Christina Rossetti, "Dante. The Poet Illustrated out of the Poem," 571.

34. Bannerjee, "Dante through the Looking Glass," 148.

35. For a full discussion of this topic, see Girouard, *Return to Camelot*.

36. For a comprehensive commentary on Swinburne's debt to this complex tradition, see Harrison, *Swinburne's Medievalism*. For discussions of Morris and medieval romantic tradition, see Silver, *Romance of William Morris*, and Riede, "Morris, Modernism, and Romance."

37. Jerome McGann, expanding upon the limited conception of estrangement articulated by the Russian Formalists, explains how the general effect of estrangement operates in literature: "The aesthetic effect of literature is profoundly related—paradoxical though it may seem—to the reader['s] . . . view of history. Aesthetic effect depends upon the distancing of the art work, the estrangement of it, its isolation from our immediacy. We say that it seems to occupy a place outside of time, as it were. But this is merely a way of saying that art works are forever placed *in* history, that is, in the vertical and horizontal circumstances which define human events" ("Keats and the Historical Method," 1026).

38. Hagstrum, *Sex and Sensibility*, 18.

39. Ibid., 20.

40. Krieger, *Classic Vision*, 56.

41. Topsfield, *Troubadours and Love*, 214. Hereafter cited in the text as Topsfield.

42. For Maria Rossetti's useful introductory discussion of the *Purgatorio* in these terms, see *A Shadow of Dante*, 107–82.

43. Singleton, *Purgatorio*, 1:3.

44. Singleton, "Dante," 44, 45, 49.

45. Ibid., 53–54. Also relevant to discussions of Christina Rossetti's work in this context is Singleton's earlier insistence on Dante's pursuit of this program despite those readers who "somehow cannot allow that good Christians, Christians who know that there is only one God of Love, could play with a convention of *venus* that had, as a central figure, either a *god of love* in no way identifiable with the God of Love of the Christian faith, or else at the center had a woman, *midons*, enthroned and worshipped in his stead (or had, more commonly, *both* figures)" (47).

46. Dante *Purgatorio* (trans. Cayley) 17, ll. 91–105; quoted in *A Shadow of Dante*, 160.

47. This occurrence is to be distinguished from the mnemonic operation of the imagination, which depends exclusively upon previously assimilated external stimuli. See Singleton, *Purgatorio*, 2:378–81.

48. Ibid., 2:379–80.

49. As Singleton further notes, "this doctrine is Platonic in origin" (ibid., 2:379).

50. Significantly, Christina Rossetti eschewed the major *stylistic* techniques

that Petrarch's most prominent imitators absorbed—Dante Rossetti among them. These, of course, included the use of elaborate conceits. In her style Christina was more austerely Dantean than Petrarchan.

51. Armi, *Petrarch*, 65.

52. Warren, "Tennyson and Dante."

53. Joseph, *Tennysonian Love*, 59.

54. Ibid., 62, 68.

55. Battiscombe records the significant reactions of friends and relations to the *Monna Innominata* when it was first published in 1881: "Dante Gabriel wrote to his mother, '[Watts-Dunton and I] are both deeply impressed by the beauty of the *Monna Innominata* series'—a sequence also praised by [W. B.] Scott, who judged the book as a whole to be 'rich in beautiful thoughts'" (*Christina Rossetti*, 169–70). Bell describes the *Monna Innominata* and the sonnet sequence, *Later Life*, as the two "chief glories" of *A Pageant and Other Poems* (*Christina Rossetti*, 253). Thomas calls it "great" (*Christina Georgina Rossetti*, 70). Stuart finds in the *Monna Innominata* "a pitch of eloquence which Christina seldom attains elsewhere, and which she does not surpass" ("Christina Rossetti," 13). Elsewhere Stuart compares the sonnets' effect to that of "a chaplet of perfectly matched pearls" (*Christina Rossetti*, 123). Zaturenska asserts that the *Monna Innominata* is "one of the great sonnet sequences in the English language, and in a handful some of the most poignant love poems in English. . . . They are, certainly, among the finest poems by any woman who has written poetry in English" (*Christina Rossetti*, 155). More recently, Bellas reminds us that "contemporary reviewers singled [the *Monna Innominata*] out for special praise" (*Christina Rossetti*, 70). And Rees deplores the fact that the sonnets, "a fine piece of work," are "almost entirely ignored by modern criticism" (*Poetry of Dante Gabriel Rossetti*, 148).

56. So far, the most thorough—but still inadequate—readings of the *Monna Innominata* appear in Rees (*Poetry of Dante Gabriel Rossetti*, 152–64, 169–75) and in Wenger ("Influence of the Bible"). Rees very usefully focuses her remarks on the formal achievements of the series, placing Rossetti's sonnets carefully in the context of English developments in the love sonnet tradition from Sidney through Elizabeth Barrett Browning. Wenger selectively identifies and briefly discusses biblical allusions in Rossetti's sonnets. Both critics make significant advances in the criticism of Rossetti to the extent that they eschew reductive autobiographical readings of these poems: "[T]o read the fourteen poems principally for biographical illumination, as has usually been done, is to fail to appreciate the author's understanding of the soul in conflict and to overlook her creative ability to translate personal experience into timeless and universal art" (Wenger, "Influence of the Bible," 15). Bellas, in his summary treatment of the sonnets, also rejects biographical readings (*Christina Rossetti*, 71). Critics who have insisted on mining the sonnets for biographical insights include Thomas (*Christina Georgina Rossetti*, 70–76), Zaturenska (*Christina Rossetti*, 155–63), Packer (*Christina Rossetti*, 224–32, 255–57), and Battiscombe (*Christina Rossetti*, 132–33)—the last despite her earlier reference to an unpublished letter of 28 April 1894, written by Christina Rossetti to William Michael Rossetti, in which she protests forcefully against "imaginative" readers construing her poems as "love personals" (*Christina Rossetti*, 54).

57. In this passage Virgil and Dante discuss the spiritual economies of renunciation. In lines 61–63 Dante asks a question of Virgil that is precisely relevant to Rossetti's sonnet, and Virgil responds:

> "How can it be, that boon distributed
> The more possessors can more wealthy make
> Therein, than if by few it be possessed?"
>
> . . . .
>
> ". . .Because thou fixest still
> Thy mind entirely upon earthly things,
> Thou pluckest darkness from the very light.
> That goodness Infinite and Ineffable
> Which is above there, runneth unto love,
> As to a lucid body comes the sunbeam.
> So much It gives itself as It finds ardour,
> So that as far as charity extends,
> O'er it increases the external Valour.
> And the more people thitherward aspire,
> More are there to love well, and more they love there,
> And, as a mirror, one reflects the other."

Dante, *Purgatorio* (trans. Cayley) 15; quoted by Maria Rossetti, *A Shadow of Dante*, 155.

58. These biblical allusions are:

Line 3:	Without Whose Will one lily doth not stand.
Matt. 6:28–29	And why take ye thought for raiment? Consider the lilies of the field, how they grow; they toil not, neither do they spin: and yet I say unto you, That even Solomon in all his glory was not arrayed like one of these.
Line 4:	Nor sparrow fall at his appointed date;
Matt. 10:29	Are not two sparrows sold for a farthing: and one of them shall not fall on the ground without your Father.
Line 5:	Who numbereth the innumerable sand,
Ps. 139:18	If I should count them, they are more in number than the sand; when I wake, I am still with thee.
Line 6:	Who weighs the wind and water with a weight.
Job 28:25	To make the weight for the winds; and he weigheth the waters by measure.

BIOGRAPHICAL EPILOGUE

1. DeLaura, "Newman and the Victorian Cult of Style," 10.

2. Pater, *Appreciations*, 17–18.

3. The Rossetti-Gemmer correspondence is now in the Frederick Koch Collection, Pierpont Morgan Library.

4. Christina Rossetti to Caroline Gemmer, n.d., Frederick Koch Collection, Pierpont Morgan Library.

5. Quoted in Sandars, *Life of Christina Rossetti*, 267. The original of this letter is now in the Spenser Collection, University of Kansas Library. See also Packer, *Christina Rossetti*, 403–4, and Bell, *Christina Rossetti*, 177.

APPENDIX

1. Reproduced from *Poems*, 2:86–93.

BIBLIOGRAPHY

Adorno, Theodor. "Lyric Poetry and Society." *Telos* 20 (1974): 56–71.

Armi, Anna Maria, trans. *Petrarch: Songs and Sonnets*. New York: Grosset and Dunlap, 1968.

Bakhtin, Mikhail M., and Pavel M. Medvedev. *The Formal Method in Literary Scholarship: A Critical Introduction to Sociological Poetics*. Translated by Albert Wehrle. Cambridge, Mass.: Harvard University Press, 1985.

Ball, Patricia. "Sincerity: The Rise and Fall of a Critical Term." *Modern Language Review* 59 (1964): 1–11.

Bannerjee, Ron. "Dante through the Looking Glass: Rossetti, Pound, and Eliot." *Comparative Literature* 24 (1972): 136–49.

Battiscombe, Georgina. *Christina Rossetti: A Divided Life*. New York: Holt, Rinehart and Winston, 1981.

Bell, Mackenzie. *Christina Rossetti*. London: Thomas Burleigh, 1908.

Bellas, Ralph. *Christina Rossetti*. Boston: Twayne Publishers, 1977.

Bentley, D. M. R. "Political Themes in the Work of Dante Gabriel Rossetti." *Victorian Poetry* 17 (1979): 159–79.

Blake, Kathleen. *Love and the Woman Question: The Art of Self-Postponement*. Totowa, N.J.: Barnes and Noble, 1982.

Bloom, Harold, ed. *Modern Critical Views: Walter Pater*. New York: Chelsea House Publishers, 1985.

Books from the Libraries of Christina, Dante Gabriel, and William Michael Rossetti. Introduction by William Fredeman. N.p.: Bertram Rota, 1973.

Bowker, R. R. "London as a Literary Centre." *Harper's* 76 (May 1888): 815–44.

Bowra, Maurice. *The Romantic Imagination*. Cambridge, Mass.: Harvard University Press, 1949.

Browning, Elizabeth Barrett. *The Poetical Works of Elizabeth Barrett Browning*. Boston: Houghton Mifflin, 1974.

Buckley, Jerome H., ed. *The Pre-Raphaelites*. New York: Modern Library, 1968.

Bump, Jerome. "Hopkins, Christina Rossetti, and Pre-Raphaelitism." *Victorian Newsletter* 57 (1980): 1–6.

———. "Hopkins, Metalepsis, and the Metaphysicals." *The John Donne Journal* 4 (1985): 303–29.

———. "Hopkins' Imagery and Medievalist Poetics." *Victorian Poetry* 15 (1977): 99–119.

Burnaby, John. *Amor Dei: A Study of the Religion of St. Augustine*. London: Hodder and Stoughton, 1938.

Butler, Marilyn. "Against Tradition: The Case for a Particularized Historical Method." In *Historical Studies and Literary Criticism*, edited by Jerome J. McGann, 25–47. Madison: University of Wisconsin Press, 1985.

Chandler, Alice. *A Dream of Order: The Medieval Ideal in Nineteenth-Century English Literature*. Lincoln: University of Nebraska Press, 1970.

Chapman, Raymond. *Faith and Revolt: Studies in the Literary Influence of the Ox-*

ford Movement. London: Weidenfeld and Nicholson, 1970.

Christ, Carol. *The Finer Optic*. New Haven: Yale University Press, 1975.

"Christina Georgina Rossetti." *The Critic* 26 (12 June 1895): 21.

"Christina Georgina Rossetti." *The Dial* 18 (16 January 1895): 37–39.

Colish, Marcia. *The Mirror of Language: A Study in the Medieval Theory of Knowledge*. New Haven: Yale University Press, 1968.

Connor, Steven. "'Speaking Likenesses': Language and Repetition in Christina Rossetti's *Goblin Market*." *Victorian Poetry* 22 (1984): 439–48.

Courthope, W. J. "The Latest Development in Literary Poetry: Swinburne, Rossetti, Morris." *Quarterly Review* 132 (January 1872): 59–84.

Culler, A. Dwight. *The Victorian Mirror of History*. New Haven: Yale University Press, 1985.

Curran, Stuart. "The Lyric Voice of Christina Rossetti." *Victorian Poetry* 9 (1971): 287–99.

Dale, Peter Allen. *The Victorian Critic and the Idea of History: Carlyle, Arnold, Pater*. Cambridge, Mass.: Harvard University Press, 1977.

D'Amico, Diane. "Christina Rossetti: The Maturin Poems." *Victorian Poetry* 19 (1981): 117–38.

———. "Reading and Rereading George Herbert and Christina Rossetti." *John Donne Journal* 4 (1985): 269–89.

Davie, Donald. "On Sincerity from Wordsworth to Ginsberg." *Encounter* (8 October 1968): 61–66.

DeLaura, David. "Newman and the Victorian Cult of Style." *Victorian Newsletter* 51 (Spring, 1977): 6–10.

[Dennett, J. R.] "Miss Rossetti's Poems." *Nation* 3 (July 19, 1866): 47–48.

DeWilde, Justine. *Christina Rossetti, Poet and Woman*. Nijkerk, Neth.: C. C. Callenbach, 1923.

Doughty, Oswald, and John R. Wahl, eds. *The Letters of D. G. Rossetti*. 4 vols. Oxford: Clarendon Press, 1967.

Engelberg, Edward, ed. *The Symbolist Poem*. New York: E. P. Dutton, 1967.

Fass, Barbara. "Christina Rossetti and St. Agnes' Eve." *Victorian Poetry* 14 (1976): 33–46.

Ferrucci, Franco. *The Poetics of Disguise*. Translated by Ann Dunnigan. Ithaca: Cornell University Press, 1980.

Ford, Ford Madox. *The Critical Attitude*. London: Duckworth, 1911.

Ford, George H. *Keats and the Victorians*. New Haven: Yale University Press, 1944.

Foucault, Michel. *The History of Sexuality: An Introduction*. New York: Random House, 1978.

Fredeman, William. "'From Insult to Protect': The Pre-Raphaelites and the Biographical Fallacy." In *Sources for Reinterpretation*, 57–80. Austin, Tex.: Humanities Research Center, 1975.

———. "Christina Rossetti." In *The Victorian Poets: A Guide to Research*, edited by Frederick E. Faverty, 284–93. 2d ed. Cambridge, Mass.: Harvard University Press, 1968.

———. "Impediments and Motives: Biography as Unfair Sport." *Modern Philology* 70 (1972): 149–54.

———. *Pre-Raphaelitism: A Bibliocritical Study.* Cambridge, Mass.: Harvard University Press, 1965.

———. "Rossetti's 'In Memoriam': An Elegiac Reading of *The House of Life.*" *Bulletin of the John Rylands Library* 47 (1965): 298–341.

———, ed. *The P.R.B. Journal: William Michael Rossetti's Diary of the Pre-Raphaelite Brotherhood, 1849–53.* Oxford: Clarendon Press, 1975.

Friedrich, Werner. *Dante's Fame Abroad, 1350–1850.* Chapel Hill: University of North Carolina Press, 1950.

Gilbert, Elliot. "The Female King: Tennyson's Arthurian Apocalypse." *PMLA* 48 (1983): 863–78.

Gilbert, Sandra, and Susan Gubar. *The Madwoman in the Attic.* New Haven: Yale University Press, 1979.

Girouard, Mark. *The Return to Camelot.* New Haven: Yale University Press, 1981.

Gorham, Deborah. *The Victorian Girl and the Feminine Ideal.* Bloomington: Indiana University Press, 1982.

Gosse, Edmund. "Christina Rossetti." *Century Magazine* 46 (June 1893): 211–17.

Gray, Donald, and George B. Tennyson, eds., *Victorian Literature: Poetry.* New York: Macmillan, 1976.

Hagstrum, Jean. *Sex and Sensibility: Ideal and Erotic Love from Milton to Mozart.* Chicago: University of Chicago Press, 1981.

Hamilton, Walter. *The Aesthetic Movement in England.* London: Reeves and Turner, 1882.

Harrison, Antony. "Cataclysm and Pre-Raphaelite Tragedy: Morris' 'The Haystack in the Floods.'" *South Atlantic Review* 47 (1982): 43–51.

———. "Irony in Tennyson's 'Little *Hamlet.*'" *Journal of General Education* 32 (1981): 271–86.

———. "Reception Theory and the New Historicism: The Metaphysical Poets in the Nineteenth Century." *John Donne Journal* 4 (1985): 163–80.

———. "Swinburne's Losses: The Poetics of Passion." *ELH* 49 (1982): 689–706.

———. *Swinburne's Medievalism: A Study in Victorian Love Poetry.* Baton Rouge: Louisiana State University Press, 1988.

Heath-Stubbs, John. "Pre-Raphaelitism and the Aesthetic Withdrawal." In Sambrook, 166–85.

Hinkson, Katherine Tynan. "The Poetry of Christina Rossetti." *Bookman* 5 (December 1893): 78–79.

Homans, Margaret. "'Syllables of Velvet': Dickinson, Rossetti, and the Rhetorics of Sexuality." *Feminist Studies* 11 (1985): 569–93.

Hönnighausen, Gisela. "Emblematic Tendencies in the Works of Christina Rossetti." *Victorian Poetry* 10 (1972): 1–15.

Hough, Graham. *The Last Romantics.* London: Methuen, 1947.

Houghton, Walter. *The Victorian Frame of Mind.* Princeton: Princeton University Press, 1957.

Hunt, John Dixon. *The Pre-Raphaelite Imagination.* Lincoln: University of Nebraska Press, 1968.

Hutcheon, Linda. *A Theory of Parody*. London: Methuen, 1985.

Jauss, Hans Robert. *Aesthetic Experience and Literary Hermeneutics*. Minneapolis: University of Minnesota Press, 1982.

Johnson, E. D. H. *The Alien Vision of Victorian Poetry*. Princeton: Princeton University Press, 1952.

Joseph, Gerhard. *Tennysonian Love: The Strange Diagonal*. Minneapolis: University of Minnesota Press, 1970.

Keble, John. *Lectures on Poetry*. Translated by E. K. Francis. 2 vols. Oxford: Oxford University Press, 1912.

———. *Occasional Papers and Reviews*. Oxford: Clarendon Press, 1877.

Kent, David. "'By thought word and deed': George Herbert and Christina Rossetti." In *The Achievement of Christina Rossetti*, edited by David Kent. Ithaca: Cornell University Press, 1987.

———. "Sequence and Meaning in Christina Rossetti's *Poems* (1893)." *Victorian Poetry* 17 (1979): 259–64.

Krieger, Murray. *The Classic Vision*. Baltimore: Johns Hopkins University Press, 1971.

La Gallienne, Richard. Review of *Poems*. *Academy* 39 (7 February 1891): 130–31.

Landow, George. *The Aesthetic and Critical Theories of John Ruskin*. Princeton: Princeton University Press, 1971.

———. *Victorian Types, Victorian Shadows: Biblical Typology in Victorian Literature, Art, and Thought*. London: Routledge and Kegan Paul, 1980.

Lang, Cecil, ed. *The Pre-Raphaelites and Their Circle*. Chicago: University of Chicago Press, 1968.

Law, Alice. "The Poetry of Christina Rossetti." *Westminster Review* 143 (April 1895): 444–53.

Lindenberger, Herbert. "Toward a New History in Literary Study." In *Profession '84*, edited by Richard Brod and Phyllis Franklin, 16–23. New York: Modern Language Association, 1984.

Lourie, Margaret. "The Embodiment of Dreams: William Morris' 'Blue Closet' Group." *Victorian Poetry* 14 (1976): 193–206.

McGann, Jerome J. *The Beauty of Inflections: Literary Investigations in Historical Method and Theory*. Oxford: Clarendon Press, 1985.

———. "Christina Rossetti's Poems: A New Edition and a Revaluation." *Victorian Studies* 23 (1980): 237–54.

———. "Keats and the Historical Method in Literary Criticism." *Modern Language Notes* 94 (1979): 988–1032.

———. "The Religious Poetry of Christina Rossetti." *Critical Inquiry* 10 (1983): 127–44.

———. "Rossetti's Significant Details." *Victorian Poetry* 7 (1969): 41–54.

———. *Swinburne: An Experiment in Criticism*. Chicago: University of Chicago Press, 1972.

Mellor, Anne K. *Romantic Irony*. Cambridge, Mass.: Harvard University Press, 1980.

Mermin, Dorothy. "Heroic Sisterhood in *Goblin Market*." *Victorian Poetry* 21 (1983): 107–18.

"Miss Rossetti's Poems." *The Nation* 3 (19 July 1866): 47–48.

Morris, William. *The Earthly Paradise*. 3 vols. Boston: Roberts Brothers, 1893.

Newman, John Henry. *Aplogia pro vita sua*. Edited by Martin Svaglic. Oxford: Clarendon Press, 1967.

———. *The Works of John Henry Newman*. 39 vols. London: n.p., 1898–1903.

Norton, Mrs. Charles Eliot. "'The Angel in the House,' and 'The Goblin Market.'" *Macmillan's Magazine* 8 (September 1863): 398–404.

Owen, Marion. "Christina Rossetti: 'Affairs of the Heart.'" *Humanities Association Bulletin* 21 (1970): 16–25.

Packer, Lona Mosk. *Christina Rossetti*. Berkeley: University of California Press, 1963.

———, ed. *The Rossetti-Macmillan Letters*. Berkeley: University of California Press, 1963.

Pater, Walter. *Appreciations, with an Essay on Style*. London: Macmillan, 1910.

———. *Plato and Platonism*. London: Macmillan, 1910.

———. "Poems by William Morris." *The Westminster Review* 90, n.s. 34 (1868): 300–312. Reprinted in Sambrook, 105–17.

———. *The Renaissance*. Edited by Donald L. Hill. Berkeley: University of California Press, 1980.

Poggioli, Renato. *The Theory of the Avant-Garde*. Translated by Gerald Fitzgerald. Cambridge, Mass.: Harvard University Press, 1968.

Poovey, Mary. *The Proper Lady and the Woman Writer: Ideology as Style in the Works of Mary Wollstonecraft, Mary Shelley, and Jane Austen*. Chicago: University of Chicago Press, 1984.

Rabine, Leslie W. *Reading the Romantic Heroine: Text, History, Ideology*. Ann Arbor: University of Michigan Press, 1985.

"Rambler, The." *Book Buyer* 12 (February 1895): 21–23.

Rees, Joan. *The Poetry of Dante Gabriel Rossetti: Modes of Self-Expression*. Cambridge: Cambridge University Press, 1981.

Review of *Goblin Market and Other Poems*. *British Quarterly Review* 36 (July 1862): 230–31.

Review of *The Prince's Progress and Other Poems*. *Athenaeum*, no. 2017 (23 June 1866): 824–25.

Riede, David. "Erasing the Art-Catholic: D. G. Rossetti's *Poems*, 1870." *Journal of Pre-Raphaelite Studies* 1 (1981): 50–70.

———. "Morris, Modernism, and Romance." *ELH* 51 (1984): 85–106.

Rollins, Hyder E., ed. *The Letters of John Keats*. 2 vols. Cambridge, Mass.: Harvard University Press, 1958.

Rosenblum, Dolores. "Christina Rossetti's Religious Poetry: Watching, Looking, Keeping Vigil." *Victorian Poetry* 20 (1982): 33–50.

Rossetti, Christina. *Called to Be Saints*. London: Society for Promoting Christian Knowledge, 1881.

———. *The Complete Poems of Christina Rossetti*. Edited by Rebecca W. Crump. 2 vols. to date. Baton Rouge: Louisiana State University Press, 1979–85.

———. "Dante, an English Classic." *Churchman's Shilling Magazine and Family Treasury* 2 (1867): 200–205.

———. "Dante. The Poet Illustrated out of the Poem." *The Century* (February 1884): 566–73.

———. *The Face of the Deep.* London: Society for Promoting Christian Knowledge, 1893.

———. *The Poetical Works of Christina Georgina Rossetti.* Edited by William Michael Rossetti. London: Macmillan, 1904.

———. *Seek and Find: A Double Series of Short Studies of the Benedicte.* London: Society for Promoting Christian Knowledge, 1879.

———. *Time Flies: A Reading Diary.* London: Society for Promoting Christian Knowledge, 1885.

Rossetti, Dante Gabriel. *The Works of Dante Gabriel Rossetti.* Edited by William Michael Rossetti. London: Ellis, 1911.

———. *The Early Italian Poets.* Edited by Sally Purcell. Berkeley: University of California Press, 1981.

Rossetti, Maria. *A Shadow of Dante.* Boston: Roberts Brothers, 1872.

Rossetti, William Michael, ed. *The Family Letters of Christina Rossetti.* New York: Scribners, 1908.

———, ed. *Rossetti Papers, 1862–1870: A Compilation.* New York: Charles Scribner's Sons, 1903.

———, ed. *Ruskin: Rossetti: Pre-Raphaelitism.* London: George Allen, 1899.

Rougement, Denis de. *L'Amour et l'occident.* Paris: 10/18, 1939.

Ruskin, John. *The Works of John Ruskin.* Edited by E. T. Cook and Alexander Wedderburn. 39 vols. London: George Allen, 1903–12.

Sambrook, James, ed. *Pre-Raphaelitism: A Collection of Critical Essays.* Chicago: University of Chicago Press, 1974.

Sandars, Mary. *The Life of Christina Rossetti.* London: Hutchinson, 1930.

Sebeok, Thomas. "Enter Textuality: Echoes from the Extra-Terrestrial." *Poetics Today* 6 (1985): 657–63.

Shairp, J. C. "Aesthetic Poetry: D. G. Rossetti." *Contemporary Review* 42 (1882): 17–32.

Sharp, William. "The Rossettis.—Gabriele Rossetti.—Maria Francesca Rossetti.—Dante Gabriel Rossetti.—Wm. [sic] Michael Rossetti.—Christina G. Rossetti." *Fortnightly Review* 45 (1 March 1886): 414–29.

Shaw, W. David. "Projection and Empathy in Victorian Poetry." *Victorian Poetry* 19 (1981): 324–39.

Silver, Carole. *The Romance of William Morris.* Athens: Ohio State University Press, 1982.

Singleton, Charles. "Dante: Within Courtly Love and Beyond." In *The Meaning of Courtly Love,* edited by Francis X. Newman, 44–54. Albany: State University of New York Press, 1968.

———, trans. *The Divine Comedy, Purgatorio,* by Dante Alighieri. 2 vols. Princeton: Princeton University Press, 1973.

Stein, Richard. *The Ritual of Interpretation.* Cambridge, Mass.: Harvard University Press, 1975.

Stuart, Dorothy. "Christina Rossetti." The English Association, pamphlet no. 378, 1931.

———. *Christina Rossetti.* London: Macmillan, 1930.

Stubbs, John Heath. *The Darkling Plain*. London: Eyre and Spottiswoode, 1950.

Sussman, Herbert. *Fact into Figure: Typology in Carlyle, Ruskin, and the Pre-Raphaelite Brotherhood*. Columbus: Ohio State University Press, 1979.

———. "The Pre-Raphaelite Brotherhood and Their Circle: The Formation of the Victorian Avant-Garde." *Victorian Newsletter* 57 (Spring 1980): 7–9.

Swinburne, Algernon Charles. *The Complete Works of Algernon Charles Swinburne*. Edited by Edmund Gosse and Thomas J. Wise. 20 vols. London: William Heineman, 1925–27.

———. *The Poems of Algernon Charles Swinburne*. 6 vols. London: Chatto and Windus, 1904.

Symons, Arthur. *Studies in Two Literatures*. London: Leonard Smithers, 1897.

Tennyson, Alfred. *The Poems of Tennyson*. Edited by Christopher Ricks. London: Longman, 1969.

Tennyson, George B. *Victorian Devotional Poetry*. Cambridge, Mass.: Harvard University Press, 1981.

Thomas, Eleanor. *Christina Georgina Rossetti*. New York: Columbia University Press, 1931.

Topsfield, L. T. *Troubadours and Love*. Cambridge: Cambridge University Press, 1975.

Tracts for the Times. 6 vols. London: n.p., 1834–41.

Trilling, Lionel. *Sincerity and Authenticity*. Cambridge, Mass.: Harvard Univeristy Press, 1972.

Troxell, Janet Camp. *Three Rossettis: Unpublished Letters to and from Dante Gabriel, Christina, and William*. Cambridge, Mass,: Harvard University Press, 1939.

Uhlig, Claus. "Literature as Textual Palingenesis: On Some Principles of Literary History." *New Literary History* 16 (1985): 481–513.

Warren, Alba H. *English Poetic Theory, 1825–1865*. Princeton: Princeton University Press, 1950.

Warren, T. Herbert. "Tennyson and Dante." In *Essays of Poets and Poetry, Ancient and Modern*. London: n.p., 1909.

Weathers, Winston. "Christina Rossetti: The Sisterhood of Self." *Victorian Poetry* 3 (1965): 81–89.

Weimann, Robert. *Structure and Society in Literary History*. Baltimore: Johns Hopkins University Press, 1984.

Wenger, Helen. "The Influence of the Bible in Christina Rossetti's *Monna Innominata*." *Christian Scholar Review* 3 (1973): 15–24.

White, Hayden. "Historical Pluralism." *Critical Inquiry* 12 (1986): 480–93.

Woolf, Virginia. *The Second Common Reader*. New York: Harcourt, Brace, 1932.

Zaturenska, Marya. *Christina Rossetti: A Portrait with a Background*. New York: Macmillan, 1949.

INDEX

226 Index

Crimean War, 138
Critic, The: review of CR (1895), 53
Crump, Rebecca W., 2, 4, 22, 41, 201
(n. 2)
Curran, Stuart, 40

Daniel, Arnaut, 165–69
D'Arcy, Ella: Monochromes, 58
DeLaura, David, 187
Dennet, J. R., review of CR (1866),
27, 52
DeWilde, Justine, 12, 41
Dickens, Charles: review of Millais's
Christ in the House of His Parents, 59
Dodsworth, Rev. William, 69
Donne, John, 77

Eliot, T. S., 204 (n. 23); "The Love
Song of J. Alfred Prufrock," 93; "La
Figlia che Piange," 160

Fass, Barbara, 11
Ferrucci, Franco, 158
Ford, Ford Madox, 39
Froissart, Jean, 161

Gemmer, Caroline, 81, 188–89, 204
(n. 32), 207 (n. 27)
Genette, Gerard, 150
Germ, The, 65, 66, 204 (n. 24); CR's
appearance in, 12, 13, 25, 29
Gilbert, Sandra, 41, 131, 140
Gladstone, William: on The Divine
Comedy, 143, 144–45
Gosse, Edmund, 105, 142; on CR's
Pre-Raphaelitism, 25, 36, 39, 40,
41, 53, 58, 62
Grosart, Alexander B.: edition of
Spenser's works, 142–43, 211
(n. 4)

Hagstrum, Jean, 164–65
Hallam, Arthur Henry, 173–74; "A
Farewell to the South," 173; "The
Influence of Italian upon English
Literature," 173; "Remarks on Pro-

fessor Rossetti's 'Disquisizioni
. . . ,'" 173–74
Herbert, George, 10, 86
Higher Criticism of the Bible, 67
Homans, Margaret, 152, 153, 155
Hopkins, Gerard Manley, 36, 39, 40,
54, 77, 80, 97
Hough, Graham, 55
Hunt, John Dixon, 26, 58, 61
Hunt, William Holman, 30
Hutcheon, Linda, 150–51

Ingelow, Jean, 14
Intertextuality, 10, 48, 85, 90, 140,
141, 148–75 passim. See also Rossetti, Christina

Jauss, Hans Robert: on Augustine's
Confessions, 136–40
Johnson, Lionel, 39
Joseph, Gerhard, 173–74

Keats, John, 10, 12, 20, 22, 43, 76,
86, 87, 88, 109, 119, 137, 140,
143, 153, 154, 170, 176, 180, 207
(n. 23), 208 (nn. 6, 8, 12); ideals of
"negative capability" and the chame-
leon poet, 16; value of "the wakeful
anguish of the soul," 17, 78; "To
Autumn," 18, 44; "Ode to a Nightingale," 18, 48, 79, 170; "Ode on
Melancholy," 78, 93; The Fall of Hyperion, 93; letter to Benjamin Bailey, 95; "La Belle Dame Sans
Merci," 117
Keble, John, 31, 65, 68, 77, 80, 143;
The Christian Year, 35, 64, 69, 75;
Tract 89, 71; on Analogy and Reserve, 73; Lectures on Poetry, 73; on
nature imagery, proper employment
of, 73; concern with suffering, 79;
"Fourth Sunday in Advent," 79; re-
view of Lockhart's Life of Scott, 82.
See also Tractarianism
Kempis, Thomas à, 89, 97, 138
Krieger, Murray, 165

Monna Innominata, 171–72
Petrarchan tradition, 89–90, 106, 135,
    152–53, 154, 155–56, 159, 160,
    164, 175–85 passim
Plato, 10, 21, 36, 82, 89, 96–101,
    109, 208 (nn. 13, 15)
Polidori, Gaetano, 12
Pope, Alexander, 160
Pound, Ezra, 204 (n. 23)
Pre-Raphaelitism: PR poetry, 2–3; aes-
    thetic values, 24–63 passim, 92–95;
    PR medievalism, 26, 36, 38, 53–56,
    70; Tractarian elements, 29–30, 67–
    88; avant-garde tendencies, 36–52,
    67; PR poets as heirs of the Roman-
    tics, 37, 143, 150; PR poetry of
    "aesthetic withdrawal," 37–38, 92–
    93, 95, 118, 159; quest for pure
    beauty, 65, 94; social values, 69;
    uses of typology, 70, 72, 76; use of
    analogy, 71–72, 76; concern with
    the details of nature, 75, 76; elegiac
    qualities of PR poetry, 76, 87, 92–
    95; PR poets as dreamers, 83–84,
    93, 118; PR artistic self-conscious-
    ness, 88; dialectic of desire and re-
    nunciation in PR poetry, 92–95,
    125–29; PR uses of Dante, 143,
    145–46, 151–52. *See also* Rossetti,
    Dante Gabriel; Morris, William;
    Swinburne, Algernon Charles
Proust, Marcel, 137
Pusey, E. B., 68, 69

Rees, Joan, 11, 41
Riede, David, 65
Riffaterre, Michael, 150
Romanticism, 35, 36, 65, 143; Ro-
    mantic "sincerity," 2, 12; Romantic
    poets and the "pathetic fallacy," 20;
    literary mythologies, 22; modes of
    imaginative expression, 37; pursuit
    of ultimate realities, 50; quest for
    permanence, 71, 76; Victorian Ro-
    manticism, 118
Rosenblum, Dolores, xi, 41
Rossetti, Christina: craving for fulfill-

ment, x, 56, 77–78, 83, 140–41,
    187–89; asceticism, x, 56, 94, 132,
    137–38, 159, 187–90; problem of
    poetic vocation, 1–22 passim; as
    craftswoman, 1–22 passim, 40–51,
    80, 188; aesthetic values, 8, 10, 12;
    ideal of "conciseness," 10, 42, 132;
    intertextual qualities of her work,
    10, 48, 62, 88, 90, 117, 118, 140–
    41, 148–85 passim; and Graves'
    disease, 14; concept of "the Poet
    mind," 16, 17, 96, 148; eschatologi-
    cal patterns in her poetry, 19, 102,
    165; aestheticist effects of her po-
    etry, 19–22, 52–63 passim, 65, 82–
    86, 94, 96–97, 102, 105, 111–12,
    113, 115, 118, 129–30, 137–41,
    150, 155, 157–58, 162, 169, 187–
    89; medievalism of her poetry, 21,
    36, 52–55, 59, 67, 161; dominant
    concerns of her poetry, 21–22, 63;
    popularity of her work, 23; Ruskin-
    ian aesthetic values, 23–36, 51; Pre-
    Raphaelite qualities of her poetry,
    24–63, 158, 159, 180, 189; typo-
    logical habits of mind, 30–36, 46–
    52, 53; and the poet as prophet, 31–
    33, 89, 100, 103, 171, 183, 188;
    and Tractarian poetics, 35, 54, 68–
    88 passim, 159; social and cultural
    criticism in her poetry, 36–37, 91,
    105, 118, 122, 124, 137, 139–41,
    149–50, 155–57, 162–63, 183,
    185, 188; avant-garde poetics, 36–
    52 passim, 155; dialogism in her po-
    ems, 41, 43–46, 89–90, 132, 133,
    139–41; concern with mutability,
    42, 57, 59–62, 112, 113, 119–23,
    135, 139, 154, 167, 180, 184; anti-
    Romanticism, 46–51, 137, 140,
    154–55, 176; sensuousness of her
    poetry, 52–63, 82–86, 98, 100,
    122, 137–39, 141, 180–81; as me-
    diator between Ruskinian and deca-
    dent aesthetics, 55; and the impossi-
    bility of fulfillment in love, 56, 92–
    95, 102–41 passim, 148; symbolist